A Map to the End of Time

Wayfarings with Friends and Philosophers

A MAP TO THE END OF TIME

Wayfarings with Friends and Philosophers

Ronald J. Manheimer

W. W. Norton & Company

New York • London

Excerpts from "Burnt Norton" and "East Coker" in *Four Quartets*, © 1943 by T. S. Eliot
and renewed 1971 by Esme Valerie Eliot, reprinted by permission of Harcourt Brace &
Company.

For information about permission to reproduce selections from this book, write to
Permissions, W. W. Norton & Company, Inc., 500 Fifth Avenue, New York, NY 10110.

The text of this book is composed in Weiss
with the display set in Braganza
Desktop composition by JoAnn Schambier
Manufacturing by Quebecor Printing, Fairfield, Inc.
Book design by Chris Welch

Library of Congress Cataloging-in-Publication Data

Manheimer, Ronald J.
A map to the end of time : wayfarings with friends and
philosophers / Ronald J. Manheimer.
p. cm.
Includes bibliographical references and index.
ISBN 0-393-04725-3
1. Aging—Philosophy. 2. Aging in literature. 3. Philosophy—
Study and teaching. 4. Philosophy teachers—Biography. 5. Manheimer,
Ronald J. I. Title.
HQ1061.M335   1999
305.26'01—dc21   98-33336
CIP

W. W. Norton & Company, Inc., 500 Fifth Avenue, New York, N.Y. 10110
http://www.wwnorton.com

W. W. Norton & Company Ltd., 10 Coptic Street, London WC1A 1PU

1 2 3 4 5 6 7 8 9 0

For Caroline, paths entwined.

CONTENTS

Acknowledgments

Many are those who have walked this path with me. First, my wife, Caroline, who helped me think through the ideas for this book and who was always willing to read aloud what I had written and help me distinguish the lively from the dull. Then the host of older students who shared their stories, feelings, and thoughts, several of whom became persistent inner voices I knew I could call upon in moments of need. My students in the College for Seniors who read and discussed an early version of this book and, chapter by chapter, showed me the steps I had yet to take. Special thanks to my colleague Denise Snodgrass for her enduring belief in the project and her ability to get me thinking again when I was inclined to grow weary. Sally Greenfield was a careful reader of an early version of the manuscript, and Kim McGuire and Peter Caufield were astute close-to-last version readers. Certain people including Sarah-Ann Smith, Rick Chess, and May Ching straightened me out on the facts concerning such matters as modern Chinese history and Jewish mysticism. My longtime friends and associates devoted to the study of the humanities and aging, Harry Moody and Tom Cole, provided inspiring intellectual exchange about many of the book's dilemmas. John Lane's enthusiasm buoyed me up when I felt most discouraged, and David Romtvedt gave me perspective on a writer's need to go the distance. John Kotre, whose "narrative psychology" broke new ground, made the initial recommendation for my authorship. Special thanks to my editor, Alane Salierno Mason, who stayed the course with me, provided objective criticism, challenged me to expand my intellectual horizons, and encouraged me to follow my instincts. To all of these people I acknowledge a debt of gratitude, reserving to myself the faults of this endeavor.

INTRODUCTION

"I am a part of all that I have met," sighs the aged Ulysses, seated beside the hearth with his aged wife. The home-bound warrior broods over the memories of daring sea voyages, heroic deeds in battle, the comradeship of fellow mariners, exotic places, rare climates, the noble and the tyrannical among leaders. He should be contented. He's both suffered and enjoyed "greatly." He's drained the cup of life "to the lees." But a wealth of experience contained in memory fails to satisfy him. He's never been good at reflection, this man of large action. And retirement from the field—"To rust unburnish'd, not to shine in use!"—does not suit him. What if, he ponders, he could turn the past, with its myriad end points, into a threshold to the future? If it were true that "all experience is an arch," through which he may yet journey, then Ulysses might once again set sail for new and distant places.

The English poet Alfred Tennyson was twenty-four when he re-created the spirit of Ulysses, the legendary Greek wanderer, to guide him through the troubled seas of despair, uncertainty, and disappointment. Tennyson worried that a family history of madness would claim him. His closest friend had just died of cholera. His talent was so far unrecognized. Feeling that he had reached an impasse, Tennyson summoned the restless spirit of a post-heroic Ulysses, whom he dubbed "this gray spirit yearning in desire."

Tennyson belongs to the great tradition of poets and writers who conjure up legendary figures from mythology or Scripture to renew their zeal for life, inspire new initiatives, or serve as guardian spirit. In fashioning his personal myth, Tennyson gave the tale a new twist. He began at the end of the story—Ulysses returned home, grown old, restless, complaining. Yet now the gray spirit is ready to forsake hearth and home "To follow knowledge like a sinking star, / Beyond the utmost bound of human thought." As if to justify fleeing the responsibilities of Ithaca, "these barren crags," he announces this time his quest is not just to seek out more experiences, "Life piled on life," but to pursue knowledge boundless as the ocean, and distant as each new horizon.

Tennyson told a friend he had written the poem to express the need of "going forward and braving the struggle of life." If his Ulysses, "made weak by time and fate," could summon the strength of will out of the stuff of memory, "To strive, to seek, to find, and not to yield," then surely Alfred Tennyson could, too. So can we.

THE ARCH OF EXPERIENCE

Tennyson's "Ulysses" is one of those classics of English literature we are supposed to read in high school or, at least, by the time we have completed college. But it was not until my early thirties that I distinctly heard how "all experience is an arch." The occasion was a poetry reading at a library in Olympia, Washington. One of the messengers, William Stafford, was on hand to read from his prizewinning volumes *Traveling through the Dark* and *Smokes Way*. The other three poets—famous, I supposed, to their friends— were local residents who looked to be in their seventies.

The room was packed with Stafford fans and with friends of the seniors. Stafford read brilliantly, captivating the audience with his ability to breathe meditation into simple language. Of "Our Life" he read,

> *We should give it away, this breath,*
> *and another, as easy as it came to us.*

We were all slightly breathless when Stafford sat down and the time arrived for the three seniors to read. I expected to hear conventional, rhymed verse. But I was wrong. It seemed they belonged to a writing workshop taught by a young poet at the local senior center. Apparently, he had succeeded in showing them the way to contemporary forms. Their work, mostly in free verse, was bold and exuberant, poignant and humorous. We heard about a stubborn horse, running away from home, a mysterious uncle, and a close call swimming in a water tank beside the railroad tracks (when the engine pulled in to take on water, the level dropped and the boys found the wooden sides too slippery to crawl out). These older folks had us laughing, even wiping away a tear.

We were invited to ask questions at the end of the reading. I had never seen Stafford in person. He was older than I had imagined. From his weathered face, gray temples, and references to his years in the Forest Service during World War II, I surmised he might have been only a decade or so younger than the other three.

On impulse, I raised my hand from the back of the audience.

Two turns later, he called on me. "Mr. Stafford," I asked, "for someone of your age, how do you manage to find new things to write about?" An older gentleman seated beside me turned and frowned. Had I said something wrong, been impertinent?

Stafford smiled, looked down thoughtfully. He seemed to be mulling over his reply. Then he looked up.

"Nothing you've experienced before is ever finished," he said, looking directly at me.

"You've got to be willing to find out what happens next, to take chances. When I was writing my poem 'Vocation,' I heard my father's voice saying, 'Your job is to find out what the world is trying to be.' If you believe that, then what you think you know starts to fade, to recede from you. It's unsettling. You want that knowledge to stay put. But it never does, really." Stafford paused, looked sideways at his colleagues of the evening.

"I wonder. Do you know the poem many of us learned by heart in school?" he said. "In it, the poet tells about an 'Idle king,' the elderly Ulysses. The poem says something about what can happen to experience." Stafford raised his eyebrows at the other three. They nodded. Without saying a word, all four pushed back their chairs and stood. Arms at their sides, facing the audience like dutiful schoolchildren, they began to recite.

> *I am a part of all that I have met;*
> *Yet all experience is an arch wherethro'*
> *Gleams that untravell'd world, whose margin fades*
> *For ever and for ever when I move.*

The four voices made the poem sound like a hymn. A silence followed; a chill went down my spine. That was the first time I tried imagining the arch—was it of stone or wood, an immaterial wisp, or invisible, a sheer idea? After the reading, when I looked the poem up in the library, I began to wonder, was I too, like Tennyson's Ulysses, a "gray spirit yearning in desire"?

Something about my own stage in life made me receptive to the chorus of voices. I was thirty-three, Tennyson's age when "Ulysses" was first published in 1842. Like his "gray spirit," I felt that the adventures of my life had ended. The wanderlust of my youth and the experiments of my college and graduate school days were over. For the first time, I no longer identified with the college students I was teaching. The responsibilities of marriage and family, pursuing my career from one short-term job teaching philosophy to another, and losing my father after his long bout with Parkinson's disease, made me feel old. Yes, the future stretched ahead, filled with obligations and uncertainties. But somewhere I had lost momentum and direction.

If past experience and a storehouse of memories could really be transformed into new adventures, I wanted to know how. If there were worlds remaining to be traveled, and knowledge that extended "beyond the bounds of human thought," then, as a student of philosophy, I believed I should make those journeys. If a mythical Ulysses could serve as a talisman for Tennyson, one "gray spirit" aiding another, what of actual older people? If a courageous old self lay hidden within each of us, then real-life seniors might be able to reveal these secrets of self-transformation and renewal. It was worth finding out.

A few weeks after the poetry reading, I volunteered to teach a philosophy course at the senior center. There I at first tended to equate aging with its outward appearance—a tuft of hair sprouting from a man's ear, the ropy skin of a woman's throat. After several months listening to my new friends' stories, I began to associate their lives with certain generational experiences—living off boiled wheat during the Great Depression of the 1930s, surviving the beaches on D day, going to college under the GI Bill. Eventually, letting go of my comfortable role as an observer, I saw myself in the mirror of their lives and recognized I, too, would grow old. Moreover, that aging and later life was fertile ground for understanding how we experience memory, change, history, our mortality, the stages of life, the work of generations—themes long embraced by philosophers.

Conjoined to a common destiny, I realized that the thread connecting these themes was what philosophers call "temporality"—inner perceptions of time that hold the power to awaken new meanings of experience. Philosophers, ancient and modern, observed that in youth the sequential time of the clock seems long, but when we are older, it seems all too short. They noted the chronological time of history, which, as we grow older, becomes compressed so that events and persons of long ago now feel as if they happened yesterday.

My new senior friends shared their descriptions of the way the birth of a child or her graduation from college could widen your consciousness of generations, drawing your concerned gaze beyond your own development and lifetime; how, outwardly, we are dated by our thinning gray hair or a tattered favorite old sweater, while, inwardly, we may feel identical to the young man or woman we were at twenty-five; and how, in moments such as providing care to our own parents, driving past a house we once lived in, remembering the loss of a loved one, we may suddenly glimpse a pattern repeated in the fabric of our personal history, or realize that some struggle or personal triumph links us to the larger movement of communal life.

Over the next twenty years, I found that Tennyson was right; there are untraveled worlds—not only of distance but of time, memory, and history. And I found fellow travelers in senior centers, public libraries, care centers, colleges, museums, family gatherings, and other places where ideas and experiences could be shared. Tennyson's arch could become the threshold to a room of eager new students, or the opening made by arms linked and raised in a circle of dancers. On occasion, it became the curved hands of a pianist or the trajectory of a philosopher's daring leap of thought. In each case, imagination—the power to consider the possible, the novel; the power to see beyond shopworn conceptions of truth, overcome impasses and barriers—charged the moment and made it eventful.

What I have discovered over the past two decades about aging, change, and qualitative shifts in our perceptions of time came through "doing" philosophy alongside teaching, collaborating with and learning from my elders. For me, these shifts in perception were turning points, just as Tennyson's aged Ulysses helped turn him from despair to renewed determination. Accordingly, I have tried to recapture my experiences the way they happened— through relationships with a wide range of wonderful, complex, and often unpredictable older persons, and with friends and acquaintances my own age or younger whose lives, when framed by the themes of aging, change, and time, suddenly looked different. The impressions I accumulated came through the stories people told me, from books I was reading, and from philosophers whose ideas and perplexing questions would suddenly blaze up in the middle of a conversation.

The following chapters, drawn from experiences of two decades, explore such questions as: Is it possible to transform the past, discover new meanings in prior events? Are there times when it is better to forget, other times crucial to remember? How are qualities such as deliberateness, reflective humor, and selflessness nurtured through new ways of perceiving the dimensions of time? Does the aim of life become clearer in old age, or does frailty mock us, unraveling the fabric of meaning we have worked so hard to weave? And are there universals of human experience, or does

diversity and multiplicity of histories make it impossible to experience a shared sense of history, become true contemporaries? With
each investigation, I found a new meaning to Tennyson's arch.

Exploring these questions, I learned that situations and relationships played a crucial role. I envisioned the little group of seekers
huddled around bunched-together bridge tables at the senior center in Olympia, Washington; recalled strolling through the parklike
cemetery surrounding a country church in Denmark engaged in
conversation with my former mentor Augie Nielsen; reheard the
enigmatic words of a Chinese cadre member and Confucian
scholar, Mr. Liu, beside Lake Wascana in Regina, Saskatchewan;
revisited a perplexing conversation with my daughter Esther on our
front porch in Asheville, North Carolina, one summer evening, fireflies glowing intermittently among the dogwood leaves.

Gathering these voices and places together, I had to confront
a recurring dilemma. Philosophers supposedly pursue timeless,
universal truths that do not depend on particular lives or specific
locales for their validity. How aging individuals—all of us,
really—are to shed the garment of our physical selves, set aside
self-interest and the distorting lens of personality, hold fleeting
thoughts steady, and outstrip the boundaries of personal history
remains a perpetual challenge to the life of the mind. Yet I could
not relinquish the features of a weathered face, the remembered
touch of a cool, small hand, or leave out the pathos of someone's
tale of hardship or his laugh of having come through life's travails.
Here I took guidance from a favorite former teacher and friend,
Oscar Sheppler, who speculated that maybe there is a way each
life and each place represents more than itself. It may be that our
experiences fulfill a timeless pattern or that we can glimpse the
timeless in the particular, if only for a moment. This, I found, was
good advice, as was his other recommendation: "Ideas and stories.
Hold on to both."

A Map to the End of Time

Wayfarings with Friends and Philosophers

CHAPTER ONE

GRAY SPIRIT YEARNING

The trajectory of a person's life, Aristotle suggests in his *Rhetoric*, can be characterized as a series of shifts in our orientation to time. Outward looking in youth, we are filled with hope and optimism about the future, whereas in old age, wearied by disappointments and losses, we turn inward to memories of real or imagined better times. Men in their prime, between the ages of thirty-five and forty-nine, according to Aristotle, should have achieved a "mean," or balance between extremes. Men in their prime should dwell in the present, neither too optimistic nor too pessimistic, too rash nor too timid, in their dealings and outlook. Though the circumstances of life may have changed dramatically since the days of Aristotle's ancient Greece, his insight that the meaning of time changes with age remains fresh. At least, that was Oscar Sheppler's view. And since he was my friend and former teacher, I welcomed his guidance as he helped prepare me for my new adventure—bringing philosophy to the elderly.

Though he's a great admirer of Aristotle, Professor Sheppler isn't pessimistic about growing old. Our lives, he says, do not follow a linear trajectory but take us through loops and spirals. If we consider alternative views of the course of life, we discover our ability to reinterpret experience and gain fresh initiative. He was talking about the process of renewal.

THE THINKER

Professor Oscar Sheppler, whom everyone called Shep, was imposing—both mentally and physically. An unusually large head sat above his massive shoulders, giving him something of the appearance of Rodin's brawny contemplative, *The Thinker*. Crowned with a mass of curly red hair that was turning gray and brown, he looked as though the fibers of his tweed sport coat had crept upward through his beard and bushy eyebrows. Adding to this image of the contemplative, Shep smoked a pipe that hung from a slot where a tooth was missing on one side of his mouth.

Shep and his wife, Sonja, a research chemist, lived in a large apartment near the sprawling campus of Wayne State University in midtown Detroit. I grew up in the Motor City, went to college there. And it was from Shep that I caught what he called the philosophy "bug."

I remember a day in his philosophy seminar. Shep was marching up and down at the front of the classroom pointing to our waving hands, calling on us to speak as though he were scattering food to hungry fish. Our morsel of the day was philosophical dualism: whether the universe could be explained by supposing the existence of two different and irreducible principles such as matter and energy, mind and body, permanence and change; or that contraries of this sort formed a subtle unity discernible only after lengthy reflection and contemplation.

One student, a member of the Young Socialists, favored dualism, pointing to class struggle and citing Hegel's theory of an invincible logic of counterforces that drove the course of history, which Hegel called "the cunning of reason." Another, an ardent environmentalist, countered with Plato's notion that all nature is akin, insisting "we are all part of a single ecological matrix." Exasperated by the Ping-Pong of opposing positions, I muttered, louder than I intended, "What difference does it make, anyway?"

Shep must have heard because he looked in my direction and raised his hand for silence. He walked toward me nodding his head and stroking his beard. "That is your problem, Manheimer," he said. I thought he was angry at my impulsive outburst. Then he smiled and went on, "Or, should I rather say"—he bent over and put his hands on my shoulders—"that now, to you, this question belongs, yes?" He stood up and announced, "Mr. Manheimer is now in charge of the question, when does a philosophical difference make a difference?" My classmates laughed, but they knew he was serious. That was his gift, what endeared Shep to us; the underlying question asked at precisely the right moment in that skewed syntax and faintly European accent you'd never forget.

I was a first-generation college student, planning to be a doctor or, like my father, a businessman. Then I caught the bug. One moment, the path of life seemed predictable—education, career, a family in the suburbs. But then a cryptic phrase, an enigmatic saying, the idea of a world presided over by dualists and monists, and suddenly a veil that hung invisibly before my eyes lifted. I grew flushed, excited, dazed by alternative realities. Before I knew it, the only thing that mattered was the quest for what Descartes called "clear and distinct ideas." The rest of life now appeared fuzzy and pale.

Now, a dozen years and a graduate degree later, while planning my philosophy class at the senior center in Olympia, I traced my route back to Shep's apartment, wondering about another kind of dualism—the old and the young. When was it that one turned into the other? Was Aristotle right in saying that the young are guided by hope and the future, the old by memory and the past?

It was the year of our nation's bicentennial, 1976, and across the country historic buildings were being saved from the wrecking ball, family histories brought out of secret drawers, ethnic traditions rediscovered and turned into public festivals. In the midst of all this preservation, I wanted to gaze through the lens of philosophy into the memories of older people's lives. Something about the elderly fascinated me. After all, weren't they in the philosophical period of life when people have the chance to revisit the past, distill important lessons? Wouldn't it be reasonable to explore how thinkers had characterized old age?

I knew I'd find Shep at home on a Sunday afternoon, in slippers and a burgundy velvet smoking jacket tied with a sash. The Shepplers were liberal Protestants. Their families had fled Vienna just before the German takeover. Their Detroit apartment was a little oasis of European culture in the midst of the industrial city. Well-worn Persian carpets covered the floors; bookshelves with titles in German, French, and English lined the walls. Shep and his wife were both accomplished pianists who spent many hours playing duets: two baby grand pianos, the curves of their mahogany bodies fit one into the other, filled half the living room.

Although he spoke excellent English and had a special fondness for eighteenth-century British literature, Shep still retained the habit of occasionally putting an action word at the end of a sentence. When I had told him on the phone about Stafford, the older poets at the library, Tennyson, and my intention to teach at the senior center, he exclaimed, "Old people? A midlife crisis maybe you're having?"

Then there was the pet the Shepplers acquired a few years ago, Toby, a stray orange-and-white-striped cat named after a character in Laurence Sterne's satirical novel *Tristram Shandy*. Uncle Toby of the novel, Shep explained, had opinions on every conceivable subject and loved to hold forth at the drop of a hat. The presence of the cat relaxed him, he said, because it had no opinions, leaving him free to wax eloquent.

REMEMBER CEPHALUS

Shep greeted me with a hug, took my arm, and led me to an armchair opposite him beside the living room fireplace. We chatted for a few minutes, I catching him up on my family and an erratic career since graduate school that had taken me to Washington State, and he filling me in on university politics, his wife's research, and Toby's latest antics. Then I mentioned the philosophy class I had volunteered to teach.

Elbows on knees, Shep leaned forward, his hands cradling his large head. "You are doing this, why? To advance your career?" He shook his head. He knew no philosophy department would take the slightest interest. "For the money?" He looked at me and laughed. "You miss, maybe, the grandpa and grandma? Flowers to the grave, you should bring."

Shep could deftly run through a set of propositions, reducing each to absurdity. Now he read my mind, scanning for a first cause, some principle or motive that had set me on this course of action.

"This is our country's bicentennial year," I began to explain, "I want to do something. You know, make a contribution."

"You could write a family history. Everyone is," said Shep.

"My aunt Sylvia's already doing that," I replied. "No, I want to do something with the ideas that have made a difference in the lives of ordinary people. Besides, I've only taught undergraduates. I was thinking, older people might bring more experience to philosophy."

He considered my answer. "A great deal of experience; it is possible," Shep mused softly. "But, my friend, perhaps you have observed. Yes? Some people repeat the same experiences—over and over. Will you find open minds capable of fresh thinking?" He rapped his pipe against his palm and brushed bits of charred tobacco into an ashtray. "Habits, Ronald," he said, "mental habits. Extremely difficult to change." Shep scrutinized the pipe bowl and refilled it from a humidor on the table beside him. He leaned back, exhaling a cloud of aromatic smoke, and asked, "So, my friend, what else has led you to embark on this journey into the realm of the elderly?"

What else? Shep was one of those people from whom you just couldn't hold back. Like other undergraduates who befriended him, I felt free to talk about my personal life as well as about philosophy. The great thing about Shep was that he encouraged us to make connections. "You know," he'd say, "the great thinkers had lives too."

"The truth is, Shep," I began, "I'm feeling older. I haven't come to terms with my father's death and, now, with the birth of our third child, Aaron, . . . I don't know." Shep knew about my father's long bout with Parkinson's disease. He waited for me to continue. "Well, I started having this dream. I'm in a trench. It's World War I. A wave of soldiers has gone forward against withering machine-gun fire. Now it's my group's turn. Another wave of soldiers fill the trenches behind us. Just before we go over the top, I wake up in a cold sweat. Even thinking of the dream makes me anxious."

Shep raised his finger, a gentle signal of response. "Shall I hand you the cliché that you are, perhaps, experiencing your mortality? That each coming generation pushes the previous one toward oblivion?" He looked at me quizzically and continued, "You are what? Thirty? Thirty-two?"

"I'm thirty-three this year," I answered.

"Ah, the Christological year. You know? The passion of Jesus?" I shook my head. No, I didn't know Jesus died at age thirty-three. Was this supposed to explain my heavy heart?

"Hmm, well, we leave this aside for now," said Shep, waving his hand. "Something else. You speak about the children. Maybe it is their vulnerability you are experiencing. After all, what can we celebrate? Vietnam, the riots, the assassination of courageous people, visible targets for hidden men? How could you not feel helpless to protect your innocent loved ones? Ronald, you are discovering your new position in life. A generation in front, a generation coming from behind, you see, a new perspective of consciousness. Until now you worried about your future. Now you can worry also about theirs. So, you see, you have an exciting new task. The work of generations."

Could Shep be right? I had focused on myself in the dream. Now, I saw, my fear, like a mist in my dream, enveloped the young recruits waiting in the trenches behind me. And the Bicentennial, yes, wasn't that a call, after the terrible upheavals of recent times, to find new meaning in the past? Older people might link me to ideals that had withstood the ravages of time. Then something else occurred to me. "Speaking of generations," I said, "I thought I would always identify with being a student. But now my students seem so young. There's a gulf between us. Maybe that's another reason. To spend time with people who would understand."

"Consolation," Shep responded. "There's a great tradition for it in philosophy. To experience healing through the music of discourse, find solace through the fellowship of a community of seekers." Shep looked over at his bookshelves, then back at me. "Much can be learned from the older generation if you are willing to learn with them. But, Ronald, this is sometimes a most uncertain proposition. Have you examined your assumptions?"

"My assumptions? That's what I've been trying to do. I'm reading about psychological development in later life. A friend gave me Jung's essay 'The Soul and Death,' where he compares the span of life to the mathematical shape of a parabola."

"Ah, Doctor Jung, scientist and mystic," said Shep, and, inscribing an arc with his finger, intoned, "In youth we long for the world, we climb the mountain of ambition in search of happiness, only to find, when we reach it"—Shep dropped his hand and shook his head sadly—"happiness lies not at the apex but in the valley below. Alas, you must reconcile yourself to finitude, accept the fact of death. And—what else is it he says?"—Shep pointed at the clock over the mantel—"In the secret hour of life's midday we discover we must liberate ourselves, must 'die with life.' Isn't that it, Ronald? Am I wrong?"

I shook my head. "So, you know this essay quite well."

"Yes. I went through a Jungian phase. Very important, his appreciation for the whole of life—waxing and waning of our lunarlike existence. You know, when he was in his mature years, Jung built a tower into which he shut himself to study the alchemy of the soul. But you, don't you want to jump out of the ivory tower of academia, not descend into some secret chamber? Are you not rather searching for fellow travelers?"

So that was his point, cautioning me from the potential isolating effects of mysticism. Shep was a skeptic. Art, especially music, was his religion. About music, he once said, "I can be a fanatic, without killing someone." But this idea of searching for fellow travelers intrigued me. It was true, I did want to find my connection to other generations. It was so easy to get lost in one's own thoughts.

Shep remained silent, then struck a match and relit his pipe. "Listen, Ronald, about the elderly you could learn a little from philosophy." A curious look came over him. "You know," he began, "we have a wonderful example of talking philosophy with old-timers. Your Plato, you remember?"

Did I remember my Plato? I searched my mind for an elderly character in one of the dialogues. Almost all those who conversed with Socrates were young men or middle-aged teachers of rhetoric, the Sophists.

"You're lucky, this I didn't ask on one of my exams, eh?" He teased. "I'm giving a hint." He looked at me expectantly and said, "The *Republic*, Book One."

The *Republic*, Plato's great treatise on the concept of justice, the ideal state, and the education people need to run that state, adopts the form of a dialogue. It begins with Socrates among a crowd of people walking back to Athens with a young friend after attending a religious festival in the port town the Greeks called the Piraeus. The opening scene describes a servant running up to Socrates to tell him that his master, a well-to-do young man by the name of Polemarchus, wants him to come to his house. Socrates agrees, and that's where the dialogue takes place.

"Book One," I said, still trying to recall an old person in the dialogue, "they've gone back to Polemarchus' home from the religious festival, and Socrates gets them to discuss the question 'What is right conduct?' or justice."

The wintry afternoon light was fading quickly. Shep reached over and switched on the table lamp beside him. He yawned and stretched. "Interesting, isn't it? The man who argued in favor of a timeless cosmic order would find the most critical actions played out on the stage of real life and recount it in the form of a con-

versation, not an abstract treatise. Yes, Socrates goes to Polemarchus' home and agrees to stay the night so that he can attend
the evening spectacle. Which is?" He started bouncing in his
chair.

"Isn't it a horse race of some kind?"

"Correct, it is a horse race," he replied, "but with a twist. Our
Greek scholars tell us that Plato is referring to a torch race on
horseback. The riders pass the torch forward as in a relay race. A
telling detail, don't you think?"

"That it should involve passing a torch?"

Shep nodded. He had taught us how seemingly trivial details
in Plato's dialogues, such as an analogy, a gesture, an innocent
word, when properly apprehended, threw new light on the play
of ideas. Still, I wasn't sure what he was driving at.

"You don't see it yet?" I shook my head. "Okay, then consider
further. With whom does Socrates hold the very first discussion
on the definition of justice?" He gave me a dour look and stroked
his beard.

"With Polemarchus," I replied. "Polemarchus argues that right
conduct is rendering every man his due. Then, when challenged,
he redefines his position, saying that right conduct is when you
help your friends and harm your enemies."

Shep chuckled. "About Polemarchus, you are correct. Socrates
gets him first to reveal his opinion, that justice is a useless commodity, and then into the position of saying justice is simply the
ability to justify taking something you want. But, remember, Plato
tells us Polemarchus inherited the conversation from another." He
bent over trying to imitate someone.

Inherited? Suddenly, I remembered. "His father, Cephalus, of
course."

"Of course, of course," Shep laughed. "The very first conversation in the *Republic* is between Socrates and Cephalus, the papa.

I'm not surprised you forgot. Usually we skip over it, believing this conversation is just a way to set the stage for the ensuing arguments. Now that you ask how philosophers regard the elderly, I am seeing for the first time." Shep touched his forehead as if conjuring up a picture. "Socrates says he enjoys speaking with the old because from them we can learn about the path of life—whether it is rough or smooth. Doesn't that strike you as significant? Why should this Cephalus, a retired businessman who shares a home with his son at the Piraeus, be the first with whom Socrates discusses justice? I'm seeing this now, Ronald, how Plato brings before us a representative of the older generation—the group you intend to teach philosophy." Shep sat forward, removed his pipe. "The plot thickens, eh?"

I nodded. The way Shep recounted a scene or argument from Plato, the action might be taking place in a living room or coffee shop around the corner. I looked past Shep at the bookshelves behind him; pale oak boards supported by small plaster replicas of Greek or Roman pillars. "So," I ventured, "the torch race is a symbol for the passing of inheritance between generations. Plato is hinting that Polemarchus may hold views similar to his father's."

Shep nodded. "Many things pass from one generation to another. Wealth, opinions, values, character traits. Clever fellow that Plato, the way he puts clues in our path."

Shep rubbed the bridge of his nose and sat silently for a moment. He bent over and spoke, "Ah, my little Toby, come hither." The orange cat, which had been lurking nearby, let Shep lift it gently to his lap.

"Let us recall," he continued, petting the cat, "Cephalus fancies himself something of a philosopher. He tells Socrates that in old age he finds the life of the mind more rewarding than the pleasures of the body. The old dualism, eh? Unlike some of his cronies who despair over their loss of energy, power, and sex drive in old age, Cephalus welcomes these changes and the moderating effects they have on his life. Perhaps he even feels liberated. Maybe he's read Jung, accepted death. No?" He laughed. "This freedom from passion, a great theme in philosophy. We would think Socrates should approve."

"Interesting," I said, "that Cephalus represents old age as a philosophical time of life. He has the right characteristics, doesn't he? Control over his emotions, the inclination toward reflection, contentment. Isn't Plato portraying the ideal of tranquillity in old age?"

"Yes, so it would seem. But the wily Socrates is suspicious of Cephalus' contentment. Maybe it's not his piety, Socrates contends, but Cephalus' wealth and powerful position in society that props up his apparent tranquillity."

"But, Shep," I replied, "doesn't Cephalus counter this, saying that some wealthy people are contented, others not? That wealth is neutral, used for good or ill. And, if I remember correctly, Cephalus tells Socrates how he has *overcome* certain anxieties about old age and death."

"Quite right," Shep answered. "Cephalus says he found contentment after a period of nightmarish dreams. Awakening, he thinks death cannot be far off. How had he led his life, how would the gods judge him in the hereafter? Yes, Ronald, the voice of conscience calling, past deeds popping up he might prefer to forget, the terror of descending into the depths of the underworld. Cephalus believes he has conquered these nighttime terrors. Offerings, he's made, at the temple, financial affairs, he's put in order. He owes no one. But—"

"There it is," I interjected, "just as Jung describes. He's made peace with death. The main thing, Cephalus argues, is development of good character. What we would call integrity. If you have that, whether you're young or old, then you've got the right stuff."

Shep gestured with his pipe, "Right stuff? Perhaps, but remember what happens when Socrates induces Cephalus to try his hand at defining the righteous life?"

"He falls flat on his face. Tricked by Socrates into stating a contradiction."

"Exactly. Cephalus cannot debate two minutes before he has to excuse himself. 'Please Socrates,'" Shep mimed in a squeaky pathetic voice, "'I am a virtuous old man. I must go to the religious festival. Here, take my son, Polemarchus. Let him inherit my place in the discussion.' And why? Because, though a moral line he espouses, under Socrates' cross-examination, we see that Cephalus cannot think ethically. He lacks the theoretical discipline to examine the principles that underlie his values." Shep pressed his thumb into the bowl of the pipe and reached for a match, saying, "Right opinion does not equal knowledge. Cephalus is not quite the philosopher after all."

"But," I countered, "isn't it possible to be a righteous and tranquil person in old age without having a disciplined mind; without knowing all the 'whys' and 'wherefores' of ethical theory?"

He gave me a look of disbelief, as if I had just uttered a heresy. "Ronald, hold your tongue," he exclaimed. "We would be out of business." Then he laughed and went on, "Of course, most people do quite well without all the mental bother of working out a set of ethical principles. In periods of relatively little change, this may be sufficient. But during periods of social and political upheaval, I can tell you personally, morality based on opinion and sentimentality is easy prey for a tyrant. By the time Plato wrote this dialogue, most of the characters were dead—brutally murdered for their fortunes or executed on political charges. Plato doesn't trust opinions. He banishes Cephalus, never to return to the great conversation. So, when you go to your old ones, this should be for you a motto: remember Cephalus."

I nodded, yes, I would try to remember, but did this mean that my older students would not be inclined to analyze their moral positions? And Socrates' question about the path of life, whether it was rough or smooth—wasn't this what I wanted to know? My life seemed anything but smooth. Married, with three small children, and moving from one short-term teaching job to another, I too woke up in the middle of the night worrying, not about damnation below but about terrestrial life—money, career, my abilities as a father, a husband.

Until recently, I had been disdainful of financial security, of middle-class respectability. I liked to take chances, try new things, travel, live on the edge. But now, pressing forward were issues of permanence, continuity, stability. Instead of identifying with my students, I was beginning to identify with my parents' lives, to sympathize with their struggles to achieve a measure of security and happiness. For their part, my parents had worried about when I would find a real job. They wanted me to be a doctor or businessman, not a philosopher; to take the path of a Cephalus, not a Socrates. Some days, I had to admit, I agreed with them.

As I sat there thinking about my parents, I glanced at the painting over the mantel—an English landscape in the style of Constable, one of those pictures of trees, barns, ponds, and cows that dissolve into squiggles and blotches when you get up close, but look completely realistic when seen from afar.

"Shep," I said, "this is very interesting about Cephalus, but how does it help me get ready to teach at the senior center? I assume they'll be ordinary, middle-class people, not wealthy industrialists."

Shep looked thoughtful and said, "Ronald, you wanted to know how philosophers regarded old age. Am I wrong?" I shook my head in agreement. This was part of my preparation. "So now, together, we are looking at the problems and opportunities you may encounter. Maybe, like Cephalus, the old have reached a time of inner calm. But don't be fooled. Integrity and good character could also be a mask of middle-class respectability and conformity. Can you tell the difference between wisdom and piety?"

Shep struck a match. "Besides," he said, holding the flame above the bowl, "from Plato we are learning many other things. This Cephalus, he represents something more." Shep paused, drew on his pipe, making the tobacco glow. "The uncertainty of change. Bodies growing old, fortunes made and lost, beliefs that fail us because they have become empty rituals. Plato points us toward the immutable, the changeless, which he implies we can attain only through rational discourse. So when you go to meet your new old students, remember they have accumulated layers of experience which, compressed by time, form crystals of knowledge, even precious gems of insight which you can help them to unearth. You may find coal, you may find diamonds."

Coal? Diamonds? Shep had a gift for irony. Which way did he see it?

SOMETHING MISSING

I was about to ask about the coal and diamonds when I heard the jangling of keys. Shep turned. Toby jumped from his lap and ran toward the foyer. The door shut, a bolt clicked, and a moment later there was Mrs. Sheppler, a tall, dignified woman in a long black wool coat, a pocketbook hanging from her shoulder, and carrying a briefcase in one hand, a bag of groceries in the other. From where I sat, I could see her kneel, hear her speak softly in German to the cat, which rubbed up against her leg.

"Herr Sheppler," she shouted over her shoulder as she walked straight toward the kitchen, *"hast du vergessen, den Kater zu füttern?"*

"Oh, goodness," said Shep, "I've forgotten to feed the cat."

"*O je, ich hab's vergessen,*" he shouted in the direction of the kitchen.

The refrigerator door slammed and Mrs. Sheppler entered the living room, rubbing her hands and looking around at the unfamiliar coat hanging over a chair. Only then did she realize Shep was entertaining a guest.

"Oh, excuse me," she said. "I did not know we had a visitor."

Shep turned to kiss her cheek as she knelt beside him. "Sonja, darling, you remember Manheimer here, my former student. Yes?"

She turned her gaze, studied me for a moment, then pointed. "Yes, the man who moved to the West Coast, got mixed up with Heidegger or was it Kierkegaard? Well, anyway, one of those dark souls. Of course I remember." She extended a hand, which I shook. "How are you? And how is your lovely wife? Didn't we attend a wedding reception for them, Sheppler?" Shep nodded. She always addressed him in this formal way, as if he were an employer or business associate. Yet they seemed a loving couple.

"It's already more than ten years ago." Shep sighed. "How the time passes."

Mrs. Sheppler sat down on the couch. "I like your wife. She is very direct, forthright. I admire that in a woman. And your children? We have seen pictures. Healthy?"

"Yes," I nodded, "the usual sniffles and fevers, but growing and active."

"Good," she pronounced. "And what have you been speaking about, if I may ask?"

Shep looked at me as if asking permission to share our conversation. I thought to relieve him of any doubt, so I spoke. "I was asking Shep, I mean, Dr. Sheppler . . ."

"He likes this name, Shep. I prefer others."

"Yes, well, you see I am about to teach a philosophy course at a senior center near where I live, and I was looking for some advice about what I might expect. So we have been discussing how philosophers approach aging."

"Hmm," was Mrs. Sheppler's response. She looked over at Shep, providing me with a view of her handsome profile, prominent chin, strong straight nose, broad forehead, and her multicolored hair of browns, grays, and a few remaining streaks of blond, all gathered up in a bun atop her head and fastened with a silver clasp.

"Sonja," Shep began, "our friend Manheimer is going through something of a midlife crisis. He's smitten by Tennyson's 'Ulysses' and is about to seek the wisdom of the gray spirits as he launches his ship into new waters."

Sonja looked doubtful. "Tennyson," she nodded, "ah, yes." She turned to me. "So, you intend to follow knowledge like a sinking star beyond . . . what is it? Oh yes, beyond the limits of human thought?"

"The bounds," Shep corrected her.

Mrs. Sheppler bowed her head to acknowledge the correction. Somehow the poem now sounded pompous, and I tried to deny the implications. "I'm just inspired by the poem."

"And well you should be," she agreed. "It is inspirational. And yet"—she tugged at the loose skin of her neck, tucked a strand of errant hair behind her ear—"and yet the poem misses something most important. Wouldn't you say?"

I did not know what to answer and looked to Shep for guidance. Before he could intervene, Mrs. Sheppler continued. "It's a man's poem. I suppose that's only natural. A man's fantasy of starting over. Full of eloquence and bravado. Today it would be the red sports car and a blonde. Perhaps a young, beautiful student, eh Sheppler?" She glanced at Shep, who frowned and shook his head. "What's missing," Mrs. Sheppler continued, "is the wife, Penelope. Tennyson discards her immediately—'aged wife' is how he puts it, if I am not mistaken. Perhaps that was the Victorian in Tennyson, downplaying the female unless to make her mysterious, untouchable, remote. But we should not forget the real thing." With fluttering hands, Mrs. Sheppler outlined her graceful figure. "Cunning Penelope, the weaver wife, faithful Penelope, loyal Penelope, mother of Telemachus, she for whom Ulysses forsakes the greatest dream—marooned on a beautiful island with the lovely goddess Calypso, never aging, abundance all around. Isn't this what you philosophers seek? This immortality? This perfection?" Shep and I exchanged glances.

"But you see, gentlemen," Mrs. Sheppler continued, "unlike Tennyson's, our real Ulysses does return home to his aging wife. He chooses history, not immortality, even if only in this Greek legend. And when he returns to Ithaca, what a time they have together in that special bed Ulysses himself designed and constructed many years before the long wandering and adventures. You know what I like, especially? How Homer says they made love and then stayed up all night talking. She wanting to know about all his trials and tribulations; he wanted to hear of her resistance to the suitors and would-be usurpers, how she wove and unwove the work of her loom to forestall giving herself to another."

Mrs. Sheppler arose, straightened her skirt, and looked at Shep. "Stayed up all night long." She raised her eyebrows. *"Du hast es nicht vergessen, mein Schatz, nicht wahr?"* Shep shook his head, looked at her admiringly. She smiled, walked behind Shep's chair, and kissed him on the top of his head. "It is very good to see you, Mr. Manheimer. Please greet your wife and children for me. And please greet the old people you will soon meet. I suspect many will be closer to Penelope than to Ulysses. From them, you can learn much to guide you through your crisis."

Mrs. Sheppler walked to the kitchen. I could hear the clatter of silverware and pots. We sat in silence, listening. The cat, Toby, licking its whiskers, returned and leapt up on the couch, taking the place made vacant by Mrs. Sheppler. Finally, Shep broke the silence. "She's quite a woman. So bright, so very bright." He shook his head, thoughtfully.

A Chinese Landscape

"I'm thinking, Ronald," said Shep, tapping his forehead, "there's another useful example about how philosophers regard us gray-beards."

I had never thought of Shep as growing old. Sure, he was my teacher, maybe even a role model. But old?

"I'm thinking Schopenhauer. You know, not many people study Schopenhauer any more. In the late nineteenth century, he was a big figure, a giant. The whole world he made a living organism, every creature, rock, war, piece of music was to him animated by a universal force, an inner Will, an energy beyond anyone's control."

"Did Schopenhauer write about old age?" I asked.

"About the ages of life he wrote, yes. Many nineteenth-century philosophers did this. They wanted to trace the development of progress and enlightenment to its pinnacle, which usually meant in their religion, their nationality, maybe even in themselves. Such hubris, eh? And here, a word of caution." Shep scratched his nose. "When philosophers describe old age, beware of ulterior motives. You see, old age, that's maybe just a canvas on which to paint the *telos*, the purpose, the culmination of life. This is it, this is what it all comes to. Like Plato, maybe you paint the portrait of a wealthy old man in a handsome toga, sitting in a stately villa. He is looking to us serene, eh? But in the eyes we see fear, we see denial, we see false satisfaction. Plato is telling us that to be a Cephalus is not the purpose of life."

"And Schopenhauer, what did he paint?"

Shep spread his arms vertically as if unrolling a scroll. "A big Chinese landscape picture, like ones painted on silk scrolls during the Sung dynasty period a thousand years ago. The kind with floating mountains and layers of mist. A cosmic order indifferent to human machinations. Tiny old men with canes inching their way along mountain paths. The human being, a mere detail, an appendage to the natural world. This is how Schopenhauer painted the panorama of his big conclusion about life—vanity, all is vanity. It is the old, he said, who finally figure this out: happiness is an illusion." Shep shrugged his shoulders. "An Oriental influence."

"Shep," I responded, "how did Schopenhauer characterize the other ages of life?"

"Schopenhauer thought every stage of life had its own mental character. For example, people your age, Ronald. They are first feeling the terrible thirst for life, after happiness yearning. But, says the pessimistic Schopenhauer, what is that but the impulse to do and suffer. Still, you forge ahead in the futile belief that happiness is something attainable."

As he spoke, Shep raised himself from his chair and lumbered over to a bookshelf where, after only a moment's pause, he extracted a slender volume.

"Listen to this, Ronald," he said as he eased back into the armchair, flipping through pages marked with annotations. "I will translate for you.

In the bright dawn of our youthful days, the poetry of life spreads out a gorgeous vision before us, and we torture ourselves by longing to see it realized. We might as well wish to grasp the rainbow!

You see, happiness is a chimera. For the pessimistic Schopenhauer, pain alone is real. But not to worry, the philosopher tells
us, I will give you compensation for the loss of your pretty rainbow. Schopenhauer, who was a great student of music, says the
later period of life is like the second part of a musical epoch.
Instead of the passionate, the Sturm und Drang, phase, like the
early Beethoven, there comes a studious reflectiveness, a simplicity, inward turning. Now instead of the crescendo, the big finale,
we get quiet resolutions, sound trailing off into silence. This pattern of life, perhaps only the old can know it, only they can
appreciate the complete cycle of the music, what Schopenhauer
calls seeing the whole of life. Disillusion, that is the chief characteristic of old age. As compensation, we get a clear, undiluted
picture of life as it really is, not the phantom projections after
which we are running."

Shep closed his eyes in silent meditation. Did he feel old? For
a moment, I drew back, as if old age were contagious.

Shep stirred from his reverie and went to the piano, where he
began playing something dissonant, eerie, like the sound track of
a science fiction movie. "You hear?" asked Shep. "No tonal centers,
no resolution of big dramatic themes. Melancholic, the music of a
wandering soul. Like Schopenhauer."

"What is it?" I asked. "Schopenhauer had a love for Wagner,
didn't he?" I was out of my depth, but took a stab. "This piece, it's
more modern."

"About music, Ronald, you have much to learn," he chided me.
"It was Schopenhauer who believed music speaks directly to the
soul, who deeply influenced Wagner, and Mahler, too. They
sought in their music the inner impulse of nature, the surging
upward, the organic energies. Then they would bring about the
great calm, the redemption of the terrible urges of nature. The
music, transforming consciousness. Have you ever heard another

piece by this composer, the revolutionary Suite for Piano, Opus 25?" I shook my head.

"Really?" he exclaimed, in a mournful voice. "A philosopher must know music." Shep continued to play. "This composer, Arnold Schoenberg, was influenced by Wagner, and through Wagner, by Schopenhauer. But he took a radical step. Since life had no conclusion, no real resolutions, why make music a drug, filled with false certainty? Schoenberg, who fled Hitler like us, to settle in, of all places, Los Angeles. Can you imagine, LA? And this is his atonal work. A wonderful blend of detachment and yearning. Perhaps the music of a displaced generation—refugees. Maybe you will meet people whose personalities float like this music." He stopped playing. "Or"—he struck a heavy chord— "like this, people firmly rooted, who know exactly who and what they are." A passionate, powerful melody filled the living room. "Beethoven," shouted Shep.

"Sounds familiar."

"The *Appassionata* Sonata," said Shep, his face hovering moon-like between the raised piano lid and the keyboard.

THREE MOONS

Later, after Shep had laid out tea and cookies on the coffee table, he remarked, "Ronald, you have made me think of an important question: Is old age a permanent condition, or has it changed so radically from the past that now we need an entirely new way to think about growing old and about the way we experience time?"

Until then, I hadn't considered this possibility. But apparently Shep had.

"This, I too have wondered," he continued. "My parents had one foot in the grave when they were the age of Sonja and me.

We don't have the same limits, the same expectations. Perhaps in old age we are now liberated from all the stereotypes, both good and bad. We can paint our own picture, eh?"

"You mean now you can be anything you want to in old age. Explore new horizons. Be all you can be," I exclaimed.

"Gray liberation," Shep laughed. "Do you know what I'm thinking?" I shook my head. "From what you have observed about philosophies of time and change, I'm thinking that maybe we have made a big mistake." Shep gently stroked the cat beside him. "You see, all along we are thinking, old, young, young, old—how is it? Opposites? Because of our use of language, we have fallen into a trap—the dualistic mode of thinking. But is it not the case that the old are just the young in disguise, as when we are children and dress up in our parents' clothing? I am older than you, and you are younger than me. But you are older than your children. So we are all both younger and older. A relative matter. To think in absolute terms, young, old, this is misleading. We are, at every moment, younger *and* older."

"True," I said, "in comparative terms. But in relation to ourselves, we are at every moment older than we were the previous moment, never younger."

Shep nodded and replied, "From a strictly chronological point of view, yes, the past always precedes the present, and the present precedes the future. But this progression, only one way to think of time. Many friends I have who tell me, 'Shep, I'm sixty now, but inside I feel—what? Twenty-five?' A denial, you might say. We are measuring on a line, birth to death. For an observer, yes, this is how it looks. But from inside the clock is different—without hands. Look"—Shep pulled back the sleeve of his jacket and displayed a wrist watch—"You see, it shows, beside minutes and hours, the phases of the moon." I looked closer and saw the gold sphere in the little arched window of his watch. "Now," he said, tapping on the watch crystal, "imagine not one but three moons."

"Only one moon circles the earth."

"One visible moon. Yes. A moon that affects many cycles on earth. But I am proposing to tell the quality of inner-time consciousness. So, a moon for memory, one for understanding, and one for hope. Three qualities of time. Orientations toward the past, present, and future. Not separate. Overlapping."

"The ultimate Timex," I laughed.

Yes, yes, ultimate," he concurred.

"To tell time out of time," I ventured. "But how does this watch work?"

"Ah, yes, I will explain. You see, when we are young, as Aristotle says, we live primarily oriented to the future, the next adventure, what we long after. So the moon of hope eclipses the other two. As we enter midlife, we become more reflective. What do all these experiences we've pursued really mean, we want to know. So now the moon of understanding begins to eclipse hope and memory. Perhaps, some period in midlife, maybe around fifty, all the moons line up. Remember, that is when, according to Plato, we are truly ready to study philosophy and be civic leaders. We have much accumulated in memory, much experience to contemplate, we have clarified our goals, what we deem valuable to seek."

"The unity of the three modes of time," I interjected.

"A unity?" he responded. "Perhaps. Let us say a harmony. Yet we cannot hold still. The moons must change again. And, as we reach into old age, memory begins to eclipse the other two. Important, though, that the three moons are always orbiting one another, just in relatively different positions. And the shadows, we must always remember."

"So aging means changes in the relative positions of these three moons?"

Shep laughed. "Well, it's a fanciful analogy, but, yes, something like that."

"Maybe, psychologically, I might feel like a twenty-year-old in a thirty-three-year-old body," I responded. "Maybe my inner self will always feel twenty. But aging is not only a psychological process. It's physical. We can't escape that."

"No," Shep replied, "this we cannot deny. But, my friend, what is it that ages, then? Have we overidentified physical aging with everything else? Notice your own words. Your body ages; your inner self remains permanently twenty. You experience both permanence and change. Why pin aging on the body? Why not on the mind or this inner self you speak of that is, somehow, ageless?" He held up his hand before I could reply.

"Wait. Let me finish. I am experimenting with an idea." Shep poked a wooden match into his ear and began fishing around. "We have identified aging with the downward slope of life, Jung's descending curve, yes?" I nodded. "We have identified growth in the young until, say, age twenty or twenty-five, with the ascending curve, development. Am I correct?" I nodded again. "Hmmm. Then when does what the ancient thinkers called the process of becoming, development, turn into aging? Or do these processes exist simultaneously? Or, better, are they one and the same?"

Withdrawing the matchstick, Shep studied the bit of wax on its tip. "Yes, aha. One and the same. Only we, as we become more aware of physical change, mistakenly identify aging with deterioration, with progress toward death, not fulfillment of life. That's where we've gone wrong in our thinking."

"I don't know, Shep," I replied skeptically, "permanently twenty? A fixed center of being that can watch all the changes and itself not change. It's almost like saying that at some point in development we attain a permanent self, fully autonomous and differentiated. I'd have to believe we were somehow already old, while we were still young."

Shep smiled, placed the match in the ashtray. "Didn't Wordsworth say the child was father to the man? Perhaps an old man or woman is already within us."

"Your idea that we are old and young at the same time?"

"Better," he replied, "like our three moons, that we harbor old age within us. And if we have the proper understanding, this inner sage is no grim reaper but a principle of life, of continuous renewal."

The Difficulty Is the Way

"You are feeling now prepared for this new venture?"

Prepared? I now realized how little I understood what first prompted me to offer my services at the senior center. Was I trying to face up to my own fears of growing older and what I might look forward to? Or was I seeking some new way to understand the passage of time, looking for some thread of sameness within the wild weave of change? Having older people for companions might give me a different perspective on my life and family. As for the contributions of philosophers, from what Shep had pointed out about Plato's characterization of Cephalus and Schopenhauer's depiction of old age, it seemed philosophers were not only characterizing older people but also viewing themselves and their ideas in the mirror of aging. Still, that too might be useful. Since I wanted a way to make abstract philosophical issues more concrete, being among the elderly might do just that. And what of Mrs. Sheppler's take on Tennyson and Ulysses? Homer shows us the sea rover giving up a paradise isle to return to the human world of Ithaca and a wife, like him, no longer youthful, yet strong and loving. A person's past could exert a powerful force. What, then, of my own history?

"I have more questions than ever," I replied.

"Good," he laughed, "then you are ready to set sail."

"Like Tennyson's Ulysses."

Shep laughed. "Yes, the 'gray spirit,' himself. That is you. And the arch of experience"—he made a sweeping gesture—"that's what you must do. Help your new friends—Penelopes and Ulysseses alike—bend the arrow of time. Reimagine the past, their memories, the weight of experience; brighten their horizons by turning experience into a threshold, an arch through which to set sail under the leadership of the young philosopher, Captain Ronald. And when you go to meet your new old friends, you may see that, like Tennyson, they will become a part of you. They will be your crew. You just need to find that span of imagination, the arch of transformation, and you will be set."

"The magical arch. Yes," I murmured, "easier said than done."

"The way is difficult," he concurred. "But remember what Kierkegaard said."

"Yes," I replied, "that the way is not the difficulty; the difficulty *is* the way."

Shep was taken aback. "This you already know?"

"From you. Many years ago."

He looked pleased. "Don't worry," Shep consoled me, "if you don't find the arch right away, eventually it will find you. You must come again and tell me what effect the old ones have on you and what you are learning from them. Pertinent information for us gray spirits in training."

I assured Shep he would be among the first to know.

As I was standing at the door about to leave, Shep gave me a hug and said, "May the wind be at your back and beautiful thoughts on your horizon. *Auf Wiedersehen*, gray spirit."

"*Auf Wiedersehen*, Shep," I shouted back as I descended the stair-way.

ONE WAY GLASS

Two weeks after my visit with Shep, I was on my way to bring phi-losophy to a group of older adults. A twenty-minute walk from my home to the senior center took me across the capital campus, a network of red tile and concrete plazas framed, on one side, by Corinthian columns and, on the other, by precast concrete façades. Everywhere, past and present, old and new, antiquity and modernity, stood juxtaposed.

A few minutes later, I arrived at the center, a modest single-story building with large one-way plate glass windows on which block letters read: SENIOR CENTER OF THURSTON COUNTY. I saw my reflection walking toward the building, but could not see what was inside. I hesitated for a moment, uncertain—was I prepared? I pushed open the door and was immediately engulfed by an unmistakable aroma—that of oven-baked chicken.

Looking to my right, I saw a living room–like arrangement. Some people were reading, others talking. I heard the clacking of billiards but could not see the players. At the end of the corridor, directly ahead, I observed a large commons area from which the sounds of a piano, fiddle, and bass were emanating. Had I stepped back in time?

I spent a few minutes looking around and decided this was probably a good place to be. I liked the vitality of the men playing pool, the ladies gossiping in the gift shop, the animated dancers swinging and stepping to the wash basin rhythms of a "kitchen band" after a luncheon of Wednesday's most popular meal—the chicken. This could be fertile soil for a sower of intellect.

Since my course was free of charge, I expected a roomful of participants. I was a little taken aback when only seven people showed up. Undaunted, I stood before the group—just as Mrs. Sheppler had predicted, six Penelopes and one Ulysses—and explained the idea of my proposed course, "Discovering Philosophy through Autobiography."

Walking back and forth before the seven people and the rows of unoccupied folding chairs, I explained how we would read passages from philosophers' autobiographical writings. "These will help us experience the ways great minds lived out their ideas through actions, feelings, and choices of daily existence. The loves, losses, and discoveries of the famous thinkers will reveal the ideas and ideals to which they had dedicated their lives. In turn, reading their memoirs will provide us with models for examining our own life experiences."

I suppose it did sound a bit abstract but, once we got underway, I was sure my older students would be enthralled. Who could fail to be moved by Saint Augustine's account of his teenage lust, or John Stuart Mill's mental crisis and subsequent love affair with Harriet Taylor, or Simone de Beauvoir's rebellion against bourgeois values and her feminist awakenings?

I went on to explain that we are all philosophers when we pause occasionally to wonder: What can I know, how can I know it, how then should I act? "These, the three big questions the German philosopher Kant said every philosophy must address, correspond to three major branches of philosophy: ontology, epistemology, and ethics. So we almost can't help doing philosophy. And when we observe a sunset, a painting, or listen to music and wonder about what makes something beautiful, why, then, we are engaged in the study of aesthetics."

"While philosophers reflect on the relationship between beauty and truth," I continued, "the arts, such as poetry and literature, also may reflect philosophical quests. Take T. S. Eliot, whose poetry is filled with metaphysical speculation. He describes time as a spiral that brings us back to previous moments in which we may have 'had the experience but missed the meaning.' Through recollection we might discover or recover those meanings, doing so with an intensity that makes it feel 'as if for the first time.' And what might have seemed a uniquely personal experience, says Eliot, when newly understood, might now speak to us not of our life alone 'But of many generations.' This, then, should be our task, this spiraling back through time to retrieve the meanings of the personal past and to evaluate their enduring value."

It was a heady speech. I thought I'd better pause to gauge the effects my enthusiasm was having on the group. The six ladies and one gentleman looked at me kindly. They smiled. Then one pushed back her chair and stood. She said she wished to make a few things clear to me. First, my class sounded like it had something to do with spiritual matters. That was unfortunate, because earlier in the week two center members had argued heatedly about religion. The center director suggested that theology should probably be debated elsewhere. Second, as to philosophy, "most older people had pretty well made up their minds by now. And, third . . ."

Had I made a mistake about these fonts of past knowledge? After all, what did I know about old people? My mother's father, a Russian immigrant, had been a bootlegger and died when I was still a child. His first wife, my grandmother, was a small, kind woman with old country ways. She had died a few years before him, and I had only faint memories of her. My only living grandmother was famous for apple pies made with dense cookie dough. She delighted me, when I was a child, by chasing her grown sons, my father included, around her house when their teasing provoked the matriarch in her. Her husband, who died before my birth, was reported by my uncles to have been a tyrant. Why, then, should I expect illumination from old folks?

"And, third, I came in here to wait for a ride from my niece, and I see," she said, pointing to the one-way glass at a figure passing by, "that she's come for me." The woman—I never learned her name—gathered her things and left. Now there were six.

I thought that would pretty much do it for philosophy, literature, and life history. A course that ended before it began. Disheartened, I sat down, uncertain what to do next. Then one of the ladies, a small, wiry redhead, turned to me, shook her head, and said, "Let's get started."

"Yes, by all means," agreed another woman. The rest nodded enthusiastically.

I had found my crew. Now would I find the arch of experience that could make the past a portal to the future?

fALLING OVER HERACLITUS

Plato and Schopenhauer would have been challenged to draw a single portrait of old age had they encountered the individuals who made up our group at the senior center. Preoccupied at times with memory and the past, at other times with hopes and expectations about the future, they ranged from a widowed farm woman with less than eight years of formal schooling to a retired college French teacher, a 1927 graduate of the Sorbonne, in Paris. Until recently, philosophers were concerned primarily about aging men. They might not have taken an interest in our group of five women, Virgil, a retired state government worker, and me.

There we were, huddled around bunched-together card tables in the center's only quiet activity room. Our closeness was partly a sign of the members' growing fondness for one another and partly a matter of necessity. The walls of the room were poorly insulated and let through the sound of phones ringing—people calling about rides to doctors, the price of a hot lunch, help for a lonely parent, or the date for the next center-sponsored dance.

A consistent pattern emerged over the weeks we were meeting. At each session, I would distribute selections from works of philosophy and literature for our subsequent discussion. I'd begin each session with a brief talk, enough to orient the group to the main ideas of the author under discussion. Then we'd go at it, just as in my college philosophy seminars.

Lately, we'd been sharing stories of prior times and wondering how much the world had changed, yet stayed the same. I mentioned the nineteenth-century German philosopher Friedrich Nietzsche, who believed that the world is subject to patterns of eternal recurrence, an endless cycle of repeating episodes. Virgil, a squat, bald man with a halo of white hair that gave him a slightly angelic look, agreed: "It's true, I tell the same stories over and over." We laughed, but he insisted, adding that nothing in life really ever changes. Our Sorbonne graduate, Dorothy, a heavyset woman with stringy hair the color of cinders, disagreed with Virgil and Nietzsche. "Our lives are unique," she claimed. "And each of us has a role to play in making the world a better place."

Despite his idea of life as a perpetual cycle, Nietzsche made some interesting observations about the value of remembering the past. We are unlike other animals, such as cows grazing in a field, whose lives are "neither bored nor painful," because they are unencumbered by what human beings cannot escape—memory. While such animals live blissfully in an eternal present, we humans cannot learn to forget. We cling to the past. For Nietzsche, to be human is to live historically.

What, then, is the value of this capacity for remembering? Nietzsche, in a meditative essay entitled "On the Uses and Disadvantages of History for Life," identifies three possible ways we can relate to history, which he calls monumental, antiquarian, and critical. We can celebrate the monumental achievements of heroes of former times, deriving comfort and inspiration from their greatness. We can collect and show reverence for the artifacts of past knowledge. Or we can set ourselves up as critics who may judge actions and actors of former times. Through such a critical relationship to history, we daringly confront our inherited and hereditary nature, in an attempt to give ourselves a "past in which one would like to originate."

For Nietzsche, history is not only a scholarly subject taught in school; it is crucial for how we conduct our lives. History should benefit mankind. Yet an excess of history, a mind that can forget nothing but beholds, like the ancient Greek philosopher Heraclitus, the stream of becoming—"everything flowing asunder in moving points"—may overwhelm us, rendering us incapable of further action. On the other hand, a deficiency of history will condemn us to indolence, repetition, wandering in a featureless landscape without the means to gauge either progress or regress.

To Nietzsche, we are all historians, each person the chronicler of his or her life. What type of history do we practice on ourselves? Are there, then, times when it is better to forget, and other times crucial for us to remember? When do we need to revere what our memories bring forth, or when to critically reconstruct the past? And what of our personal heroes, indebtedness to traditions, angry judgment of deeds done to us, remorseful judgment of things we have done ourselves?

Dorothy insisted that liberation movements gaining prominence during the bicentennial showed we could no longer be satisfied with monumental or antiquarian types of history, because they tended to reinforce the status quo. We were just beginning to hear about the histories of women and ethnic minorities, which underscored Nietzsche's emphasis on critical history. Virgil wasn't too sure. He'd grown up on stories about the founding fathers and the achievements of America, and felt we needed to secure our future by promoting patriotism. He'd vote for antiquarian history.

Somewhere in the lively debate that followed about history and memory, Dorothy burst out with the line "In my beginning is my end." That silenced the group. What did she mean? "It's from T. S. Eliot," Dorothy explained, "from his poem the *Four Quartets*. Our future is already wrapped up in the past."

The poem, a lengthy meditation on time encountered in memory and through imagination, weaves together elements of Eliot's personal history, Christian and Hindu spiritual outlooks, and reflection on the language and function of poetry. Filled with scholarly references, the poem could be heavy going. Yet it might serve our group as a guide to making similar connections in our own lives. "Should we try reading some of it?" I asked the class members. They were enthusiastic. After all, our esteemed Dorothy found it worthwhile.

FOUR QUARTETS

"Today," I began, "we're going to begin discussing the *Four Quartets*, written between 1935, when Eliot was forty-seven, and 1942, the darkest period of the war in Britain. Each section of the *Quartets* examines a moment in the author's life when he arrived at certain personal and philosophical insights about time, history, love, and salvation. Four place-names in England supply the titles of the poem's four sections. 'East Coker,' for instance, was the homestead of the Eliot family before their emigration to America in the seventeenth century, and 'Little Gidding' was the resort of an Anglican community to which Eliot was attracted in his conversion to the Church of England. The first *Quartet*, 'Burnt Norton,' our topic for today, is the name of an abandoned house with garden and reflecting pool in the Cotswold Hills area that Eliot once visited with a lady friend, and where he had some sort of visionary experience."

"Visionary?" interjected Virgil, his mischievous blue eyes sparkling above the half-lens glasses that had slid down behind the ball of his nose. "You mean he had trouble with the bifocals? It happens, you know, around that age. Pres-by-opia," he pronounced slowly. Then, with a satisfied grin and raised eyebrows, he cast a glance from side to side. In his vintage, double-breasted brown serge suit and short, wide polka-dot necktie, Virgil was something of the class clown.

"Now, Virgil, really," came an exasperated voice, "I'm sure the poet was not talking about bifocals, or even"—Mary removed her own silver frames, held them up to the light—"or even trifocals." A former high school teacher who knew how to handle attention-seeking students like Virgil, Mary was a tall, handsome woman with long grayish-brown hair she braided, wound, and pinned atop her head like a crown. She usually came to class primly attired in paisley-print dresses and white-lace collars. I picture her extracting a handkerchief from her long sleeve. Then the room would smell like lilacs or violets. Now she wiped a lens on her sleeve, saying, "The poet must have had a mystical experience. Isn't that it?" She looked at me for confirmation.

"Yes," I said, "some would call it that. We'll get there in a minute. But first let's listen as Eliot presents us with several hypotheses about time." Speaking professorially, I intoned, "'Time present and time past / Are both perhaps present in time future.'" I glanced at the expectant faces. "'And time future contained in time past.'" Mary smoothed the skin of her cheek. I felt as if I were leading them into a carnival hall of mirrors. "'If all time is eternally present /'"—I hesitated, then lowered my voice for the conclusion—"'All time is unredeemable.'"

Someone let out a sigh. It was Effie, a proud former Kentucky woman who called herself a "briar," a hillbilly. She looked up at the clock on the wall as if searching for clues to the poet's meaning. Tight, curly, bluish-tinted hair and a tanned, leathery complexion made Effie look both glamorous and worn. She'd left school in the eighth grade, which everyone in the group except me knew was common for many people of her generation. Was asking Effie to consider abstract metaphysical statements about time more than I should have expected?

There was no turning back. I plunged onward, giving dramatic emphasis to the line " 'What might have been is an abstraction.' " Grace fingered the string of pearls around her neck. Like Effie, Grace had quit school after the eighth grade. A rather dour person who, we learned over the weeks, had grown up on a farm in Idaho, Grace had married a farmer, moved to Washington State, where they raised wheat in the Palouse of eastern Washington, and had a child, Billy, who was born developmentally disabled. After her husband died, she and the boy moved to Olympia, where they lived in an apartment building downtown. Grace was devoted to Billy, a hulking, happy-go-lucky fellow, now in his forties. She would bring Billy with her to the center, where he played pool with the older men. They were tolerant, in part because he was a terrific pool player, in part because he wasn't ashamed to express his affection for them.

" 'Remaining a perpetual possibility,' " I droned on, " 'Only in a world of speculation.' " I looked at the petite and sinewy Hildegard, who nodded as if Eliot's words were the most obvious statements in the world. In Hildegard, matter and energy were inextricably woven. Her every gesture and expression had an exuberant quality, a purposefulness. She left no doubt who was the helmsman of her life. Hildegard was the only one of the women who wore pants to the center. It was she I most admired, maybe because of that take-charge, life-affirming energy I sometimes felt missing in myself. Watching Hildegard was like being hooked up to a battery.

Encouraged, I continued, " 'What might have been and what has been, / Point to one end, which is always present.' " Dorothy leaned forward, resting her chin on her folded hands, and gave Hildegard a conspiratorial look. In retirement, the erudite Dorothy now supplemented a modest teacher's pension by running an animal kennel on the edge of town. Looking at Dorothy, I'd think of the philosophical theory that body and mind exist in a dualism. Her mind was sharp, insightful, daring, dashing. But her body, usually covered in loose-fitting, printed dresses, was shapeless; her bones prone to fracture because of osteoporosis; her right eye, she once showed me, partly veiled by a cataract. Perhaps she had been married, perhaps she had always lived with another woman, as she did now.

I looked nervously at the faces. It was probably going to take a lot of explaining to untangle this metaphysical conundrum.

"Ron," said Dorothy, "you do understand what Eliot's talking about, don't you?" Dorothy sat back, putting her massive arms behind her head. I had prepared a set of notes about the poem's various references and meanings, but over the weeks I'd found that our discussions were more successful when members of the group played an active part in making sense of the readings. I nodded to Dorothy that she should continue.

"Yes, well, I just thought since you, I mean being Jewish, you might not be as personally familiar with Eliot's Anglicanism— you know, his theology—as some of us raised closer to the tradition." I did know something about Eliot's theology, but Dorothy was right, mine was an outsider's knowledge. It wasn't a challenge, but an offer of assistance. I would let her run with the ball.

Dorothy glanced at Hildegard, whose husband, Al, we learned recently, was a minister before studying to become a psychologist. Hildegard smiled knowingly at Dorothy.

"You see," said Dorothy, her hands pressed together as if in prayer, "the view of time unique to Christianity is that the beginning and ending points are already established." She leaned forward, resting her elbows on the table. "This isn't necessarily my belief. I'm just telling you how things stand in the traditional Anglican view. You see, the end"—she extended her left hand, pointing with the index finger—"that's the return of Christ, the time of redemption. And the beginning"—she extended her right hand, pointing in the opposite direction—"that's the Annunciation, when Mary learns she will give birth to a being who is both a god and human."

Dorothy wiggled the opposing fingers and continued, "These are the fixed, we might even say, timeless points between which our lives"—she bowed her head toward the invisible line between them—"are located." Then she shrugged her shoulders, "Of course, we have our own parents, our trials and tribulations, beginnings and endings. That's our story. But, from Eliot's point of view, that's less important. You see, dear friends, our little story can only be understood as part of this big story. The story of the fall of man into sin and his, or should I say her, redemption from sin. That's the story Eliot takes to frame personal history. So, you see, the end, the culmination of time, well, in this sense, I guess you could say the past and the present already foretell the future."

I glanced around at the others and saw mixed expressions of awe and bewilderment on several faces. Dorothy was way ahead of us.

"Dorothy, aren't you leaving something out?" asked Mary. "What about this idea that if time is eternally present, why then it's unredeemable? Now, what do you suppose that means?"

Dorothy looked at me. Shrugged. "Ron's the philosopher."

"Mary," I responded, "I think I can clear that up. You see, in the tradition of people who believed in the great myths, such as the ancient Greeks, time was cyclical, like the seasons. Everything repeated over and over, just as Nietzsche was to believe. In that sense, as Plato says, time is a moving image of eternity. Our individual lives are part of a never-ending cycle, and no power can be found that might disrupt the unchangeable pattern and modify it. So the flow of time cannot be altered, events undone. In Judaism and Christianity, a divine being enters history at unique, unrepeatable moments, like his God appearing to Moses on Mount Sinai, or like Jesus talking to the Roman soldiers. The cyclical pattern is broken open so that the past can take on new meanings and hold new possibilities."

We were wading into some pretty deep theological water; maybe even breaking the center director's stricture against discussing religion. I noticed Virgil drumming his fingers on the table, a sign that he was about to speak. "Teacher," said Virgil, who persisted in calling me that, "teacher, haven't we overlooked something?"

"Yes, Virgil," I replied, "what is it?"

"What are these funny hedges along the top of the poem?"

"Funny hedges?" At first I didn't understand. Virgil held up his copy of the poem and pointed. Now I saw; he meant the two epigrams from Heraclitus at the beginning of the poem. I guess, if you weren't familiar with them, sentences in Greek script might resemble rows of prickly vines. I had planned to skip over the epigrams until we'd gotten further along; the Greek would intimidate some of our members. Yet I knew Virgil would insist that we put first things first.

"Virgil," I said, "those are quotations in Greek from the ancient philosopher Heraclitus. The one Nietzsche mentions."

Virgil raised his eyebrows and asked, "Harry who?" Virgil had been cooped up for years in one of those state office cubicles shuffling papers and writing numbers all his life. Now, free to meander, he wanted to know about everything.

"Her-a-cli-tus," I responded, sounding out the name, only to realize a moment later that Virgil, now grinning, was teasing me. I continued, "All we have of his writings are fragments preserved in commentaries by other philosophers, mostly those living before Plato's time. The first fragment translates to something like 'Although the logos is common to all, most people live as if each one had a private understanding,' and the second says simply, 'The way up and the way down are one and the same.' The brevity of the fragments makes it difficult to understand what Heraclitus might have meant. Some scholars think he does that on purpose, puts these statements oddly, like riddles, so you have to figure them out."

"I don't understand, Ron," said Effie, pursing her lips, her arms folded, "what's a Greek got to do with it?"

"Eliot was a well-educated, scholarly sort of person. He may have chosen the epigrams to notify the reader that his poem will deal with ancient wisdom and esoteric knowledge about unchanging truths. Though Eliot is one of the pillars of modern poetry, he doesn't accept modern ideas about progress that might lead us to undervalue the past and think that only the present is important. Maybe he's using Heraclitus to remind us that even though things change, some things stay the same. We need to pay attention to the timeless as well as the temporal."

"You mean we should stop pretending we're know-it-alls?" said Mary, looking pointedly at Virgil. Mary and Virgil were always going at each other. Still, I sensed they liked each other, liked fussing at one another.

"Well," I replied, "or question whether what we know is all there is. The second epigram suggests that even though things may look different, depending on whether you're ascending or descending a path, really, it's the same path. Maybe Heraclitus was thinking of a circle. The ancient Greeks symbolized life by a wheel divided into four quadrants. Each life completes a circle."

That seemed to make sense to the group, so I went further. "Heraclitus believed in a theory of cosmic change, that all matter is in a state of flux. There is a downward tendency through which fire, the highest element, turns into water, which turns into earth; and a countermovement in which earth moves upward through water and fire. Did Heraclitus mean this literally, or was he speaking in metaphors? It's something of a mystery to me."

"Teacher, teacher," Virgil was bouncing up and down in his chair, "now I get it."

"Oh?" I said.

"Harry what's-his-name is right," exclaimed Virgil; "the way up and down are the same." He started talking about elevators, escalators, mountain climbing, digestion, double-entry bookkeeping, bank balances, the stock market, the rise and fall of civilizations, sleeping and waking. God, I thought, he's spinning out of control. Falling over Heraclitus, I'll never get us through the poem. I looked over and saw Dorothy gazing at Virgil, her mouth hanging open. Then, to my utter surprise, she started to clap her hands, applauding him.

"Bravo, Virgil," she said. "You've got it, you're living up to your namesake."

"Namesake?" I asked. I looked at Virgil. He didn't know what she was talking about either.

"Oh, come now, gentlemen, the famous Virgil, the author of the *Aeneid*. Remember Dante's *Inferno*?" asked Dorothy. Virgil, dubious about what was to follow, eyed Dorothy above his half-rim glasses.

"It's the Latin poet Virgil who comes to guide Dante into the underworld, where he's going to gain moral truths from real and legendary dead people about the mistakes and sins they've made in life. So, you see," said Dorothy, "our very own Virgil is doing the same for us. He's got the basic insight from Heraclitus that if

you have the courage to go down into the depths of your soul and face all your fears, phobias, weaknesses, and vulnerabilities, then you can come back up a better, stronger, and smarter person. The way down and the way up, don't you see, they're connected."

I marveled at Dorothy's ability as a teacher to find the vein of gold in the mass of dross and bring it out so even a rascal like Virgil began to look like a sage. Dorothy helped people experience their own brilliance, helped them shine. A great gift for an educator. And it certainly worked with Virgil, who, beaming with pride, announced, "I stand at the zenith of a long line of Virgils." We all laughed.

Of course, Mary had to respond, "Virgil, this just proves the ancient Greek's truth that your top and your bottom are connected." We all laughed again. This time Virgil wasn't pleased, and I knew he was going to fire off a blast at Mary unless I could keep us on track. Fortunately, Hildegard stepped into the breach.

VARIATIONS ON A THEME

"Dorothy, from what you've told us, don't you think that Heraclitus, like Eliot, could be talking about how we experience time?"

Dorothy gave Hildegard a quizzical look. Sometimes it seemed they had rehearsed these routines. "Yes," said Hildegard, who spread her hands on the table, "when I look at my hands, I see my mother's hands. And lately, when I'm in a conversation, it's like my father is talking through me. I'm saying things he'd have said, having his thoughts. Of course, we are different people from different generations. Everything changes, like Heraclitus says, it's all in flux, but there's a pattern . . ."

Hildegard paused, holding us in suspense, and then came forth with this question: "Isn't it possible that the past repeats itself through us? That what Heraclitus means by the road up and down is not literally direction in space but the past and the future?"

After Hildegard made her point, it was like a rabbit let out of the gate. We went running after it.

"I like that idea," said Dorothy, "and it probably fits Eliot's viewpoint that what really matters is what stays the same despite change, like God's enduring love for mankind, the possibility of redemption, the incarnation of Christ that brings eternity into personal history."

"Yes, that's just what I mean," Hildegard responded, "what's always present. We think we're each different, unique, and we are. But how important are these differences? We put so much emphasis on being individuals. Then, eventually, we realize we're living out a familiar pattern, not the same one exactly, but we've got a lot more in common with our folks and their folks, and with one another than we thought earlier in life when being different seemed so important."

Dorothy responded to Hildegard like the cello to the violin, "But, dear Hildegard, aren't we responsible for our own lives, responsible for what we each have to be and do? I love that line from Simone de Beauvoir where she says she was born to fulfill the great need she had of herself. We each have our own special mission in life that only we can perform. That's why I disagree with Eliot's narrow Christian view. I think we redeem ourselves, our pasts. Look, for example, at what we women have done to liberate ourselves. Would Eliot's God have done that?" Dorothy shook her head. "Some progress is real, despite Mr. Eliot."

The conversation was getting pretty heavy. Could the rest of the group follow? I was relieved when Effie and Grace decided to join the conversation.

"Speakin' of childhood memories," Effie started in with her mountain girl accent, "when I was a mere slip of a lass on our farm in Kentucky, I had a favorite horse I'd ride all over tarnation." Effie tapped the eraser end of a pencil on the table.

"One day," Effie continued, "my horse, Chester, up and breaks his ankle by tripping over a drainage ditch. I loved to take him out jumping over low bushes and stumps. You see, there was a thin layer of snow on the ground, and he'd not spotted the ditch. Served me right for taking him out in such weather. One moment we was up, the next I was on the ground. Thrown, though not badly hurt, just shaken up. I was a tough kid back then. The horse had to be done in, and I was real sad. Oh, I cried and cried over that horse, and blamed myself. But my daddy said, 'Honey, he'd be glue someday anyway. Weren't your fault, neither, 'cause you're not in charge of all that happens in this life.' My daddy was a kindly man," said Effie, but you could see traces of pain in the lines around her eyes, "though he could be rough at times, specially after he'd taken a few too many nips of the jug."

Then, in the way Dorothy and Hildegard played off each other, Grace like a viola responded to Effie's second violin part. We didn't often hear from her; she tended to sit quietly, arms folded as if in judgment. But today she was another woman.

"Effie's got it right," said Grace. "There's a lot from our early days worth remembering. Fresh like when it first happens." Grace pulled out the photocopied pages I had distributed the preceding week. I could see what looked like crayon markings all over the text. She had drawn lines around the section of "Burnt Norton" right after the philosophical part about time.

"Now, I don't have much schoolin'," she told us, "and I'm not comfortable with all that high-minded stuff, but I hear these footsteps. I really do." She pointed to an underlined section beginning with "Footfalls echo in the memory," where Eliot takes the reader down the passage and through a doorway into the rose garden. He describes staring down into the dry and cracked reflecting pool and seeing a mirage. The pool is suddenly filled with "water out of sunlight." And from the depths of that water, he envisions a lotus flower floating silently to the surface. The poem conveys an intense feeling of joy. A moment later, a cloud passes over and the vision vanishes.

Grace explained, "See, I once had a beautiful rose garden my husband, Gene, God rest his soul, and me used to love to walk in. Well, it didn't have no door or gate, like that. But just hearing the poet tell about it, about what could've been but, maybe didn't cause, well . . ." And here she paused and swallowed hard.

"He died young," she continued. "TB. Weren't no cure for it back then. Terrible sickness." Wiping something from her eye, she said, "It pains me to recollect, but it helps a deal, too." Then she pulled herself upright, lifted her chin, and kind of nodded to herself. She had said enough.

Grace took Eliot personally. He was talking directly to her about redeeming the past, working through sorrow over life's disappointments. What could be a better connection to Eliot's Christian view? And as for Heraclitus, wasn't Grace connecting her private pain to something common, something everyone in the group could understand, could feel?

My own education had made me expect a certain level of response, more conceptual, more scholarly. Yet that was one of the things I often complained about, how remote and disembodied I found intellectual encounters with colleagues at conferences. I wanted them to personalize their knowledge, wanted to do the same for myself. Yet, with my senior center group, it was often the other way around. I wanted them to intellectualize.

After Grace talked about her husband and the rose garden, there was a moment of silence. Then Virgil turned to me and asked, "What about your footfalls, Ron?" He looked around at the others, for moral support, I suppose, because he went on, "What is it that would make a nice young fellow like yourself come spend time with a bunch of old folks?"

"You're not that old," I said, falteringly. It was a foolish remark. My turn had come to open up.

THE USES OF THE PAST

"Like Eliot," I said, "I've been wondering about the meaning of the past. Somewhere in my middle teen years, I began to have the feeling that I was a visitor to life, a wanderer just passing through. I held myself slightly aloof, which made me feel free, feel superior. I had a secret belief: nothing could be possessed, only borrowed. History? That was just a series of random events. The things that happen to you." Wasn't it arbitrary that I had been born to a particular set of parents named Irving and Marion, grew up in a neighborhood of two-story brick houses where silver maples made pools of cool shadow on summer lawns?

"By the time I got to college, I had decided that growing up meant the past was something you needed in order to push off into the wider world. It receded behind you; you only looked ahead. I discovered that this attitude was not unique to my generation. My parents had fled their past, or at least the parts that were demeaning. I remember the stories. An alcoholic, abusive father, undignified work, superstitions from villages whose names had long been forgotten, prejudices against Jews and ones they turned against themselves.

"My father became a businessman, he wore white shirts, was kind to us children. Ours was a life of regularity. We ate dinner at an appointed hour. My mother, who had worked from childhood in an outdoor market, became a modern housewife. Unlike her own immigrant parents, she never raised her voice or her fists against kith and kin. In their new life, seemingly freed from the past, our parents had bestowed the gifts of sufficiency and security upon my sister and me. But, to me, these gifts became walls. An ungrateful son, I sought to escape the boredom of a predictable middle-class life. Overly cautious, I yearned for adventure."

I paused, studied the faces of the people I now viewed as fellow seekers. How small and heroic their faces looked against the drab background of pale green painted walls lit by overhead fluorescent bulbs. I had never given a thought to or appreciated the sheer strength of survival or that, despite personal losses and disappointment, these individuals had kept the flame of interest and concern burning, if at times only faintly.

"My illumination took another form than Eliot's reflecting pool," I continued. "Rather, returning home from college for visits, I would leaf through family photo albums and school year books. There I was, page after page, year after year, laughing, poised, happy—a satisfied smile playing on my lips. What I now saw beneath the glossy surface of those pictures was an unformed self, one who's lost, adrift, perpetually daydreaming. I'd sought the freedom to invent myself, but a weight still dragged at my heel.

"One day, fantasizing about my possibilities, I awoke and saw myself. I was part of the past.

"In graduate school, I came across the phrase 'Becoming historical to oneself,' in a book written by the nineteenth-century Danish philosopher Kierkegaard. Like the words of Heraclitus, this phrase had in it something enticing, mysterious, almost magical. The words could form a riddle: 'Who is it that becomes historical to himself?' A maxim: 'Seek ever to become historical to yourself.' An incantation: 'Become, become, become . . . yourself.'

"Kierkegaard's phrase, I learned, referred to a life transformation occurring around the age when the dreams of youth fade and the visions of adulthood arise—probably somewhere in one's middle twenties—which I was, just then. For the generation of young men with whom I grew up, life in youth and early adulthood was filled with meanings to discover and purposes to invent. Meanings were garnered through romances, travel, education, political action, aesthetic experiences. We lived for the moment, wandered like nomads, journeyed on heroic quests for higher consciousness. Eventually, these experiences lost some of their glamour and vitality. The journey brought us to predictably similar destinations: choices about partners, jobs, places to live, children, religion, money, happiness."

I paused again. Would this make any sense to them? Probably only Dorothy and Hildegard had heard of Kierkegaard. I was so middle-class, compared with Grace and Effie. The tests of my life were literally that, college quizzes. But in recent years my life had gotten tougher. I knew what it meant to be out of work, the humiliation of applying for food stamps, the worry that a child's illness and doctor's bills might mean a late mortgage payment. Had Kierkegaard, who had neither wife nor children and lived on a small inheritance, troubled himself over such mundane matters, or only over weighty issues like the "teleological suspension of the ethical" he pondered in discussing the biblical Abraham's "leap of faith"? No, Kierkegaard knew hardship. Just a different kind.

"Kierkegaard was right," I continued. "A life lived for the intensities of each moment would eventually grow tiresome because moments are fleeting and the results desultory. Experiences accumulate only to vaporize. What did I have to show for myself; what endured? For me, life was a series of rehearsals, but no opening performance." Philosophically, my state of becoming lacked belonging, continuity, a lasting sense of selfhood.

"I know that becoming historical to oneself sounds awfully academic, terribly self-conscious. Still, the phrase beguiled me, calling, 'Step onto your unique path; feel it press back against your feet.' But I resisted, answering, 'The image of a single path is an illusion.' I thought of all the detours I'd taken in life, often with divided intentions, fostering multiple selves. And I'd rarely taken the paths alone. There were my parents, sister, friends, lovers, my wife and children, grandparents, my ancestors. To me, the single sojourner was an abstraction.

"I knew I was resisting Kierkegaard's exhortation 'Choose yourself. Give birth to yourself.' But I was reluctant, answering, 'I am a wanderer, a parentless child.' Yet there was something I couldn't deny. However arbitrary many of my meanderings and however random my encounters, over time they became the ones I had, and not others. I heard Eliot's exhortation, at the end of the *Four Quartets*, never to cease exploring, yet to arrive where I had started, 'And know the place for the first time.' Could I now possess the streets, houses, people, the shadows, toys, books, the emotional ties, even the distances . . . possess them as though for the first time?

"That's what drew me to Kierkegaard's theory that we are each drawn, by stages, toward a unique future, a destiny which we are free to embrace or reject. How simple an idea, that by choosing it, I could change my personal history from a weight to a source of energy. Choosing was action, not reaction. So I said yes to my past, chose it. And, almost at once, I felt new energy course through my body and mind."

With that, I paused. Like Grace, I felt I had said enough. There was more I could not say. How that energy had taken many forms: producing finished essays and articles, joining with my beloved in an enduring relationship, bringing forth children, choosing an occupation. It had meant working out my inherited destiny with its bootlegger grandfather and apple pie grandmother, an uncle bumped off by the mob (after whom I was named), my parents' lives and my father's death, a sister from whom I had grown distant, a religion from which I had fled, the houses, sidewalks, streetlights, the memory of which shaped me in more ways than I could ever fully comprehend.

I now realized what had drawn me to the senior center to teach this class. I wanted to feel the weight of history, bear it gracefully; to place my life in the context of generations, to understand that becoming a self, achieving individuality, also meant belonging to the world and to others. With her comment on Heraclitus, Hildegard had put her finger on a truth about the uses of the past: sometimes the way back is the way forward.

Our origins, families, legacy of the past can be a weight from which we try to free ourselves. But forgetting doesn't work. We have to make the best of what we've got, to turn it, as Nietzsche says about critical history, to our own advantage.

ONE OF US

After my little speech, the room was quite still. Mary took out one of her handkerchiefs and enveloped us in the scent of lilacs. The members of the group studied me. What was it they now saw?

Then someone broke the silence. "Mama?" It was the voice of a child-man. "Mama, we gotta be goin' now." He had been standing in the doorway, quietly, patiently, for I don't know how long—Grace's son, Billy.

"Yes, Billy," said Grace. "But, first, come over and say hello to your friends." She motioned him to come nearer.

"Hi, everybody. Hi, hi," said Billy. He seemed delighted to see us and walked full circle around the table, touching the backs of each person's chair until he stood behind his mother. Grace looked up at him and smiled. "My gift," she said. "Don't know what I'd do without him." Grace gathered her papers, put them into a large handbag, arose, and took Billy's hand. The rest of us started to put things away, to push back chairs.

We said our good-byes. I told them I hoped we could continue with the poem next week. "I think I'm going to learn Greek," said Virgil.

I was closing up my briefcase when Hildegard came over to me. "That was good," she said. "You're letting people get to know you. To know your mind." She reached out, took my hand between hers and held it for a moment. I felt her cool skin, the bones of her thin fingers. Then she craned her neck, looked up at me, and whispered, "Now you're one of us."

CHAPTER THREE

PHILOSOPHERS IN LOVE

In the *Quartets* Eliot urged old men to "be explorers." Yet he used old age as a symbol of frailty and finitude, contrasting the "folly," "fears, and frenzy" of the elderly to the timeless world of spiritual inwardness. Eliot was skeptical about progress and self-improvement, dual ideals inherited from eighteenth-century humanism and empirical science; the goal of establishing a rational, secular society was anathema to him. He regarded the idea of movement toward a perfect society as an illusion of modern times. Self-improvement was impossible, Eliot believed, without surrender to the will of a higher being. He admired the spirituality of the Middle Ages, when church and community were bound in close communion. Yet who wanted to return to a society dominated by church authority or to live under rigid class and gender norms? Certainly not the women in our group.

Someone—I think it was Mary—suggested we'd had enough of religious piety and political conservatism. "How about a radical type?" she asked. Then, someone else—Virgil, I believe—said he thought we'd spent too much time talking about our pasts. "It's fine what we old people have to say, but what about young folks? Why don't you bring some of your young college students to the senior center?"

Responding to Mary's request, I suggested we read a chapter from the autobiography of a nineteenth-century radical political thinker, John Stuart Mill. I explained that Mill, in contrast to Eliot, favored self-improvement and social progress without the aid or interference of religion. He had crusaded for women's rights, free speech, public access to information on birth control, and broadened participation in the democratic process. In our era of liberation movements, wouldn't he be a good choice for our consideration? Besides, we could compare Mill's championing the future with Eliot's allegiance to the past.

There was some hesitation. "I've had to teach his difficult essay 'On Liberty' in high school," said Mary, skeptically.

"But," I responded, "have you ever read Mill's account of his mental depression and how he fell in love with a married woman?" Mary shook her head.

"Okay," she demurred, "you know how I love 'soaps.' You've got me hooked."

Then I agreed to Virgil's request, which the others seconded. I would see whether some of my students at the college might want to join our group. I wasn't sure that members of the younger generation, many of them counterculture types, would find it worthwhile to spend time with the "gray spirits," as we dubbed our members. I figured that, like me at their age, they'd have little interest in people of their grandparents' generation. But when I made the invitation to my class at the college, I discovered I was wrong. Almost at once, a handful of willing adventurers came forth.

THE COMING OF YOUTH

My students entered our little classroom at the senior center like characters stepping out of history. Two of the young women, Hannah and Sue Ellen, were attired like Indian maidens in fringed garments and wore their hair in long braids. Two of the men, furry black-bearded Daryl and blond-goateed Frank, could have been pioneer farmers or wilderness preachers in their tattered jeans and faded work shirts. Two others, Diane and Richard, looked entirely different. The downtown restaurant where she worked required Diane to dress in a white blouse and a black short skirt. With her black tights and jet-black hair gathered into a ponytail secured with a ribbon, she looked like a member of the Beat generation. Richard, with his long, narrow, clean-shaven face, cardigan sweater, and khakis, looked 1950ish Ivy League.

The students were enrolled in a year-long freshman course in Western civilization I cotaught with a team of faculty members at the college. We traced early Western civilization from tribal village kinship systems to the fortified cities of ancient Greece and Rome. Pausing along the way to make the course "relevant," we compared kinship patterns and civic tribunals with hippy communes and recent civil rights trials. The students' lives echoed Freud's theme—"civilization and its discontents." Many of them were caught between family traditions and aspirations for social liberation. During office visits with students, I learned that Daryl was gay but hadn't found a way of telling his parents. He had been active in the youth movement at his hometown church and was sure that both his peers and God would reject him. My student Hannah worried about an older boyfriend, soon graduating from college. He wanted her to drop out of school and go live with him on a communal farm in Vermont. "I love him," she told me, "but what about my life goals?" Frank talked to me about his desire to enter a Buddhist monastery in California. A few years earlier, taking time off from school, he had made the trek to Kathmandu. A part of him never returned.

Was there something about these students that attracted them to the senior center? Could they imagine finding their wanderlust and search for intimacy or spirituality engaged by a group of old people? Anything's possible, I thought. After all, it was working for me.

The students took their places in folding chairs around now six pushed-together card tables. Their youthful presence gave the senior center furnishings an even more temporary look, as if the whole place was a stage for a traveling theater group that might pack up and move away in the night.

This was probably the first time my young students had been in a setting dominated by the older generation. I later learned that most hardly knew their own grandparents, though a few had been raised by grandpa and grandma because their parents were divorced, estranged, or unstable. The college students looked clean and wholesome, even with their long hair, beards, bandannas, peasant skirts, beads, and the occasional odor of patchouli oil. They were on good behavior, as though taken for a family visit. My seniors were their usual selves—candid, eager, and rambunctious.

Mill's Depression

After an initial round of introductions, I began, "Consider the following situation. A philosopher and social activist, John, falls in love with another bright social activist, Harriet. Reciprocally, Harriet loves John. However, Harriet is married and has young children, whereas John is a bachelor. Moreover, John is dominated by a father who has devoted long hours home-schooling the lad in Greek, Latin, algebra, economics, political theory, and history, making John a child prodigy. He feels duty-bound to his father in helping him promote an agenda of major social reforms. The father, James, worries about the scandal likely to be visited upon his son since the situation arises in the third decade of the nineteenth century; the place, Victorian England. What would you do in John's or Harriet's place?"

Silence. Who would go first? Frank spoke up. "Rechannel the love by finding a project to work on together that will benefit others."

"Mm, yes," I said, "a very moral thing to do."

"Just be good friends," said the levelheaded Effie.

"Right, that would keep them out of trouble."

"Write a book about it and go on a television talk show," said the indomitable Virgil, grinning broadly to all at the table, especially at Diane, seated beside him.

"Well," I responded, "they had gossip columns in some popular newspapers then. But if you wanted to set people straight and tell your own story, the next-best thing would be to write about the relationship in your autobiography." A few heads nodded. "That is why I've given you a chapter of Mill's life story."

I began by explaining that John Stuart Mill's story was inseparable from his father's. James Mill was born into a poor, rural Scottish family, from whose limited circumstances he escaped thanks to a wealthy benefactor who recognized his intellectual gifts. James Mill went to college and studied to become a minister. He soon discovered his lack of skill in and enthusiasm for preaching. Changing careers, he became a journalist and immersed himself in the laborious project of writing a massive, three-volume *History of India*, which eventually landed him a life long position with the British East India Company, a quasi-governmental bureaucracy that managed trade relations and treaties with India during the colonial administration.

James Mill married Harriet Burrow and proceeded to keep her pregnant. She bore him nine children in twenty years. James disparaged what he believed were Mrs. Mill's lack of intellectual talents. For her part, Mrs. Mill accepted the role of a hardworking, submissive wife. She did her best to manage an ever-growing household while struggling with limited financial resources as her husband worked away at the multivolume history.

James Mill, under the influence of a good friend, the British philosopher Jeremy Bentham, held the theory that a child's mind was a blank slate, a "tabula rasa," upon which experiences left permanent impressions. He reasoned that if a teacher could exercise full control over a pupil's experiences and impressions, through careful guidance and encouragement, then that child would grow to possess an intellect free of false opinion and ungrounded beliefs. There was no limit to what a properly conceived education could do to prepare a young person—regardless of class or gender—with an ideal mind and character. A whole society of such unencumbered, freethinking individuals would fulfill the vision of a liberal society.

It was just that perfect mind and character that James Mill set out to create. By virtue of his considerable native intelligence, the son, John Stuart, received a precocious education under his father's tutelage—one that gave him, he writes in his autobiography, "an advantage of a quarter of a century over my contemporaries."

John Stuart's father's daring educational experiment began with teaching him Greek by the age of three; Latin, at seven; logic, at twelve; and natural sciences and political theory starting at age thirteen. Instead of college, the young Mill joined various clubs of intellectuals who pursued further learning as intellectual co-mentors. John, like his father, espoused what were then called Radical causes promoting new or expanded freedoms. He was a champion of parliamentary reforms, including election of the prime minister, abolition of the monarchy and the House of Lords, establishment of the secret ballot, and appointment of civil servants by competitive examination. While John Stuart, like his father, favored representative government, the elder and the younger Mill differed on the issue of women's suffrage.

Despite this amazing home schooling, writes Mill, he "suffered from a flaw in the theory upon which his education rested." It was all intellect and no feelings. "Real feeling" says Mill, was not just neglected in the family household; it was positively banned. Mill's father possessed great contempt for passionate emotions of all sorts, regarding them as a form of madness. He valued, rather, a concise, factual use of language corresponding to a strictly materialist and empiricist view of reality.

In chapter 5 of the *Autobiography*, Mill describes a near–mental breakdown, the result of a certain set of reflections. He had, he says, relied for his ideal of happiness on the distant outcome of social betterment for which he campaigned. "But the time came when I awakened from this as from a dream," says Mill. He describes an encroaching state of psychological ennui in which he was "unsusceptible to enjoyment or pleasurable excitement." And in this frame of mind he posed to himself the following question. Suppose that your goals in life were realized; that all the social improvement you were looking forward to could be fulfilled at this very instant: would this bring great joy and happiness to you?

Mill says the uncensored reply welled up in him: "No!" The goals for which he was striving "had ceased to charm," and, consequently, he fell into a deep depression.

Mill sought to snap out of this dark mood by reading his favorite books, "those memorials of past nobleness," but to no avail. His feeling of isolation was further intensified when he realized he had no one to turn to. His friendships were not intimate. He couldn't discuss his problems with his father, since James Mill's psychological theories ruled out the possibility of the son's unhappiness. Mill had nothing left but to turn to himself.

He explains that his studies led him to believe that all mental and moral feelings and qualities, of both good and bad kinds, were the result of psychological associations. James Mill had raised his son to associate pleasure with "all things beneficial to the great whole, and pain with all things hurtful to it." But the theory had failed. The association between pleasure and social benefit went no deeper than an intellectual habit of mind. And this tenuous association could not withstand Mill's powers of critical analysis. Thus, Mill despaired: "to know that a feeling would make me happy if I had it, did not give me the feeling."

I paused in the middle of my mini-lecture because Mary was shaking her head. "Mary, is something about this bothering you?" I asked.

"Well, yes," she replied, placing her palm across her forehead. "Was Mill really depressed? I mean seriously? Wasn't he having a typical identity crisis of young adulthood?"

It was a good question. Mill's *Autobiography* is written in a factual, dispassionate style that only occasionally rises to a pitch of emotional expression. "Let me give you an interesting example of Mill's mental state," I said, "then you decide." Mary yielded, for the moment.

"It seems," I continued, "Mill had a great fondness for classical music, especially Mozart. At the onset of his depression, he was tormented by the thought that pleasures are not inexhaustible. He reasoned there are only so many possible combinations of musical notes in creating music. Given all the great composers, most of the combinations had probably been tried. The chances were slim of anyone coming up with wonderful new musical compositions. Musical innovation was at an end. Now, would you call that . . . ?"

Mary frowned. "I'd like to say I'm sympathetic," she said, "but I can't imagine getting worked up over such speculations."

"Okay," I conceded, "at first glance it seems like a minor issue. But, in the context of Mill's life story, it has a larger meaning. His premonition of the end of music was a symptom of his gloom and his sense of the foreclosure of possibility."

"The what of possibility?" exclaimed Virgil.

"Foreclosure," I responded.

"He shouldn't have missed his mortgage payments," Virgil teased, playing to his new audience.

"Right. The bank takes away your house, takes away your chance to own your residence. Only, in Mill's case it was happiness not property that was taken away. The future was sealed shut; the possibilities of life, cut off. An unspoken assumption about life as progress toward a better world, reaching for the goal of happiness . . . suddenly collapsed. Think of it, music, an invisible medium of expression residing solely in time; and the time of future music comes to a halt. Only the musical past remains, glorious as it is. Isn't that one way to describe depression—feeling that advancement is futile, that nothing new can happen? You discover that the world has reached a dead end but everyone around you remains indifferent?"

"Well, maybe," Dorothy intervened, looking around at the others. "Maybe, given his father and his upbringing, Mill might have been clinically depressed. He's not very successful at communicating depression, though he gets the idea across to us. But what troubles me, Ron, is the even more unconvincing story Mill tells of his recovery." I saw several others, including my students, nodding their agreement.

I suppose Dorothy was right. Mill describes breaking the closed circle of depression by turning not to religion or psychology but to literature. Almost accidentally, he happened to be reading the *Mémoires* of Marmontel, a minor French playwright of the eighteenth century, when he came to a passage in which Marmontel describes his father's death and the young son's inspiration to assume the family protector role—to become the surrogate father. "A vivid conception of the scene and its feelings came over me," writes Mill, "and I was moved to tears. From this moment my burden grew lighter."

Mill leaves the reader free to interpret the meaning and mechanism of his catharsis, and various scholars have indeed speculated on Mill's oedipal complex and "death wish" toward his father. Despite his considerable self-reflective powers, Mill does not explain his miraculous transformation, simply implying that he tapped the energy of suppressed emotion locked tightly within his own psyche. What he does tell us is that his liberation from depression and despair produced three major effects on his opinions and character.

First, he altered his life philosophy. No longer would happiness be his direct goal. Instead, he would focus on aiding in the happiness of others, on the improvement of mankind, and on art and other pursuits that he now treated as an "ideal end," not a means. Happiness would now be a by-product of pursuing these goals, not the goal itself. "Ask yourself whether you are happy, and you cease to be so," writes Mill.

Second, he decided to put greater emphasis on the "prime necessities of human well-being, to the internal culture of the individual." He turned his attention to the cultivation of feelings, setting about the task in the best way he knew, through a methodical study of poetry, particularly the Romantic poets of the English Lake District, his contemporaries Wordsworth and Coleridge. Mill adopted the view not that feelings are innate but that the capacity for feeling is intrinsic and can be cultivated and refined through the arts so that feelings become an organic part of one's very being, not merely a set of learned associations.

Mill reached a third conclusion. Instead of regarding his mental crisis as a strictly private and idiosyncratic event, he decided the flaw in his life must be "a flaw in life itself." Mankind, especially his British compatriots, must suffer from a similar deprivation of feeling and deficiency of inner culture. Among his reformist goals, then, should be to champion the value of poetry and imagination as a part of education and the cultivation of feeling. The free development of individuality became Mill's rallying cry.

The corrective Mill gained from Wordsworth's poetry was to find joy not only in political struggle or in the effort to overcome imperfection, the crusader's preoccupations, but in attempting to attain, as he prosaically put it, "states of feeling, and of thought colored by feeling, under the excitement of beauty."

Noticing my young student Sue Ellen fidgeting, I paused again and looked toward her.

"Wow!" she exclaimed. "Is this how philosophers work out their problems?" She gestured nervously with her hands. "Sure a good thing Mill didn't have to see a shrink. He'd never have come up with any of this stuff. They'd give him, like, all these drugs. Make him calm down so he could adjust to society, not change it." Sue Ellen shook her head, the long braids falling across her shoulders. Was she speaking from experience?

"True," I said, responding to Sue Ellen, "there were no mental health counselors to go to then. Beer and gin were popular. Interestingly, opium was being tried by some of the Lake poets. But Mill doesn't seem to have indulged in anything stronger than tea."

"I like the part," interjected Frank, "where he says the flaw in himself was a flaw in society. He turned a mirror of self-scrutiny into a telescope to investigate the planets of society." Frank had a penchant for analogies.

"Yes," I replied, "Mill didn't regard his personal situation as unique. It was something to learn from and apply the lessons to the world around him. Subjective states of mind held important social meanings. That's why he considered his recovery important enough to write about. I think Mill makes it clear that this episode marked his turning away from his father's influence and toward his own independent thinking; away from a life based almost exclusively on intellect, toward one balanced by feeling; away from a psychology resting on a narrow and reductivist set of principles of human nature and toward a broader, more holistic psychology that regards human relationships as not simply competing self-interests, but containing the very real potential of affection and intimacy made possible by individual liberty—that is, the possibility of intimacy between a man and a woman where each is a complete human being of equal worth."

"Ron means," interjected Dorothy, "Mill was turning into a real person with feelings and sensitivity toward others. Isn't that his main message?"

"Yes, succinctly put, thank you," I replied. "But there's something else going on here that links us closely to Mill's life and times." I looked at Hildegard and met her warm smile and encouraging nod. "What Mill discovered," I continued, "was the power of the imagination."

"Where does he say that?" asked Mary.

"He doesn't say it directly in the *Autobiography*. But by quoting the poets Wordsworth and, especially, Coleridge, he conveyed to his contemporaries his belief in the theory at the heart of the Romantic movement, that imagination holds the power to enlarge the world as we know it. Coleridge spoke of a 'shaping' or 'combining' power that enables us to take diverse impressions and meld them into surprising new relationships that sometimes make us feel joyful. When Mill found he could still be moved by literature, he realized a deep inner resource that hadn't been put there by his father. It was truly his own. That was the seed of his recovery. Now he could imagine a different outlook on happiness, on social improvement, on his own combining power. He was liberated."

"Liberated," exclaimed Mary, "by what? By fantasies?"

"Imagination, to Mill, didn't mean fairy tales and probably not Victorian erotic literature. It was the ability to transform the given, the conditions of life, into the possible, the ideal. In one of his essays on religion, Mill claimed that art and imagination open up new ideas and possibilities to which people otherwise would remain blind. My guess is that his experience reading Marmontel didn't immediately resolve his mental crisis. More likely it was an epiphany, one of those illuminating moments. Mill discovered his ability to find meaning in strong emotion."

"And that's just when he met his ideal woman, Harriet Taylor," said Hannah.

"Yes," I responded, "Mrs. Taylor, the beautiful, clever, and passionate Victorian lady with three children whom it should not have been possible for him to love, except perhaps as a friend."

"But with the power of the imagination, he took the plunge," said Hannah.

"And, the music went on, and on," sang Mary.

"The music went on," I agreed.

"And the consequence," said Dorothy, "was that Mill had to decide whether to follow imagination—his combining power—or stick with intellect."

I nodded.

"But how does that link us to Mill?" asked Sue Ellen.

"I think I understand," said Frank. "Aren't we like romantics in an age of scientific reason? We're taught we should be creative, have imaginative thoughts. But when we try to express those thoughts, we're told they're irrational and unacceptable because they threaten the status quo."

"Ron," said Sue Ellen, "you mentioned Mill disagreeing with his father about women's right to vote. How does that fit in?"

"It's part of the imagination problem. You see, Mill could imagine a society that did not yet exist; one that, to most people, seemed implausible. James Mill believed married women's interests were identical with their husbands'. So they didn't need the vote. John Stuart understood that, without self-representation, you missed the opportunity to exercise your liberty—an essential experience if you were to develop fully as a human being. Perhaps this knowledge grew from his own struggles to become a full and separate person. Years later, he would write an essay, together with Harriet Taylor, called 'The Subjection of Women,' in which they claimed that because of women's limited opportunities to exercise their influence and develop full personhood, women were so underdeveloped that, as they put it, 'we hardly know who they are.' "

"But Mill could imagine this future," said Mary.

"Yes," I said, "and that made life both exciting and difficult for him."

"That's like us," said Virgil. "We hardly know who we are."

"Speak for yourself, Virgil," retorted Mary. "I know perfectly well who I am."

Virgil was about to respond, but Hannah jumped in, "You didn't tell us about the love affair between John and Harriet. How did they meet?"

The group began to dissolve into several conversations. Frank was talking to Hildegard, Hannah to Dorothy, Diane to Virgil. Effie stared into space. Grace looked bewildered.

"People, people!" shouted Daryl, trying to bring order to the situation. "Can we slow down for a moment?" he asked. I had never seen Daryl assume the role of moderator, but he managed to get their attention.

"Thank you," I said. "Yes, let's take it one at a time. First, Virgil, I'd like to know what you meant about not knowing who you are?"

Virgil covered his mouth, feigning embarrassment.

"Go ahead, Mr. Keller," said Diane, who seemed to have developed an instant fondness for Virgil, "tell them what you told me."

Virgil, pretending to submit to Diane's insistence, spoke up. "I just meant that we old people are like the women before they got the right to vote. Everyone treats us as if we've had to behave a certain way because we're old. You know, the cute little-old-man, little-old-lady business. I go into a store and I'm treated like I don't exist. Like I'm invisible. They can't see past our wrinkles, gray hair or"—he patted his head—"no hair. But, deep down inside, we're like everyone else." Virgil turned a pleading face toward Diane, who patted him on the shoulder.

Mary wasn't going to let Virgil charm the unsuspecting Diane. "Well, fortunately, Virgil, we know who you are deep down inside," she taunted, "an old goat."

Diane was shocked. The other students didn't know whether Mary was serious or joking.

"Goat or no goat," I teased, "Virgil has an interesting point. Stereotypes do create prejudices and sometimes coerce people into playing roles that suppress their talents and abilities. The women's movement is helping to change that. Do you think an old person's liberation movement is next?"

"Elderlib, is that it?" asked Effie. "I don't know about that. I'm an old woman, a grandmother, onetime rancher and housewife, a widow. I can't imagine myself one of those chorus-line girls—whatcha call, Rockettes?—all of a sudden." Effie laughed, as did the others.

"You'd be a great Rockette," said Dorothy, "a fully matured Rockette. I only wish I had a body like yours."

Effie blushed. We rarely talked about our bodies in the group, except when someone showed up with a visible bruise from a fall, or a blister where suspected cancer cells had been frozen and then scraped from a cheek, nose, or forehead.

"Don't there have to be limits to imagination?" asked Frank, who tugged at his beard. "If we were all completely free to do and be anything we wanted, there would be utter chaos. There must be some principles of harmony, of what is right for people to do at certain times of life." Frank looked around for support.

"There's some truth in what you say, Frank," said Dorothy. "The problem is, who decides on the principles? In the past, people claimed it was nature that dictated what was normal and proper behavior. Now we know it's society, economics, laws, vested interests, religious propaganda. I would think you young people could see that better than us old folks, because imagination gets worn down over the years by disappointments. There's no such thing as natural. There's only history and the people who make it up." Dorothy folded her arms in a gesture of defiance. "That's what Mill and Taylor were all about. They were Unitarians at a time when that meant something quite radical. They defied the conventions of their day because they regarded them as hypocritical, even immoral."

"It's interesting that you should say that, Dorothy," I chimed in, "because John and Harriet subscribed to the views of the utopian visionary Robert Owen, who said that chastity was sexual intercourse with affection, and prostitution was sexual intercourse without it."

Grace raised her hand. "Maybe they were just trying to justify their own foolin' around. People are always trying to make their sins look honorable."

At this, Hannah practically leaped out of her chair. "What did they do that was so bad?" she asked looking straight at Grace. "Isn't love, when it's really true, more important than what other people think? If you suppress your feelings, then you turn into someone like Mill. You get depressed."

"You get depressed when everybody thinks you're an old fuddy-duddy," answered Virgil, with a glance at Mary. I saw I had better head off another barbed interchange.

"Hannah asked about the love affair between John Stuart Mill and Harriet Taylor. Maybe their story is useful here. You see, Harriet Taylor, though married to a successful businessman with whom she conceived three children, was a restless wife. She was stirred up by the political and intellectual disputes of the time— about the institution of marriage, divorce, women's rights, the plight of the working class, free speech, freedom of religious expression. She went to see her minister, the political activist and Unitarian leader William Johnson Fox, to whom she complained that she lacked an intellectual companion with whom she could discuss these issues. Her husband, a kind and good person, was lacking in intellectual and artistic tastes. In short, she was bored by him.

"Fox suggested she might like to meet John Stuart Mill, and arranged for Mill and some of his friends to attend a dinner at the Taylor home. Almost from their first meeting, a deep bond of friendship and intimacy sprang up between them.

"Mill was ready for an exchange of feelings and affection. And in Harriet Taylor he found the perfect partner, except that she was married. Of an unconventional disposition, Harriet insisted on her right to spend time with Mill, and he likewise sought her company. Although her husband, John Taylor, objected—out of jealousy and fear of social castigation—Harriet persisted. Eventually John Taylor gave in, allowing the couple to spend periods of time together at her country house and on vacations to France. Still, as far as is known, theirs was a purely Platonic relationship, passionate but chaste. It lasted this way for twenty years, until John Taylor died and Mill and Harriet Taylor married. By then they were both in poor health, the effects of slowly developing tuberculosis—the dreaded disease they called consumption in the nineteenth century. Harriet died eight years later and was buried beside a cottage they owned in Avignon, France, where the couple lived in relative seclusion. And there Mill remained for fifteen years, tended by Harriet's daughter, Helen.

"Throughout those twenty-eight years, Harriet Taylor exerted tremendous influence on Mill. In fact, he claimed his most important ideas came from her. They also wrote essays and articles together. You could certainly say they lived out the philosophical ideas they had championed. But they paid a heavy price for their love and their intellectual life together, distancing themselves from friends and family to avoid further gossip and embarrassment."

"What a sad story," Hannah sighed.

"Why do you think it's sad?" asked Hildegard.

"They waited too long to really enjoy each other. All this denial of emotions, of physical attraction. Was it worth it?"

"Yeah," said Daryl, "they should've just done it. That's what people thought was going on anyway."

"You don't believe two people can experience a spiritual relationship that goes deeper than sex?" asked Hildegard.

"Not without sex. No," replied Hannah, shaking her head.

"Maybe you're right," said Hildegard, "but I found that intimacy can take many forms. When my husband, Al, was sick, we stopped having intercourse. We slept together, touched each other, and sometimes we lay awake late into the night silently looking into each other's eyes without speaking. Those were some of the most tender, intimate moments of my life. We came closer to each other than at any other time in all our married years." Hildegard smiled at Hannah, who put her hand on Hildegard's arm.

"But, what about before that?" said Hannah. "You had all those years of, well I don't want to pry, but, well, didn't you make love? I mean, you had children, right?"

Hildegard laughed. "Yes, of course we made love. And had children, too. But you get a different perspective. I don't know. Is it all right to talk about this?" Hildegard looked at me, then at Dorothy.

"We've become liberated, Hildegard. We can talk about anything," said Dorothy.

"I don't see what this has to do with John Stuart Mill's philosophy," said Richard, who had been quietly making notations in the margin of his text.

"You wouldn't," piped up Sue Ellen.

"Wait," I said in Richard's defense, "Richard has a good point. Is it right to evaluate a thinker's ideas in relation to his or her personal life?"

"If Mill hadn't written this autobiography, we wouldn't be discussing his sex life," said Dorothy. "I don't want to reduce philosophy to personality, but when a philosopher is in love with a woman his equal and she in love with him, and when he's written about personal liberty, individuality, and women's rights, well, that does make you want to know more about the connections. It's like he's turned his ideas into characters in a play, and we're the audience."

"I understand that," said Richard. "But we've been talking about people's sex lives." Richard turned toward me. "Yet you've told us probably Mill and Taylor never had sex. So isn't it a moot point?" Richard folded his arms.

"Maybe we're defining sex too narrowly," I responded. "Con-

sider this. Mill gave us the definition of happiness as a prepon-
derance of pleasure over pain. But he rejected the Benthamite
position that pleasure and pain could be quantified by what Bentham called a hedonic calculus—like assigning units of pleasure or
pain to various acts. Mill argued that some pleasures were higher
than others. He favored a qualitative approach to pleasure and
pain. Who would decide on the rating system? Probably the theorists, the educated classes. Mill apparently rated intimacy and
friendship higher in quality than physical sexual experience."

"That's just how he saw it," said Dorothy. "Once you open the
door to individual freedom and rate pleasures quantitatively or
qualitatively, there's no stopping the process. Everyone is going to
come up with different calculations."

"Right," I replied. "I suspect Mill knew that would happen.
Look at his views on individuality in his essay 'On Liberty.' He
says people have a right to experiment with how they want to
lead their lives. He praises spontaneity, originality, and even
desires and impulses. You have to realize that much of the history
of philosophy consists of suppressing these characteristics as inferior to the human power of reason. Mill himself supports the historical view that there was a time when men of strong bodies or
minds acted too much from impulse and the desire to dominate.
So you needed the iron rule of the church and the king to curtail
these excesses. But now, says Mill, the problem is not excess but
deficiency. Reflecting on Victorian England, Mill saw pervasive
censorship, conformity, suppression of feeling, and imitative
lifestyles rather than true individuality. As long as people do not
cause harm to one another in their experiments, he argued, they
should be free to pursue them."

"Unleash the imagination, tear down the barricades," exclaimed
Frank.

"To an extent, yes," I responded. "But Mill believed these acts of exploration leading to diversity of character would actually strengthen society, not weaken it. If people are more fully alive because they are more fully themselves, they will make more of a contribution to society, he reasoned. Also, because we do not know which ways of life will prove best for advancing human progress and the perfection of society, it's a good thing to have diversity. Who knows which way of life will prove most fruitful?"

"That's incredible," said Hannah. "That's exactly what I believe. I mean, I never thought it out like Mill, but he's said it the way I feel." She shook her head and looked to her friend Virgil for affirmation. But Virgil, a confirmed bachelor, was in a state of red-faced shock. This open discussion about sexuality and personal freedom had him tongue-tied.

"Ron?" asked Dorothy. "Which came first, Mill's libertarian views or his relationship with Mrs. Taylor? Isn't that the question we've been circling around?"

"Mill dedicated 'On Liberty' to his friend and wife, Harriet, and said it resulted from their collaboration. Harriet's 'great thoughts and noble feelings,' wrote Mill in the dedication, were his inspiration. The essay was published one year after her death."

"Do you see it then as an *apologia pro sua vita?*" asked the sophisticated Dorothy.

"An apple orchard?" Virgil had regained his power of speech.

"An *apologia*," said Dorothy, "that means an apology. Lots of great thinkers and writers wrote them. Kind of a defense of their lives and views. I just wonder whether Mill wrote his essay 'On Liberty' as a justification for his and Mrs. Taylor's controversial lifestyle. Or that they were able to break social taboos and conventions because they already had firm convictions that they were in the right and that's what most mattered."

"I suspect the latter is correct," I responded.

"Does it really take a liberation movement to be an individual?"

asked Richard. "I feel pretty individualistic in my views and goals. But it hasn't meant rebelling against my parents or society." Richard studied the circle of faces for support.

"Good for you," said Virgil, "a young person should respect his parents. And if you think you can do better than them, more power to you."

"Don't you have to rebel just a little?" asked Sue Ellen. "Otherwise you don't have your own identity. You're, like, just conforming." Sue Ellen glanced at Richard, seeming to comment with her eyes on his button-down shirt and cardigan sweater.

"I don't have to look different to be different," Richard retorted.

"We're all products of our environment and society," said Frank. "Identity is an illusion," he added, tapping his pencil on the tabletop. Frank's comment seemed to bring the conversation to a halt. Were we incapable of originality? Were our views and beliefs simply products of upbringing and the accidents of birth and history?

A Game

"I have an idea," exclaimed Hannah, "let play a game."

"A game?" said Richard.

"Yes, let's not just talk about what Mill said and did; let's do it ourselves. Let's take turns trying to imagine an ideal time in the future, a better world and what we'd be doing in it."

"Half of us would probably be dead," said Dorothy.

Hannah frowned. She hadn't thought of that. Then she perked up. "But you wouldn't have to die. Not unless you wanted to. Use your imagination. Maybe in your ideal future they'll have a drug that stops aging and keeps people healthy. You could live almost forever."

"Oh, my," gasped Dorothy, putting a hand to her bosom.

"Forever is a very long time," sighed Virgil.

"Oh, come on," she beamed enthusiastically at the others, "don't be a bunch of stick-in-the-muds."

"It sounds cool," said Daryl, "I'm willing."

"I'd give it a try," said Effie.

And so, reluctantly, we agreed to follow the exuberant Hannah. Since she came up with the idea, insisted Richard, shouldn't she go first? Hannah accepted the challenge. She folded her hands and bowed her head as if in meditation. While we waited, Virgil began whispering something to Diane; Grace dragged her huge handbag to the tabletop and began rummaging inside. Finally, Hannah looked up.

"Jeez," she said, "this is harder than I thought."

"You couldn't do it, huh?" said Richard.

All eyes were on Hannah as she turned toward Richard and smirked. "Yeah, I could do it," she said, adding in a tiny voice, "Sort of."

Virgil looked at Hannah over the top of his half-rim glasses, and Grace groaned as she lowered her handbag to the floor. Hildegard gave Hannah one of her encouraging smiles.

"Okay," said Hannah, "I'm not a John Stuart Mill or a Harriet Taylor. But here's the future I see." She raised her hand to her brow as if sighting a distant horizon. "In my future, no one's either fat or skinny."

At this pronouncement, we all broke into laughter.

"It's not funny," insisted Hannah, but tears were already flowing down Mary's face and Richard was bent over holding his stomach.

"Listen up, folks," shouted Daryl, who had suddenly become protective of Hannah, "let her tell her future."

We managed to bring our laughter under control, and Hannah continued. "Okay, it sounds funny. But think of it. Today the two greatest ills in the world are not having enough to eat and eating too much. I'm not referring to gluttony, exactly, but to overconsumption. See, some people have too little and others too much. Some are skinny from malnutrition, others fat from overindulging. You'll have to admit that it takes a leap of imagination to picture a future in which people are neither skinny nor fat. Everyone's fit."

"But some of us," insisted Dorothy, "are both fat and poor."

"Maybe," said Hannah, grown serious again, "you can overconsume from being poor. You fill up on substitutes." That comment sobered the group. "The future I want," she continued, having regained our attention, "is one where everyone has enough nourishment, enough proper food." Hannah surveyed her audience. "You know what I saw when I tried to picture the future?" We waited in silence. "I saw my grandparents' table, saw us sitting down for dinner. They lived on a farm, and I lived with them from the time I was eight to about fifteen, when I went back to live with my mom, after she remarried. My grandparents ate what they grew. We had lots of fresh vegetables, lots of squash and beans and peas and corn. Sometimes we ate chicken. And Grandma baked breads, pies, cakes, Sunday morning waffles. And Grandpa made syrups, cured olives, put up pickles and made his own beer, which he'd give me in little sipping glasses on Friday nights. They weren't rich, that's for sure, but they weren't poor either. They just seemed to have enough. And that's what they gave me," said Hannah, casting a challenging look at Richard, "enough, and not too much."

"Boy," said Grace, "I sure can identify with that. Livin' on a farm. It's hard work, but there's good in it, too."

"Almost impossible nowadays," said Effie, "them big industrial farms have changed all that."

"So it's really not a realistic future," argued Richard.

"Well," countered Hannah, "it's my future if I can imagine it. You can imagine your own."

"Maybe Hannah's future shouldn't be taken quite so literally," conjectured Hildegard. "She has projected a world of sufficiency for everyone. Her grandparents' dinner table could be a metaphor, something from her past that inspires an ideal for the future."

"But people will always be both fat and skinny. There will always be the haves and have-nots," insisted Richard. "Unless you're suggesting a communistic world with neither rich nor poor but everyone the same, everyone working for the state. Is that it?" Richard shot a challenging look at Hannah.

Hannah pondered Richard's question, then shook her head. "No, I'm not in favor of everybody being the same or having their lives regulated by Big Brother. I want everyone to be free, like Mill says, free to pursue their own idea of individuality. But I want a world where people value each other for what they are, not for what they can do for you or for the pleasure they can give you. This will sound funny, I know, but I want a world that can be summed up in me asking Grandma to 'please pass the mashed potatoes,' and her saying, 'Here Hannah, I made them especially for you.'"

"I believe I rest easier knowing there's young folks like Hannah about," said Grace, with a sigh.

I knew what Grace meant, but I couldn't help wondering if Hannah was for real or whether this was a command performance from a very talented actress. Richard, too, studied Hannah; a mixed look of skepticism and admiration on his face.

"Dear Hannah," said Hildegard, rescuing the conversation, "don't ever let go of your dreams." Hildegard shook her head and continued looking at Hannah, who seemed embarrassed by all this attention. "But as you dream," continued Hildegard, "remember that's also where responsibility begins. Like this couple, these philosophers, Mill and Taylor, there is sometimes a high price paid for trying to turn your dreams into reality. After a few setbacks early in life, most of us give up or become indifferent. We accept somebody else's dream and take responsibility for it. We can be very serious, hardworking, loyal, devoted. Still, the dream is never ours. And one day we wake up and realize it's too late, our time has run out for following our dream, or maybe we can't even remember what it once was." Hildegard continued to watch Hannah, who, fiddling with her braids, returned a childish smile. I felt I should say something. But what?

"Hannah has a good point about mashed potatoes," came Virgil's impish voice. "They're so soothing. Much better than baked, boiled, fried, or even au gratin, I'd say. Sometimes I even dream of mashed potatoes." He described with his hands an invisible mound of the stuff.

"Oh, come now, Virgil," quipped Mary, "you do not."

"Yes, yes, I do," insisted Virgil. "I picture myself whipping up huge globs of potatoes like sand castles at the beach. Then I serve them to all my friends at a big party. I put lots of melted butter in the moat and sprinkle paprika on the turrets." Virgil's eyes shifted from side to side as he looked over the top edge of his glasses to watch for reactions.

"I believe you, Virgil," said Dorothy, " and I would love to attend one of these mashed potato feasts." Dorothy laughed and her bosom shook. Then she leaned forward on her heavy arms and said, "Hildegard, did you ever really stop dreaming or living out your dreams? Because I can't think of anyone more faithful to her own vision of the future than you."

"No, I haven't stopped dreaming, I guess," Hildegard replied. "But I've gotten tired of worrying about world peace and children in poverty. I need to feel others are going to take up the banner."

"Well, I see a likely group of new recruits, right here," said Mary, pointing at the students.

Hildegard nodded, but she didn't look convinced.

"There's a big difference between us," said Daryl who watched me carefully. "Between our generations, I mean."

"A generation gap, is it?" said Mary.

Daryl looked confused. "Sort of. It's just the people here at the center seem so patriotic. Just coming in for the first time, I overheard people talking about unemployment, world peace, poor children." He hesitated. "You know, like, big problems. And we—well, me, anyway—I worry about the things that affect me directly, what I care about. The big issues out there in the world just don't turn me on. My causes are things like people cutting down trees on campus, or discrimination against, um, less conventional groups. Stuff like that. Always real personal." Daryl put his hand on his chest.

I wondered whether anyone would ask him to explain what he meant by "less conventional groups," but no one did.

"That's true," said Richard. "We tend to get involved in what's personal to us. Is it age, I wonder? Something we won't understand for a long time? Or is it our generation. We don't get involved just because people say some cause is important. Only if we can relate it to our lives. When people our age go around saying they're worried about peace or starvation—with the exception of Hannah here, I tend to think, like Hildegard said, it's not really them, not really from the heart. It's somebody else's dream or cause, and they're just mimicking."

"Maybe there is a generation gap, then," said Dorothy. "I've assumed the idea of a chasm between generations was just hype. I often feel I have more in common with young people than my age peers. But Daryl may be onto something. The way we were raised, you were expected to give to charity and help support the poor and patronize the arts because it was expected of you. At least in my family that was how it was. World War II made patriots of us all. Korea made us a little confused. And Vietnam really scrambled our beliefs. But the idea of only helping because it feels good—Dorothy wrinkled her brow—well, that doesn't give me much assurance that important needs will be met."

"We're hopelessly subjective and self-centered," said Frank. "It's all ego. Me, me, me, me."

"But, I feel sympathy with the hungry, the downtrodden," exclaimed Hannah, recovering some of her lost verve.

"That's just it," said Frank, "sympathy. Sympathy is just pity. You don't experience another person's pain as your pain. Deep down inside you're saying, 'Wow, I'm glad that's not happening to me.' Compassion, that's what the Buddhists preach. Seeing you're no different. Your plight is the same because everyone is part of you. We'll die. We will all die." Frank pointed his finger at us. "We all suffer fear, anger, disappointment. But we're shut up in our own little cocoons."

"Jesus felt the same way," Grace put in, "taught it in the parables."

"Summon the little children unto me," Virgil intoned.

"Amen, brother," responded Grace.

"And a-women, too," laughed Dorothy.

"Haven't we gotten awfully far afield?" asked Richard. "I guess it's partly my fault, Ron. It seems like we've lost track of John Stuart Mill."

"Not really," I answered. "Mill conjured up an ideal future society. He believed history reflected an evolutionary process with periods of great social progress and periods of setbacks. His father, James Mill, believed history was governed by laws of human nature, that everyone was motivated by self-interest. He thought altruism and self-sacrifice were myths. But John embraced change. After all, he could change, so why not society, countries, the world? Maybe that's what we're asking ourselves by arguing about the future. Hannah challenged us to open our dreams up to each other. That's harder than sharing our doubts, our skepticism."

"Spaceship earth," exclaimed Daryl.

"Not space. Time," insisted Dorothy. "That's the final frontier. We're time travelers. You're looking at a bunch of sojourners soon to step across the threshold of the finite."

Time travelers, yes, that was a good way of putting it. Though belonging to different generations, we shared a common destiny. Here was Tennyson's arch, once more. The power of imagination to turn a limitation into a possibility. Mill himself admired Tennyson and wrote some of the first reviews praising the poet, then in his youth. And here we were, a crew assembled of different generations, making the voyage together.

"Every generation has its unique experiences of history and wears the mantle of its special causes," I said.

"I never though of myself as a crusader or part of social change," reflected Daryl.

"Doesn't seem there's much about us that's really one of a kind," said Grace. "I mean, that's somehow just our own, nobody else's."

"Oh," said Hildegard, "we're unique. Each, one of a kind. Just look around this table."

We looked at one another. Virgil was drumming his fingers, Diane fastening her hair, Mary ferreting in her pocketbook, Frank tapping his pencil on the tabletop, Daryl scratching his beard, Dorothy chin out, looking thoughtfully at the ceiling, Sue Ellen fidgeting with her bracelet, Effie humming, Hannah writing intently in her notebook, Richard studying his fingernails, Grace, eyes closed, fingers interlocked. Hildegard was watching me, and I was watching Hildegard.

CHAPTER FOUR

WAVE OF MEMORY

The idea of the self or soul is a legacy of the ancient past. The Greeks called it *psyche*, and Plato claimed it had three aspects: appetite, spirit, and reason. Appetite could mean hunger or lust; spirit was an essential ingredient of courage and honor; reason was the noblest, according to Plato, because it provided the individual with the means to discern true and worthy goals and pursue them by reining in appetite and spirit. If someone achieved a unity of the three parts, he or she was equipped to look into the eternal order of being and see the soul's immortality reflected. By contrast, several major schools of twentieth-century Anglo-American and European philosophy have abandoned the idea of a timeless core or inner self. For them, the self is simply a classifying term for a collection of traits and attitudes attributed to the physical person or a linguistic usage equivalent to the personal pronoun "I."

Theories of the fundamental principles of reality, metaphysics, were traditionally based on the notion that the visible world is grounded in the invisible. Knowledge gained through the senses depended on prisms of the mind, immaterial ideas and concepts, which filtered experience, making it intelligible. Early and middle twentieth-century schools of philosophy rejected this dichotomy in favor of the visible. They sought to embrace scientific and empiricist standards and methods. The self, like the terms "soul" or "spirit," lacked anything we could actually see—it referred to an inaccessible form of subjectivity, a hypothetical "I" that could never be directly perceived except through purported moments of intuitive insight or mystical contemplation. It had to go. So it was replaced by the notion of a conceptual self, knowable indirectly through reflection and constructed out of what others perceive about us and we report about ourselves. This gave rise to notions of the ideal self, self-evaluation, self-esteem, self-image, and the many other hyphenated concepts of self that could be measured through quantitative tests to rate people on a scale of low to high.

For some, the demise of the unhyphenated self signified a general trend toward secularity and denial of the spiritual dimension of life; for others it meant progress through new methods to bring modern science into the psyche. Perhaps these issues seem merely academic—let the philosophers, psychologists, and theologians untangle issues about the self! But for me, the subject is crucial. Several years after I started teaching at the senior center, one particular situation brought this home.

WAVE OF MEMORY

"Like a wave, it comes over me," Hildegard said. I had spent so much time with my older friends that their joys and sorrows, frailties and strengths, seemed familiar and understandable. But this was something new.

"Is it like water?" I wanted to know. "Is it blue?"

"Blue?" She looked puzzled. "No, there's no color. Not water, more like breath. It bathes me, touches everything. My bed, the table and lamp, the pictures on the chest of drawers."

"Does the feeling make you afraid?" I was worried about her, but I was not expecting the note of panic in my voice as I studied her and wondered whether she was preparing to reunite with what the Greek philosopher Plotinus called the flame of eternal being, or was slowly disappearing before my eyes.

"Afraid?" she asked and looked at me, amused. "Should I be afraid of what gives me pleasure? Mornings like this I awaken before it's light outside. That's how it is with many of us. We waken early. Do we get out of bed?" She shook her head. "I don't get up. Don't have to. No one needs me to do anything for them. I only need myself, now."

Hildegard looked at me from across the kitchen table. She had been telling me about early-morning reveries, spontaneous waves of memory that swept over her. To me, they sounded overwhelming; to her, a synthesis of—what? Sadness? Joy? Could it be an aftereffect of the stroke? She also told me she'd been dreaming in German, the language frequently spoken on the streets of Baltimore during her childhood.

Friends advised her not to work long hours gardening in the heat of midday. But Hildegard is strong-willed. Dehydration may have been a factor in the stroke, the doctor said. "My mother's always been like that," her daughter complained, "stubborn." Fortunately, she bounced back. Only a little paralysis remained, and her speech was fine, though sometimes she had to search for the right word.

"So I lie in bed and let the past flow through the present. The memories, they're—oh, what's the word? Unbecome?" She shook her head. "No, beckon. Yes, they're *un*beckoned." She looked pleased, repeated it softly. "Unbeckoned. That's how it is. Pictures from my life, painful, happy. Funny things I hadn't thought about in years. Our first car, my mother's hairbrush, my sister and I at the beach. The waves bring them to me. They're mine, or I am theirs. All of a part, flowing together. Or is it that I am"—she paused, cocked her head—"floating . . . flowing? Can you understand this, Ron?"

I nodded, but did I understand? I remembered my grandmother, in one of our rare adult conversations, telling me how, when she went to sleep at night, it was like entering a movie theater. Her life, featured on the screen, with scene after scene passing before her eyes. "Not a dream," she said. I never asked what she meant.

The skin on the back of Hildegard's hands was almost translucent. The vessels, muscles, tendons, and bones that supported her life were on prominent display. Still, she looked handsome in her striped blouse and pale blue wrap-around skirt. The look of a perpetually delighted child played across her wizened face. Her red hair had gotten thinner. Already petite in stature, she was growing ever smaller.

From the time I first met Hildegard at the senior center, she had been a friend, even a mentor. She was one of those people I picked out as a role model, the sort of "gray spirit" I wanted to be in old age—to be, even now.

The quick, decisive way she spoke and moved communicated her personal qualities: independent, decisive, caring, accepting, skeptical of authority, secure despite her open admission of doubt and uncertainties about religious beliefs. She was by no means infallible, and some of her attitudes appeared to me to be contradictory, but she was the sort of helmsman I most admired. I wanted to know how she had achieved these qualities. Was it something I could learn?

On another occasion, a few weeks before we talked about the

wave of memory, I was sitting in her kitchen and Hildegard showed me a magazine published by the Hemlock Society, an association providing information about how to take your own life.

I was shocked. "Would you really do this?" I asked.

Hildegard nodded. "If I felt that I could no longer live life with my full spirit, I would not want to continue," she said. There was no sadness, no anger in her voice.

I wanted to object that reserving the right to determine your own death assumed that living was a matter of personal choice. Hildegard had espoused the view that life was a gift, that it did not belong to us like a property. Her present attitude seemed to contradict that. She wanted to be in control. Still, she was in the situation of having to face serious disabilities. It was her quality of life that was at stake. Shouldn't the choice be hers?

Hildegard also told me that if it ever came to pass that she would no longer be able to read, her life would be unacceptable. I didn't know whether to praise her courage or try to talk her out of a position that could have stemmed from depression, not an uncommon condition after a stroke. And who was I to advise Hildegard that she should follow the path of acceptance in relation to her life situation? Given my own view that autonomy is the essence of personhood, freedom to determine our path in life the most important factor, I had to respect her willful position. In fact, it was one of the character traits I most admired in her. But it did not seem fair for her to remove herself from the lives of those who loved and cared about her. Where did that fit into my concept of self-determination? Uncertain, I remained silent.

The times I spent with my older friends brought a growing sense of urgency to wrestling with ideas about memory, selfhood, freedom, and finitude. Until I got to know older people personally, I assumed there was ample time for working through philosophical problems. Now I felt a heightened tension between the heady speculations of great thinkers and the practical, emotional, and even physiological issues of everyday life.

I was drawn to philosophy because the world of ideas enlivened life. Each thinker I studied revealed new possibilities of meaning and self-understanding, presenting keys to a treasure trove of ideals for which generations of people had lived and died. Traditional philosophical dilemmas were wonderfully manageable when they remained bound between the covers of a book or within the pages of a scholarly journal. You could open and close them at will; you could set aside time for reflection and writing. But for my older students, the distance to the horizon of the future was shrinking. There would not be endless opportunity to pursue metaphysical uncertainties or ethical quandaries about the purpose of one's life. In the quest for timeless truths, time was running out.

Through the seniors, I imagined my own later life, my eventual eleventh hour—however close to the present it might be. In the final reckoning, where did I stand, philosophically, and what difference did my stand make in how I conducted my life, related to people, and participated in my community?

Are We the Same?

About five years after our conversation about the wave of memory, Hildegard had several more small strokes. She had become frail, confused, and could no longer live independently. Her daughter, a psychologist in Seattle, persuaded her to give up the home she and her husband, Al, had built for their retirement years. Al had passed away several years earlier, after a short bout with cancer. Now Hildegard was living in what they call domiciliary care, with a small group of residents in a homelike setting. Most do not need skilled nursing, but they cannot manage on their own.

I hadn't seen her for several months and was apprehensive about my visit. When I telephoned the home before coming over, the director warned me, "She probably won't recognize you." The thought disturbed me. Maybe now the wave of memory had pulled her under. I had so thoroughly identified Hildegard with her energetic self-determination, I worried, what would remain?

I arrived at a pleasant-looking large house located in a residential neighborhood only a few miles from Hildegard's former home. At the door, I was greeted by a man and a woman, the couple who ran the facility. Several people were seated at a kitchen table playing cards. Bill Morgan, the director, pointed toward the adjacent living room. On a couch in the sun-filled room sat a hunched-over figure in a handsome blue-and-black plaid blouse, the type you see in sports fashion catalogs. Her head was bowed, and I could see her scalp through the thin hair. If she was asleep in the middle of the afternoon, should I waken her? Would she know who I was, would there be anything to talk about?

Cautiously, I stepped forward. Suddenly, lifting her head, she gave me a beaming smile, stood up, and stepped lightly toward me. "Here you are," she exclaimed, "you just walk in like that." She took my hand, exactly as she had done on so many other occasions. Then she led me to the couch. "Sit down," she said. "They said he was coming." She looked at me. "You're the same. Am I the same?" she asked. Were either of us the same?

Though I had spent many hours and days with people at least twice my age, some of them quite frail, others more robust than myself, I was still unprepared for how to be with Hildegard. Did she really know who I was? What could I assume about our shared knowledge of the past?

Hildegard had not taken her life, but had adjusted to the gradual onset of disability, accommodating to the limitations, until she would no longer be capable of carrying out her own demise.

Whether this was a conscious decision on her part, I could not determine. Perhaps she had discovered that, despite what had earlier seemed unacceptable conditions, there was some worth in continuing to live. However it came about, I was grateful to be with her.

I searched her face and gestures for signs of that fullness of spirit without which she would not want to live. I was looking for that spark of transcendence that would lift both of us from ourselves and join us to each other. Once again, I was the novice, well-intentioned philosopher at my first senior center class.

If I couldn't be sure whether Hildegard really knew who she was talking to, what assumptions could I make about how to communicate with her? As we talked, I noticed her speech was much more disjointed than after the first stroke and lacked the specificity of names and places. But there was the characteristic good humor and animation in her voice and gestures.

"He came here too. Just like that, walked in," she said. But I didn't know who "he" was. "And he knew it, just like you knew it. I don't know what happened to the other girls, but one died. Maybe he died too." When she used the pronoun "he" it was unclear whether she meant me or a merging of other male and even female friends and acquaintances—perhaps an effect of the aphasia that frequently follows multiple strokes. Hildegard paused thoughtfully and then, with that characteristic sparkle in her eye, went on. "Isn't that something? Do you know it too?"

I wished I did know it, or maybe I did and had forgotten. Here was my friend Hildegard, who wanted to know whether or not I knew. And here I was thinking, Is the real Hildegard gone? Dispersed by leaking arteries in her brain, retreated into the past of distant memory, mimicked by residual habits of gesture and voice? Yet there was a certain continuity of personality, unmistakably Hildegard. Or were these character traits now detached from that core of being whose unity was Hildegard? Had Hildegard lost her self but retained the externalities by which I ordinarily recognized her? So many questions, but such precious little time with my friend.

THE AGING SELF

Just a few weeks earlier, I had begun to prepare a talk for a gerontology conference on the topic of the aging self. A friend doing research on how certain key terms were used by different academic disciplines when applied to old age had suggested this topic. Now, sitting beside Hildegard on the floral-patterned couch, I felt caught in a struggle between the opposing philosophical views I had surveyed.

We continued to look at each other. I mentioned some of our old friends from the senior center like Dorothy, Effie, Mary, Grace, and Virgil. With each name her eyes lit up. "Yes," she exclaimed, "yes, you knew him too." And she would tell me of some event—the time he argued with the director, broke a leg, told a funny story—though whether these had occurred years or days ago, I could not be sure. Had Virgil come to see her just last week? That, I knew, was not possible. I stretched my legs and shifted my position on the couch to better assess Hildegard's whole body. If the self was a collection of behaviors, then here was Hildegard, a physical presence, a collection of familiar gestures. I should feel at ease. Instead, I thought of Simone de Beauvoir's criticism of how younger people treat the elderly.

In her scholarly treatment of aging, *The Coming of Age*, based on a study of diaries and journals written in later life by French novelists, painters, playwrights, and philosophers of the past several centuries, de Beauvoir strove to demystify aging as neither a remarkable accomplishment of accumulated experience condensed into memory and crystallized into wisdom nor an inevitable form of social obsolescence. Old age was something private that happened between you and the mirror in which you beheld an aging body surrounding a much younger, even ageless, mind. Public old age was a conspiracy perpetrated on the elderly forced to look into the mirror of social attitudes.

The French philosophers with whom de Beauvoir associated were especially fond of the idea that a good deal of nonverbal communication, with metaphysical significance, occurs in *le regard*, the "glance" that takes place between people. The exchanges of the eyes say it all. As we get older, argued de Beauvoir, our inner identity, who we are to and for ourselves, does not really change. Yet the way people choose to look at us lies beyond our control. For them, we are an artifact, a collection of behaviors, a stereotype. In de Beauvoir's eerie account, this projected image is "a cluster of rays of intentionality directed through an analagon towards a missing object." In other words, people no longer see us as unique persons but, generically, as old men and women. In their glance we see ourselves reflected—an "analagon."

Old age is a conspiracy into which we are reluctantly drawn. The only way to contend with the glance of others and the threatening image we behold in the mirror is to refuse to withdraw from society, disclaim the role of the old-timer, and avoid slipping into the self-deception that you are as others see you, a repository of memory, living primarily in the past, a passive agent incapable of further willful action and decisions. We must, exhorted de Beauvoir, continue to pursue projects of action that impel us toward future accomplishments. If we lose our raison d'être, our purpose in life, we lose our *être*, our being. Neither frailty nor the inner life of spirituality has a place in de Beauvoir's schema. Hildegard was no longer capable of pursuing projects. Did that mean, according to de Beauvoir, she was no longer really there?

Now I was the conspirator looking for the "missing object," the Hildegard whose voice, insights, and gestures emanated from a hidden source of being—hidden because never before had I had to seek it. Hildegard had always been the keeper of her self. Now I was injecting myself into the confusion of her flawed grammar, trying to repair her sentences.

As I perceived Hildegard slipping away from the world, I felt drawn into the empty spaces she left behind. Her stories from earlier years had become mine: about growing up in Baltimore when German was as commonly spoken in the streets as English, of her childhood visit to Germany when she had watched from a balcony the parade of soldiers marching off to the battlefields of World War I and, unlike her cheering relatives, had cried out and fled into the living room; of a brother who had taken his own life and her father, a Lutheran minister, who had done the same. Only now did I realize that Hildegard's thoughts of suicide had family precedents.

Until now, I could count on Hildegard to be the repository in whom these memories dwelt, while I was a witness, a secondary memory. Now I found myself inhabiting two positions—mine and Hildegard's. I grew fearful at the prospects of my own obliteration, that somehow Hildegard would take me with her into the unconsciousness of dementia and death.

I had to care for her stories and to be the life, the consciousness, that would fill the emptiness of her disappearing mind. When Hildegard was gone from the space of the world, a part of her lifetime would remain with me, be part of my memory, coexisting in time. I was becoming Hildegard, maybe even colluding in her disappearance. As if I were throwing out a lifeline, I put my hand out to hers. I needed to feel her physical presence, to anchor her, and myself, in the moment. I felt the soft skin and sinews of her hand.

I felt my hand in hers. We looked at one another in silence.

Sometime afterward, I left.

IN SEARCH OF THE AGING SELF

A few weeks after my last visit with Hildegard, I flew to San Francisco for a conference on the theme "Aging, Memory, and the Self." The meeting was held in one of those big conference hotels decked out with a lot of mirrors, marble, brass, and soft music—a place so incongruous with the senior center as to make me wonder what I was doing. But there I was, about to explain to the audience how the revised, hyphenated self had trickled down from the logical positivism movement of the 1920s into the social and psychological sciences of the 1950s and 1960s. Eventually, it trickled into textbooks on gerontology where you might find the supplanted, subjective self transformed into four objective selves: self-concept (what you think you are like), the ideal self (what you think you should be like), the evaluative self (what you should not be like), and self-esteem (how you feel about the fit between the first two). Tests had been devised to study, measure, and chart on scales the manifestation of the four objective selves.

The behavioral hyphenated self found application in textbooks for practitioners. In one on gerontological nursing, even self-concept received a downgrading as the authors explain, "Self-concept is one means of organizing existing data on personality change throughout the lifespan." While the authors reduce the concept of self to little more than a handy category, they discover additional facets of the observable self—body image and physical identity. These, they argue, along with the acceptability of expressing pain and the role of illness in one's family, are influenced by cultural attitudes that make it difficult to separate self-concept from one's cultural background. For example, when an elderly Latina woman complained to her doctor about chest pains and he was about to order an electrocardiogram, a Latina nurse stopped him, explaining, "She's heartbroken over the loss of her husband, Doctor. She needs consoling, not tests."

These practical insights about the self were designed to help turn aging into an empirical science. I could appreciate their utility, though I marveled at the ease with which they had dispatched two thousand years of investigation, speculation, and debate. However, the question of the self's meaning and philosophical status was far from settled. After all, recognizing that our sense of physical selfhood is influenced by cultural (and, I should add, religious) traditions underscores both the relativism of the concept and its rich and dynamic spiritual aspects.

I entered the assigned meeting room for our session and strode down the center aisle to the white cloth-covered head table, which reminded me of a hospital gurney. I took my seat alongside two other speakers who were making last-minute changes in the papers they were about to read. As the rows of seats began to fill up, I thought about Hildegard. My experience of shared subjectivity ran against most of the philosophical and psychological theories of selfhood with which I was familiar. They were based on the premise that each of us is a discrete psychophysical entity whose boundaries form an impermeable membrane around us. We are able to conjecture about other people's thoughts and experiences, but never feel or know them directly. We can identify the body of another person as that of a thinking subject, like ourselves. But we are always more aware of the separation than of the relationship that conjoins us. Even the view of someone like the great social psychologist George Herbert Mead, who proposed the concept of the "me," an identity that emerges through the ways I see myself in relation to others, is still an analysis that focuses primarily on what happens inside the mind of an individual.

When my turn came to speak, I decided not to read my paper but to present my findings in a fairly conversational way. I began by commenting that frailty and vulnerability, important issues in advanced old age, are also conditions that may befall people at other times of life, as poignantly evinced in the famous cases of the young women Karen Quinlan and Nancy Cruzan. Issues about competency, personal autonomy, and dignity, as well as attitudes toward care, stem from our basic understanding of what it means to be a person and on our conceptions of the self at any age. The situation of the elderly seems to have the effect of dramatically highlighting certain perplexing questions.

I could appreciate the current dominant influence of the behaviorist approach to the self because of the importance of prediction and control, which were deemed the most important outcomes of research. Limiting your focus to observable and measurable actions and products of the individual as an active agent enabled you to find practical, concrete ways beneficially to intervene in people's lives.

The danger, I said, is what happens when benefits are narrowly defined only in terms of behavior. What of the inner experiences that are less obvious to an observer? What of the danger that we train caregivers to think behaviorally about their own actions? They may become contrived, mechanical, artificial. I pictured the pseudo-cheerfulness of nurses, doctors, social workers, and myself in the company of the frail. The behaviorist approach might result in artificiality and distance that could lead to a denial of the fuller meaning of selfhood—one's own and that of the other person.

What other approaches to the self might we consider, and what would be the consequence? I asked, all the while holding in my mind a picture of Hildegard on the floral couch.

The Linguistic Self

An unusual and poignant article in the British journal *Ageing and Society* brought this issue home. The Oxford University philosopher Rom Harre and the Georgetown University psychologist Steven Sabat decided to study the status of the self under extreme conditions—in Alzheimer's disease. They wanted to see whether by analyzing how Alzheimer's sufferers talked and acted they could glean empirical evidence for the self's presence or absence. They discovered that the self of personal identity "persists far into the end stage of the disease."

This claim intrigued me, coming as it did from researchers trained in contemporary psycholinguistics and thereby influenced by theories of how language shapes our views of social reality. What sort of a persistent "self" had they discovered under conditions of mental frailty and vulnerability?

Initially, they were surprised when listening to spouses, other family members, and professionals who work with Alzheimer's patients when, in the presence of the patient, they would refer to Mr. A or Mrs. B as a "former" lawyer, accountant, businessman, and so forth. "Former" did not just mean retired. Since the Alzheimer's sufferer's disorientation and memory impairment seemed to preclude self-identification, "former" implied a past life disconnected from the present.

Sabat and Harre then conducted interviews with the Alzheimer's patients and found that despite mental confusion and problems of orientation in early and middle stages of the disease, these individuals in numerous instances used self-referential language that made it clear they still identified themselves with certain professional roles and still felt in possession of other personal attributes denied to them by others. Influenced by the analytic tradition that discounts notions of an inner, subjective self, Sabat

and Harre found a linguistic self in the speech or "discursive prac-
tices" of people with moderate to severe degrees of dementia.

Since analytic philosophy, and subsequently psychology, of
this sort tends to restrict itself to what can be known in and
through language, especially ordinary language and the scientific
use of concepts, their revelation was both significant and
poignant. They made it clear that while families and helpers too
quickly discounted the relevance of socially important attributes
of the Alzheimer's individual, the Alzheimer's person himself or
herself nevertheless retained a vestige of selfhood, detectable in
careful listening to and analysis of speech and language use.

Sabat and Harre were cautious not to commit what, for their
academic disciplines, would constitute a heresy—lapsing back into
the rejected metaphysics by implying a core inner self. Instead,
they defined the primary self of personal identity, as differentiated
from the secondary selves or personae derived from and dependent
on social roles, as an experienced "continuity of one's point of view
in the world of objects in space and time." The persisting self can
be found in the fragile discourse even of someone suffering severe
dementia. It is not in the content of that discourse—which can be
unintelligible at times—but in the use of the first-person pronoun
"I" and in other words that imply personal agency.

As a practical consequence, Sabat and Harre recommended
that people close to Alzheimer's patients resist presupposing that
because the Alzheimer's sufferer seems like a shadow of his or her
former self, the former self no longer exists; instead, the shadow
self is still a self and deserves appropriate recognition, respect, and
treatment. To use language about the other person as though that
person no longer exists is a conspiracy, like de Beauvoir's *analagon*.
It has the effect of further fraying an already fragile thread that still
connects the dementia sufferer with a sense of personhood.

The presence of the linguistic self, under conditions of frailty, provides some comfort to philosophers and social scientists who rule out access to the metaphysical self of traditional, pre-twentieth-century philosophy. And in Hildegard's gestures and speech, I too could be comforted, because whatever Hildegard may have perceived in my speech and behavior, she was still unmistakably herself.

Perhaps, then, I could find comfort in thinking of the preserved self of my friend in her very manner of telling her life, even if the telling was somewhat fragmented. What I missed in Sabat and Harre's account was reflection on their own roles. By responding to the plight of the Alzheimer's sufferers they interviewed, did they help to maintain, or even revive, the person's sense of self? And how had that affected them? They were remarkable listeners, yet limited their roles to confirming and helping preserve the selves of social personae, while indirectly observing the "I" as reflected in conversation. They wanted to promote a linguistic concept of the self that was not simply a composite of other people's perceptions of us, or dependent on "intact recent or remote memory recall." Dependency on others would only confirm our social identities. Emphasis on memory could imply that the self was some form of timeless subjectivity—a mysterious, behind-the-scenes stage director. These views would make the self either too external or too internal. For Sabat and Harre, the solution was to embed the self in language as a linguistic reference point positioned in acts of speech, including inner narratives.

But I continued to wonder what Sabat and Hare's relationship to the people they studied was. I wanted to know if stepping inside the subjective experience of the relationship with a frail person meant that you would lose objectivity and succumb to your own biases, or that you would gain a truly vivid understanding of the multidimensional reality of that person and yourself. Could you embrace both perspectives?

The concept of the linguistic self confirmed my sense that Hildegard was still present despite her mental frailty. That was a comforting thought. Yet I wanted an account that would include my position as her friend, someone who shared her stories and his own. This led me to the theoretical framework of the self as inner story.

THE NARRATIVE SELF

I was familiar with the idea of the narrative self that had grown out of literary and philosophical work during the 1970s and 1980s. We are all aware that states of thinking and feeling are like voices in our minds. If we "talk" to ourselves, is that not proof of an inner presence? And when we talk to one another, are we not exhibiting our selves through narrative? Hildegard was telling me herself, and my listening, my being there for her, was my narrative self responding. I am still responding.

The narrative idea encouraged me to think of Hildegard as a self centered not exclusively in a willfully acting individual but in characteristics and values that she shared through gestures, speech patterns, and stories, and in my knowledge and memory of this radiant diffusion of personhood. According to this framework for understanding the self, we had given parts of ourselves to each other years earlier. That could never be changed: our selves were commingled in sharing our narratives. For what would be the point of narrating one's self if there were no others to listen? The idea of the narrative self—a self distributed to others in words, stories, and other forms of expression—brought us closer because it confirmed the self as essentially related to other people.

Theories such as that of the distributed self make sense intellectually and even have an aesthetic importance—for example, when we look at an artwork, say, the famous van Gogh painting of his room. The objects—a bed, table, candleholder, wooden floor—are commonplace, hardly the subject matter of great art. There's not even a person in this setting. Yet van Gogh is able to suffuse through the pigments that make up each object (chair, table, window) a powerful intimation of the person to whom these things belong. The energy, emotion, and artistic sensibility of the artist are transferred onto the canvas and made accessible to viewers willing to allow him to speak to them.

The distributed self of narrative theory held an exciting warmth and intimacy I missed in other outlooks. But its heavy dependence on literary theory conjured up an image of Hildegard and me as open pages of books set across from each other on a table. The theory's explanatory power brought me closer to my life with Hildegard—but only as close as one gets to a character in a novel.

I glanced at the audience and saw a few heads shaking in disagreement. There would be questions and counterarguments. Several older women sat in the front row. What if Hildegard were actually here, listening to me? Well, why not? Wasn't my goal to bear witness to our relationship and to find a framework that honored our closeness?

THE RELATIONAL SELF

Martin Buber, who invited people to think of experience as fundamentally relational, turned the attention of early twentieth-century philosophy and theology to the intuitive, almost mystical communion possible between people when they are open to one another. Drawing on research in the psychology of perception that emerged during the first decades of this century, and combining it with his penetrating understanding of the eastern European Hasidic tradition of storytelling, he explained in *I and Thou* the powerful role of dialogue.

Buber proposed a distinction between apprehending people, nature, animals, even oneself, as object-like (which he called an "I-It" relationship) and apprehending these as intimately and simultaneously part of oneself and yet as subjects in their own right (an "I–Thou" relationship). He presented a peculiar idea: that in a truly I–Thou experience, the quality of exchange could be located not in either of the relating minds or beings but "between" them. In the immediacy of consciousness, the relationship itself becomes a third and inclusive consciousness. An example might be the feeling of compassion.

For Buber, compassion meant that one experienced a relation from both sides: that the presupposition of separateness was transcended in a fundamental sense of belonging both to each other and to something ineffable, some ground of being that made such an experience possible—a unity that preserved the personhood of both individuals. Running against the mainstream of early twentieth-century philosophy, Buber was criticized as obscure in his use of language, unscientific in his epistemology of intersubjectivity, and prone to mysticism. He had a deep and lifelong interest in the Jewish mystical and communal Hasidic movement, and he spoke of endowing with a sense of the sacred, or "hallowing," the world and life itself.

Yet in his discussion of compassion, Buber was making a practical, even empirical, observation. As finite creatures, we all share a destiny. That common end—the fact that we all die, that life is not endless, is a third element in such an exchange, a "ground of being" on which we all stand. In moments of closeness to the pain, vulnerability, and frailty of others, we can impose an artificial distance, a denial of relatedness, or we can draw near in recognition of belonging to a unity of life.

And how was this notion of dialogue different from narrative theory? Buber emphasized the transcendent quality of language: that speech, above all, brings us to silence. And in that silence, the most important experiences take place. Thus narrative is only a means, not an end. With Buber, we must take a leap. The truth we are to discover, said Buber, is that the self is fundamentally relational. The singular self and the hyphenated selves of modern philosophy and psychology are, for Buber, constructs of denial, deceptions of pseudo-science useful for manipulating the world and other people, but misleading in causing us to deny the living sacredness of each moment, each encounter. A reality too intense, perhaps, to bear.

My time was almost up, my paper not at all conclusive, simply a series of stepping stones with no final destination. There was so much more I wanted to say—that at the beginning and end of life there is fragility, vulnerability, and dependence. Each of the twin twilights of life, dawn and dusk, has its special beauty and its own perplexities, its own blurring of the sharp outlines. An infant's frail life announces future strength and independence. An old person's announces dependency and death.

Hildegard revealed to me that dignity resides in the relationship of one person caring about and for another. When one person declines, the other has the opportunity to honor, to preserve that person's worth. The bestower of worth does it for the sake of the other, for his own sake, and for what is common to both.

Dignity, as a quality of worth, no longer registered as identical to autonomy, the individual recognized as self-governing. Hildegard was no longer in control of her life. To argue that she should be treated as though she were in full possession of her decision-making capacities would be an act of self-deception. But Hildegard was my worthy friend. And this is where the ideal of autonomy, probably the most cherished value of a society enamored with the concept of individuality, begins to falter.

What happens when the autonomous self collides with the reality of dependency? For some people, a dependent state of existence is so unacceptable that they would sooner take their own lives. To insist on one's fundamental autonomy at the expense of one's essential relatedness leads to an impasse from which there is no escape. Once a philosophy or a psychology establishes the autonomous self as its focal point, it must find a way to link that self to others. Often there is no adequately convincing way out.

Perhaps I should have turned to Buddhism and embraced the idea of the self as an illusion of separateness based on certain commonsense but erroneous preoccupations with the world of appearances. Many years later, I would find in Stephen Levine's *Who Dies?* just such a Buddhist approach to compassionately caring for the terminally ill person as my compatriot in death. But for the moment, I was stuck. The best I could do was to recognize the fundamentally relational concept of self and to notice, paradoxically, how difficult it was for me to endure moments of true belonging to another person.

I sat down. The next speaker was already at the microphone.

Q AND A

After the next talk, there was time left for questions. The first— really a monologue in disguise—was addressed to the last speaker, who, wisely, just nodded and thanked the commentator. Then a dignified-looking gentleman in a handsome blue pin-striped suit rose and cleared his throat.

"I have a question," he said, pointing at me, "for Manheimer." I nodded and prepared to make notes on my yellow pad for my reply. "You have reviewed several concepts of the self but avoided one very important one. What about the notion of multiple selves? Don't some people argue that an individual is the locus of successive selves? After all, we have a significantly different outlook at twenty than at forty or eighty. Why assume one master self?"

Again I thought about Hildegard the vibrant woman I first met at the senior center and Hildegard the frail, confused woman in the domiciliary care home. Would it have made matters simpler to assume multiple Hildegards? If so, why shouldn't I assume multiple Rons?

The idea of multiple selves makes sense when we look statistically at how poorly most people plan for retirement and old age, shortchanging the older self they will become for the younger self they are now; or when we look at the promises we make about the future, when we're younger, that we fail to keep when that future catches up with us. It makes sense of certain choices, perceptions, and judgments we make that suggest we hold quite different outlooks at different times. Yet I wanted to argue that instead of multiple selves, we recognize the self as a process. "What we call self is really our capacity to reimagine the past in order to adapt to the present and prepare for the future," I said. "The poet T. S. Eliot has the famous line 'We had the experience but missed the meaning'—a later, older self grasping what an earlier self could not. I don't agree. We get a meaning the first time but revise and rediscover other meanings at later moments because the overall picture changes. We reintegrate the meaning according to our changing situation, sometimes preserving, sometimes canceling out earlier meanings. Our capacity to reimagine the past is the key to our ability to live creatively."

Maybe it would have benefited me to adopt the multiple-self framework. Then I could more readily have accepted the frail Hildegard as a new and different person, could have let go of expectations stemming from my insisting on some thread of continuity with the past. And I would have been free to be a new person myself in this changed context. Yet I preferred the tension of the frayed thread.

Two turns later, a woman raised her hand and said, "This is a question for Manheimer. Really, a concern. In your appraisal of the relational self, don't you run the risk of denying your individuality and your integrity of selfhood in your rather mystical suggestion of union with another person?"

That was a tough one. I wasn't sure how to answer. Before I could try, our moderator suddenly looked up from his notes and announced, "I'm sorry but we've gone way over our time, and I see another group waiting to come in for their session." As I gathered up my things, I looked around for the woman who had asked the question, but she was gone.

THE REBUKE

Later I thought about the unanswered question. Would I have to suppress the memory of my communion with Hildegard's future death in order to embrace my wife, laugh with my friends, play with my children? Could I still read and write about philosophy? In that moment, I heard Hildegard's voice within me: "Of course you can. I'll take care of my death. You take care of yours." This is the paradox of the self, hyphenated or not.

Our lives may be experienced as streams flowing into a common river. But to blur all the outlines of personhood and meld with another is another kind of illusion or fantasy. Though we shared turns at the helm of a common vessel, I had to follow my direction; Hildegard had to follow hers. She had been among the group who stood reciting Tennyson that eventful evening at the

public library, and now, more Ulyssean in spirit than I could ever
hope to be, Hildegard was making her journey toward a vast new
sea that I could not fathom. Maybe we can never pass through
someone else's arch of experience, only our own.

The spatial metaphor of the journey of time and self cannot do
justice to the experience of commingled searches or shared histories. In space, even the closest things stand only side by side. But
the meeting in time is the experience of an inexplicable moment
in which here and there, self and other, dissolve. Then the spatial
metaphor of time reasserts itself. Insight slips away in forgetfulness. Still, the memories of such encounters return to me from
time to time, often unbidden, like Hildegard's wave.

CHAPTER FIVE

SARAH'S LAUGH

Is it strength of character or some impulse of self-preservation to laugh in the face of adversity? Despite Hildegard's loss of her husband and her decline into frailty, a certain twinkle, even merriment, continued to shine from her eyes. When I conjure up her voice now, I cannot help hearing a gentle, teasing laugh that is like an arm around my shoulder. I have heard other laughter from the brink of anguish. An older friend told me of her shock when, in a conversation with her husband about a wilderness trek they had taken the year before, she discovered he couldn't remember anything about it. They knew he had early signs of dementia. Faced by this terrible reality, she began to cry. But her husband stilled her tears with a laugh, telling her, "Honey, don't be sad, I'm sure I had a wonderful time!"

In a recent "Doonesbury" cartoon series, Garry Trudeau depicts Lacy Davenport, an elderly California member of the House of

Representatives and an eccentric political activist, who is compelled to give up her seat in Congress because of the onset of Alzheimer's disease. The comic strip makes fun of Lacy's memory lapses and brings out reactions of both concern and anxiety in those around her. Trudeau allows Lacy to jest about her own predicament, asserting her humanity in a time of adversity. With an element of lightness, he makes public a plight that befalls and will befall many in this new age of extended longevity. Like my friend's husband and like Hildegard, Trudeau softens the hard edge of misfortune through a lens of humor, transforming indignity to dignity.

Freud, early and late in his career, investigated the hidden recesses of laughter. He observed that deep humor, unlike other forms of the comical such as satire and parody that depict the castigation of human folly, acknowledges human weakness and vulnerability while refusing to accept human suffering. For Freud, humor is the noblest of our ego defenses. Like the safety valve of a steam engine releasing pent-up pressure, a laugh can transform pain into pleasure and liberate the individual from the wounds of life. With his concept of the tripartite psyche, Freud pictured the otherwise stern and demanding superego taking on a consoling parental voice, telling the wounded ego, "Look here! This is all that this seemingly dangerous world amounts to. Child's play— the very thing to jest about!" How much more dangerous the world appears to us as we age, and how much greater our need for the soothing balm of humor.

From my earliest contacts with those treading the path of life before me, I began to notice important differences in the meaning and expression of humor. I admired, and longed to develop in myself, the quality of humor displayed by people who could laugh at their foibles and shortcomings and accept the truth that, for them, time was running out. Self-reflective humor seemed to help my older friends put their lives in perspective while increasing their tolerance of others. However, I recognized that in contrast to the positive humor coming from these older persons, much of the humor about aging and old people was negative.

There were the silly "over the hill" birthday cards poking fun at someone's turning forty or fifty. There were the innumerable jokes such as the one about the old man who picks up a magical frog—a beautiful princess who offers to gratify his every desire if only he will kiss her. Putting the creature into his pocket, he comments, "At my age I'd rather have a talking frog." Humor is always about the most serious matters of life—forgetfulness, impotency, and death being prominent among the topics related to aging and old age. Most attempts at humor about aging and the elderly are defensive, not in Freud's sense of making light of adversity, but through denial, distancing us from the reality of suffering and finitude, helping us avoid anxiety about sickness and death.

Whether by the elderly or about them, the humor of aging rests on the very real issue of time. Where Freud spoke of the wounds of life, we could just as easily say "wounds of time," because aging and later life mean greater awareness of personal vulnerability, proximity to death, and consciousness of the limits of one's body. The longer we live, the more exposed we are to loss, accident, and decline. We are slow-moving targets for adversity.

In light of these examples, should we say that humor is a defense mechanism, a quality of character, the emergence of a latent resource, or possibly a manifestation of wisdom? Humor related to aging can work in all these ways. I felt I had the most to learn from those whose ability to turn humor on themselves enabled them to embrace rather than resist the impact of time and change, to turn regret or bitterness into self-forgiveness, thus loosening the bonds of emotion. It was clear that, for some, the lesson of survivorship could be expressed by Tennyson's Ulysses, who says, "Though much is taken, much abides."

Maybe the lens of humor they applied to life would help me to understand what Kierkegaard had in mind when, in his theory of life stages, he placed the outlook of humor in an intermediate position between the ethical stage (the individual's obligations to society) and the religious stage (his or her surrender to divine authority). He was thinking not of lightheartedness or escapist humor but of accommodation to incompleteness, a form of humility and self-acceptance that exceeded ordinary (though difficult to achieve) moral maturity. Kierkegaard's humoristic hero was Socrates, in whom wit and wisdom were entwined. Still, for Kierkegaard, enlightened humor must always fall short of the ultimate goal: transcendence, redemption, the promise of a life free of suffering, immune to time. The humanist in me balked at this presumption; the spiritualist in me yearned for it.

In line with Kierkegaard's theory, the humor of several older friends reminded me that spiritual insight is sometimes heard in the laugh, the jest, the comic parable of traditional spiritual elders such as Zen masters, Hasidic rabbis, and Sufi sages. Though their eyes are said to burn with mystic fire, they are often portrayed as laughing. But why? Sometimes it seems their wisdom is nothing but recognition of the limits of their own knowledge—a profound ignorance of which they had previously been unaware but which now so delights, so tickles them that it cannot be contained. "Listen," we hear them call out in koans and parables, "have you heard the one about the wandering monk, the beggar's shoes, the haughty crow?"

If humor could be an expression of wisdom, a heightened stage of consciousness, a philosophical outlook, then I wanted to know its secret powers, grasp its internal principles, learn the lessons it could offer about liberation from suffering and from the ravages of time. Along the route of my investigations into the varied expressions of humor, I was to find that the laugh of wisdom could resound in unpredictable places and emanate from unlikely people, that it might echo in a phrase, a gesture, an object. That it might occur at a bar mitzvah I attended when visiting home in Detroit came as another surprise.

UNCLE JOE

My brother-in-law's uncle Joe did not appear to be a sage or spiritual master. For most of his adult life, he had been a kosher butcher. Although I'd heard he was a pious man, to me, Joe was the man who loved cigars. He'd enter a family party with a nice Upmann or Don Tomas clenched in his jaw. Never once could I remember him striking a match or clicking a lighter, and yet by the end of the evening it was gone. The whole night he'd be laughing and talking, rarely removing that stogie from the corner of his mouth. With his black slicked-back hair, small shining black eyes, wide jowls, and thick neck, he exuded a sense of warmth and good will.

So ubiquitous was Uncle Joe's cigar, his wife, Suzie, told me, that once when the neighborhood baker passed him on the street and Joe was cigarless, the baker failed to greet him. The man later apologized, explaining, "I didn't recognize Joe without that cigar."

I'm pondering the enigma of Joe's cigar as I sit next to him one night in the late stages of a bar mitzvah party—after the cake cutting, the speeches from the child come of age and the proud parents—having consumed cups of strong coffee to wash down the rich desserts. My wife, Caroline, and others from our table are off visiting or dancing. Joe, four fingers worth of smokeless cigar jutting from his lips, wears an amused look on his face as he watches the younger couples, shoes kicked aside, cavorting on the dance floor of the synagogue social hall.

"Uncle Joe," I say, though he isn't really my uncle, you just want to call him that, "Uncle Joe, you look like you just heard a good joke."

Uncle Joe nods, inspects his gold cuff links, spreads his hairy-knuckled fingers on the white tablecloth, now stained with drops of wine, gravy, and coffee, and looks up at me. "Well, I tell you," he begins, tucking the cigar to the corner of his mouth. "I was just thinking about a visit I paid to a men's clothing establishment a few days ago." He looks at the dancers, taps his hand to the beat, looks back at me.

"See, I need cuff links. So I drive over to Marcus Men's Clothing one afternoon. I come in the store, there's only the old tailor standing there. The other salesmen are busy with customers. So, I says to him, 'Excuse me, sir, I'm looking for a . . .' But, before I can finish, the old fellow throws up his arms, grabs both my shoulders, looks me in the eye, gives a big sigh, and says, 'Yes, my friend, and I'm looking, too.' " Joe laughs. "I'm looking for a pair of cuff links, and now we're looking for the messiah, or something." Joe's belly shakes with laughter as he repeats, "And I'm looking, too."

"Was he serious?" I ask. "I mean, was he just joking?"

"Joking?" Joe stares at me, a gleam of mirth in his eyes. "Who isn't joking? Jews are always joking—about God, about forgiveness, about luck, about each other. What tickled me is the way he said it. Right out of the blue. Of course, I understood immediately."

"Because you're Jewish?"

Joe nods yes then shakes his head and says, "You appreciate some things as funny when you get a few years on you." Leaning forward toward me, he adds, "You should understand this. You're a philosopher, aren't you?"

"I think of myself as a student of philosophy."

Joe shrugs his shoulders as if to say, "So what kind of answer is that?" He removes his cigar, crosses one short leg over the other, and leans back. "You know," he says, looking at me straight-faced, "Jews invented laughter."

"Invented?" I exclaim. "How's that?"

"It's in the Torah, the Five Books of Moses. You know, the first book, Genesis?"

I had heard that Joe had steeped himself in talmudic scholarship, hoping to become a rabbi when he was young. But the family could not afford the necessary education, and Joe, after returning from overseas duty during World War II, went into the meat-cutting business with a buddy.

Seeing my look of puzzlement, Joe explains, "You know the story of Abraham and Sarah, right?" I nod. "Well, that's a pretty old story. Just a few turns of the scroll from where God creates the heaven and earth, Adam and Eve, Cain and Abel. Not much further after that we get Abraham and Sarah. Am I right?"

I'm not sure what he is driving at, but I stroke my beard as if in acknowledgment.

"Sure, that's right," says Joe. "God has promised to make Abraham the father of a whole people, so, of course, he needs the help of his wife, Sarah. But try as they may, the couple don't succeed in having a single kid. By now he's pushing a hundred, and she's no young chickadee either at ninety. So much for promises. But then there come three men wandering in from the desert. Nomads maybe. Maybe not. Abraham welcomes them, and gives them to eat and drink, and they tell him, 'Abe, the time has come, your wife, Sarah, is gonna have a kid, no foolin'.' Well, he doesn't know what to think. Imagine someone telling me and my Suzy, here in our seventies, that I'm going to get her pregnant. No way, José." Joe slaps his hand down on the table and chuckles. "And it stands in the Torah that Abraham laughed in his heart. Yeah, he kept it quiet. But now, Sarah, she's an altogether different cookie. She hears this, too, from where she's hiding in her tent. And she gives a laugh, but a good one. Naturally, they hear. 'Abe,' the angels tell him—see, by now he knows these are no ordinary guys—'Abe, this wife of yours, she doesn't believe us, she's mocking us.' But Sarah denies it. 'No,' she says, 'I wasn't laughing at you; it was a joke I heard from one of the ladies in the next tent.' "

Joe looks away for a moment, grabs the hand of someone passing by. "Lou, you're looking good out there on the dance floor." The tall, gray-haired man smiles, pumps Joe's hand, and walks on. Meanwhile, my mind has wandered to another pair of Jewish oldsters who experience a surprising surge of romantic energy late in life—a frail, reclusive doctor of philosophy, Nahum Fischelson, a bachelor living in a garret room on Market Street, and his unlikely paramour, his neighbor, the spinster cleaning lady, Black Dobbe, whose dark complexion and mood have landed her that nickname.

"You know the rest of the story, huh?" asks Joe, snapping me back.

I do know. Sarah becomes pregnant and has a child, Isaac, whose name in the Hebrew, Itzak, means "he laughs." Given my rationalist Hebrew school education in biblical history, I offer the usual explanation. "There's a folklore explanation about the name Itzak, connecting her laughing with his name."

"That's what they taught you in Hebrew school?" Joe shakes his head in disappointment. "Modern rabbinic nonsense," he says. "That's the easy way out." Joe scoots his chair closer. I can smell the pungent, unlit cigar. "If the Bible was that simple," he continues, "people would have lost interest in it thousands of years ago. Folklore, ha. No, boychick, let me tell you how it is."

Joe rests an arm on the table, puts his other hand on his knee. "This is Genesis, the book of creation, we're talking about. Every year when we reroll the Torah scroll, we start with 'In the beginning.' You know how it goes. And every year, we hear the same litany. How are Abraham and Sarah going to fulfill the prophecy when he can't get her pregnant, or she can't get pregnant, who knows? We've heard the story over and over. We know how its gonna come out. Still, every time, the suspense builds. I sit there in *shul* following the story, and it's like I've forgotten. God promises and promises, Abraham obeys and obeys, and still no baby. It's never gonna happen. Then"—Joe slaps his knee— "bingo."

"She gets pregnant," I say.

"No," Joe fixes me with his black eyes. "No, she laughs; Sarah laughs," he exclaims. "That's the first laugh in the Bible, maybe the oldest laugh ever recorded. I dunno. Possible the Chinese have an older one. I'm no expert. But I can tell you, when I hear that laugh, it goes right through my *nishama*, my soul. You know why?"

I shake my head. I've never heard anyone interpret Scripture quite like this.

"Because it's the miracle of creation all over again." Joe taps his knuckles on the table. "If God can make a universe out of absolutely nothing—a huge miracle, you'll admit—he can make Sarah and Abraham fruitful. When Sarah laughs, that's the miracle happening to a real person, a human being. Sure, it starts out as the laugh of doubt. At her age, who wouldn't doubt? But then"—Joe grips my arm—"it becomes the laugh of joy, the surprise of creation. You see, the more unlikely the story, the bigger the laugh." Joe grins, and I see gold caps gleaming on the molars clenching the cigar stub. "And you know something, mister philosophy student?" Joe raises his heavy black eyebrows. "Sometimes, right there in *shul*, when I hear this story chanted, I laugh, too."

I smile. Shake my head in admiration. Joe nods, removes a handkerchief from his suit pocket, and wipes his forehead. Two little girls in white dresses—great-nieces, perhaps—come up to Joe, giggling, telling him something about their teacher and friends. Joe seems to know all about it. He teases and asks questions. They love his attention, like that of a friendly bear. Again my mind wanders to Fischelson and Black Dobbe. The place is Warsaw; the time, the eve of World War I; the teller of the story, another Itzak, Isaac Bashevis Singer. I read the story years ago. A comic tale, of sorts. Fischelson has devoted thirty years of his solitary, impoverished life to studying the Latin text of Spinoza's *Ethics*. As a young man, he had hoped to publish an essay defending Spinoza's philosophy against the criticisms of Kant and his followers. Somehow a promising career eluded him. The years ebbed away, leaving him with a tattered book and a stomach ailment that, he believes, could be cancer. Fischelson remains fixated on Spinoza's concept of an impersonal God, an "absolute infinite Substance." Through his intellectual contemplation of this God, Fischelson speculates, his own infinite Substance could not be destroyed. Yet, lying on his bed awaiting the angel of death, he feels pangs of doubt. At just this moment of remorse enters not an angel but a messenger in unlikely garb, the old crone Black Dobbe. She wants Fischelson to translate a letter she's received from relatives in America. Seeing his state of distress, she decides to look after the eccentric old man, who, she has heard it whispered, might be an apostate.

So a precarious beginning at a late stage of life for a couple whose lives are barren of children, hope, or riches. Yet the story creates a sense of promise. Was Singer thinking of the patriarch and matriarch in the desert wilderness?

HUMOR AND AGING

"Uncle Joe," I begin, "you mentioned appreciating humor differently as you get older. Do you think there's a connection?"

"Let me tell you, sonny, there's nothing funny about getting old." He pats his chest. Maybe he's had bypass surgery.

"No," I respond, "I guess not."

"On the other hand," says Joe, "maybe you learn to accept some of the disappointment and surprises life hands you. You learn to laugh at what you can't understand."

Joe had a point. Though not everyone develops a deep sense of humor in growing older, from my experience with older friends, I've noticed some use humor to lighten feelings of loss or physical discomfort. They become more tolerant of the contradictions and paradoxes of life.

"Humor could express a kind of wisdom," I say.

"Now that," says Joe, "I will go along with." He gives me a scrutinizing look. "Obviously, you've thought about this, Mr. Philosopher. What else have you learned?"

The band has just broken into the "Macarena," and there's a scramble to get in line for the dance.

"I've learned, Uncle Joe, that you're right about how laughter is related to the unlikeliness of the story. It's in Aristotle."

"Good," he says, "I like Aristotle. He had quite an influence on Maimonides, you know."

I knew that Maimonides, the twelfth-century Jewish physician and religious scholar, had adopted many of Aristotle's methods of analysis for reasoning through complex issues. "Aristotle," I continue, "says comedy and tragedy are similar and different. Both, he says, involve a collision of wills between a human being—usually a prominent leader, like Oedipus, or a warrior, like Agamemnon—and the gods."

Joe looks at me quizzically. Maybe he wonders whether I've given myself over to pagan beliefs. "The gods, you see," I'm quick to explain, "represent powerful social and cosmic forces related to tribal taboos, family allegiances, codes of war, and political controversy." Joe takes a sip of coffee. "In tragedy," I continue, "a hero's character flaw—like excessive pride, vanity, or greed— leads painfully to disgrace, downfall, and death. The cosmic order asserts its dominion over human destiny. But in comedy the heroic individual, drawing from a bag of tricks, painlessly triumphs over humiliation, failure, and degradation. The comic hero's flaws— foolishness, impulsiveness, or naïveté—can become redeeming qualities that turn the tide."

"Aristotle says that?" asks Joe, putting down his spoon. "Maybe he'd seen a lot of Chaplin movies, eh?"

"Chaplin, yes," I affirm, "or Woody Allen. But probably he was thinking of some comedies he'd attended down at the local amphitheater."

"So the little schlemiels of the world come out on top?"

"Yes, that's how it goes. Not only do they manage to survive but, according to some interpreters, they reenter society with a new and higher status."

Joe nods, "Like this great-nephew of mine, huh?" He points to a boy awkwardly dancing with his mother. "The bar mitzvah kid, Stevie. Such a little meshuga. Who'd have thought he'd pull this off without some prank. Well, I guess when it's your bar mitzvah, you'd better behave."

"Yes," I exclaim. "I never thought of it before, but a bar mitz- vah is like the weddings and festivals at the end of lots of famous comedies, as in Shakespeare, when they have the big parties that feature the comic hero in his new role. See, now your nephew Stevie is an insider, not just some kid. Do you think he's ever danced before with his mother?"

"So you're saying a bar mitzvah is a comedy?" Joe laughs. "You got a point there. Look at that little *pisher*. He chants a few words of Torah," Joe snorts, "and now he's a man."

"He can now be counted for a minyan," I reply. Joe shrugs, and

I go on, "Besides, Aristotle says comedies always deal with contradictions and plots that deviate from the expected. Overnight, a boy becomes a man and starts dancing with his mother. The whole thing is a ritual designed to incorporate surprises and why laughter . . ."

"Mr. Philosopher," Joe interrupts, waving his cigar, "Bar mitzvahs and weddings are for young people. Didn't you say humor had something to do with getting old?"

The connection had slipped my mind. "Well, yes," I answer, getting back to the point. "See, as we get older"—Joe gives me a dubious look, as if suggesting I haven't qualified yet as a peer—"we learn that a lot of the things we expected to get resolved or settled—like, can there be happiness without sorrow, good without evil—can never be fully resolved. We learn to accept many of the contraries in life, make our peace with time. We can look at ourselves and laugh at what formerly troubled us and made us anxious. We accept our humanity."

"Peace with time," Joe muses, "that's a good one." He snaps his fingers. "I have an example."

"Yes?"

"Sure. I was in a meeting just a few days ago, a club I've been a member of for God knows how long. And a guy gets up. What's his name? Yeah, Curly Shapiro. Curly"—he points to his full head of hair—"because he's bald. So, you see, right there, what you call a contrary. Yeah. Well, this Curly, he's chair of the long-range planning committee. Every organization's gotta have one. So Curly gets up to give his report, and he says, 'Boys, before I give my report, there's something I gotta tell you.' And he pauses, real serious-like, making us wonder—'What's happened? Is he sick?' Then Curly goes on, 'Boys, for me, long-range planning means what am I gonna eat for breakfast." Joe breaks out laughing, "What am I gonna eat for breakfast? Well, he had us, you know?"

"You're right," I say, "that's a good example. He knows he could die tomorrow, yet here he is working on long-range planning and can laugh at that. That's what I mean by 'making peace with time.' "

"Maybe," Joe snorts, "but don't be too sure."

"Why not?"

Joe takes a sip of water. "Mr. Philosopher," he says, pointing a stubby finger at me, "you think all this humor business is about accepting the fact that life is short but meetings are long?"

"Something like that."

"And we, the *alter cockers* of the world, accept this fact. We make jokes about it. Who knows what tomorrow will bring. Am I right? Okay. But let me tell you something, boychick. The secret of humor is not just accepting the ticking of the clock." Joe shoots his sleeve and shows me his gold watch, then shakes his head. "Not only time, my friend," he leans forward, cups his hand around his mouth, and whispers, "timing."

"Timing?"

"Timing," he repeats. "The secret of telling a funny story is timing. Without timing, nothing. Take my friend Curly. Suppose he'd said the identical thing but hadn't given us the big sigh and the long puss? We wouldn't have started feeling uncomfortable, feeling like maybe he was gonna tell us something bad. Just when he's got us real worried, he springs it on us. So, you see, that's what your Aristotle left out. First danger; then safety. The right timing."

"Well," I respond, "okay, how you tell the story is important. But you still need the tension of opposites."

Joe considers this. Chews on his cigar. The band shifts from waltzes and rock and roll to Jewish dance music, signaling the party's finale.

"You play golf?" asks Joe.

Is he annoyed, changing the topic of conversation? "Golf?" I exclaim. "I played in high school and a little in college, but with all my traveling and having to haul around the clubs . . ." Joe puts his hand on my wrist.

"Fine. So you know, maybe, a little about golf."

"A little," I nod.

"Well, golf is like humor."

"It is?"

"Yes. Wait a little, I'll explain." Joe takes the end of a spoon and etches a curving line into the tablecloth. "When you're young and strong and full of yourself, you swing a golf club in a big arc. Like this"—he points at the tablecloth inscription—"You give the ball such a *zetz*, it goes from here to tomorrow. Right?" I nod. "But when you get to be an old-timer like me"—Joe retraces the line with his spoon—"you got a few aches and pains, maybe you've had a few places sewn up, so you don't wind yourself up like a clock each time you swing. See, I got these golfing buddies, been playing with them for years. And I notice, like me, Lou and Herman, they take the club back only to about here." He cuts the curved line with the spoon. "And they follow through only to about here." He makes another cut of the arc. "It's like Darwin said, survival is 90 percent adaptation. We don't look so good up there on the tee. Lou, he contorts himself like a pretzel. Herman, he's just the opposite. Makes himself stiff as a general. Nothing bends. But"—Joe takes the cigar from his mouth, gestures with it—"here's the secret. They still got the timing. When that club head meets that little white ball, glick."

"Glick?" I ask. "Not, click?"

"No, these are Jewish golfers; they got Yiddish balls." He grins from ear to ear, his eyes sparkling. I laugh.

"And this is why golf is like humor?"

"Well, can you imagine anything funnier than three old duffers trying to hit a little white ball down the middle of the fairway?" I shake my head. "Of course," he continues, "that doesn't happen every time."

"I wouldn't think so."

"No. But seriously," he says, "isn't this like what Aristotle says—opposites mixed together? I'm saying that our threesome plays a funny game of golf. We look like we might be in pain, and sometimes we are. Like what we do is contrary to nature and the laws of physics. But we've figured out ways to adjust to our little infirmities."

"And the glick?"

"The glick, the timing. You still got it. Because, even if you're a *shtarker*, you know, a strongman?" I nod. "Without timing, you might as well be a weakling."

I could see his point. If humor means accepting your limitations but not giving up, overcoming an obstacle that, in this case, is an aging body, then maybe a golf swing—one of those little triumphs of the human spirit—can be a kind of humor. Maybe timing is the essence of humor, not the content of a story or, as Aristotle has it, the structure. But this would mean that almost anything—said in the right way—could be comical.

Uncle Joe certainly embodied the idea that a sense of humor, especially about oneself, could liberate the spirit. His tales reminded me of Norman Cousins' description of how watching film comedies helped him recover from a serious illness. Getting on the humor therapy bandwagon, some researchers had been showing comedies in nursing homes to bolster the spirits of residents; this seemed to help most people adjust better, but they also found that some people became more depressed. Maybe the researchers forgot that comedies deal with some heavy topics and that these might have triggered unhappy memories.

As Uncle Joe looked about, I noticed he was wearing his yarmulke, a small disc of knitted yarn held to the crown of his head with a bobby pin. He was *frum*, an observant Jew. Maybe I could ask him about whether Kierkegaard was right, that humor not only was a means of accepting the limits of one's life but pointed to a religious understanding.

TRANSCENDING HUMOR

Joe's wife, Suzie, a short, stocky redhead wearing a pair of large green eyeglasses and bright red lipstick, returned to the table. She put her purse down and slid into the chair, giving Joe a gentle elbow for him to move over.

"Ronnie, are you still talking to this old guy?" She looks at Joe. "Don't believe anything he tells you."

Joe winks at me. "Of course, he doesn't believe anything I say," he tells Suzie. "He's a philosopher. They're supposed to doubt everything. Right, boychick?"

"That's right, Uncle Joe."

"Good," says Suzie, "because with Joe you never know." She elbows him again, and Joe laughs. Then another woman arrives at the table and sits beside Suzie. "My cousin," she explains, and immediately the two plunge into conversation. Uncle Joe and I sit in silence.

"Uncle Joe," I begin, "there's something I've been wondering about."

"This is about humor, still?" he replies. I nod. "So, *nu?* Ask."

"Well, you know, as a philosophy student, I studied the Danish thinker Kierkegaard."

"I've heard of him," says Joe. "An eggs-a-stench-alist," he mouths carefully. "Have I got it?"

"Right. A religious existentialist, not one of the atheistic branch. He believed that every life mirrored that of Jesus because in every person there was something finite and something infinite,

something mortal and something godly. All our lives we try to figure out how to bring the two parts into harmony."

"This is very true. You'll find the same idea in our books. You
know, Ronnie," he looks at me sternly, "why do you waste your
time with this Kierkegaard? You could be learning Torah, reading
Hillel and Schamai and the other sages."

I don't know how to answer. My studies had brought me to the
conclusion that every path has its truths and that all paths ulti-
mately lead to the same place.

"That's a long story, Uncle Joe," I say. "It was something I got
onto in graduate school—how philosophers thought about
human development, about what was possible in life. Kierkegaard
had some interesting things to say."

Joe nods, thoughtfully. "And what were these interesting
things?"

"Well, Kierkegaard believed that humor was a kind of transi-
tional life stage that came between what he called the ethical and
the religious."

"He was a golfer?" Joe teases.

I laugh at the thought of Kierkegaard playing golf. "No, but he
was a rather comic figure; spindle-legged and hunchbacked—the
Copenhagen tabloids of his time made fun of his looks."

"Now they sell porno in vending machines. Right on the
street!" Joe exclaims. Apparently, he and Suzie, who were fond of
traveling, had visited Denmark. "But this Kierkegaard, he sounds
like Lou."

"Physically, perhaps, but he wasn't an old man, not chronologically, anyway. My point is this. Kierkegaard has these life stages.
He says that when you're about middle-aged, you've reached a
stage in life when you've tried to do your duty to society to
become a respectable person. You're not a young romantic any
more, living for peak experiences and infatuations, but now you've

come to realize that the things that make for continuity in life, like marriage, a career, close friends, maybe children—that these give your life depth, permanence, a meaning that endures against lots of the unexpected changes, hardships, and disappointments that happen to everybody." I look at Joe to see his reaction.

"*Nu?*" he shrugs. "This we need a Kierkegaard to tell us?"

"Well," I say, "he has a very original way of bringing out the issues." Joe shrugs. "Anyway, Uncle Joe, here's the interesting part. You see, for Kierkegaard, development does not stop with the ethical. Kierkegaard says that in the ethical time of life, we can't help feeling that somehow, despite trying to live a righteous life, we're still not complete beings. We're not fully in control of our lives, we're never completely independent, and we still have long-ings that fulfilling our obligations to society never quite satisfies. And, as we get older, we realize more and more that each of us falls short, in some or many ways, of an ideal we have of a happy life. Call it contentment, completeness, or . . ."

Joe waves his cigar. "I know exactly what you're saying. I used to feel exactly the same way."

"You did?"

"Yes, right after the kids went off to college. *Shesh!*" Joe shakes his head. "See, at first I can't wait for them to leave. A little peace and quiet for once we'll have. But after they're gone. Ah," he sighs, "I look around at the house. All of a sudden it's big and empty. Me and Suzie look at one another, and I think, you know, is this it? Sure, the kids will be back; there'll be weddings and grandchildren and lots more to look forward to. But is that all there is? I ask myself. And I start thinking, 'What does my life amount to?' All day long I'm han-dling meat. A tenderloin, ground round, a leg of lamb. It's what I know. And let me tell you, there's not much funny about meat." I nod, picturing Joe expertly slicing into a side of beef. "Okay," Joe continues, "I'm a good father, a good husband. Sure. But I know something's missing. Call it a midlife crisis. Who knows? All I know is that's when I got the idea I should start going to *shul* like I used to when I was a young fella. Now I'm gonna look into the teachings of our prophets and the great sages. And you know what?"

"What?"

"I find they have a lot to say to me. Before, I used to think, well, these people in the Bible, only rabbis and scholars really understand them. Me? A butcher? I'm just an onlooker. They'll tell me what it means, how I should live, I should be a good person. But that way, I'm not part of it. But something happens. I'm hearing voices in my head. I never put myself into Torah. You know, let myself be part of what's going on. Now I start listening in my heart. I hear the laughing and the crying, the joy and the sorrow. I don't want anybody getting in the way unless he can help me listen better. It's not that I was unhappy before that. I had a lot of *naches*, a lot I should be grateful for. But I didn't feel part of God's creation. I mean, a real player."

"You had a feeling of imperfection?" I ask.

"Imperfect. Sure, who's not?"

"I mean, did you feel that you hadn't achieved some goal, hadn't lived up to some ideal?"

"Maybe." Joe tilts his head. "What are you saying?"

"I was thinking about Kierkegaard. He says that humor comes before faith. Humor is an outlook. You accept your flawed nature, but you don't give up, because there's something that keeps gnawing at you. That's your godly aspect. The potential."

Joe rubs his chin. "Was he a psychologist, maybe? He went around with a tape recorder asking were you in a good state of humor today?"

"No, he wasn't scientific at all. He did talk to people, read, make observations. But he was interested in subjective truths—how people felt inside. He didn't think feelings were meaningless.

They were your values and beliefs about the world. Kierkegaard was especially fond of describing Socrates. You could say that Socrates was his ideal of the humorist." Joe grimaces, shakes his head. I've lost him. "See"—I lean forward to make my point— "Socrates is wise enough to know that he doesn't know about certain really big issues—like what virtue is, or human excellence. He's great at pricking holes in other people's inflated ideas, especially smug, know-it-all types. He traps them into making contradictory statements. And this way of working from paradox to paradox gets people looking into themselves for answers. According to Kierkegaard, Socrates induces people to talk about their ideals, pushes the limits of what we can know with certainty, 'intensifying their existence.' Where he hints that even though we are mortal beings, we should try to grasp timeless, immutable ideas, that's where Kierkegaard thinks the humor comes in."

I sit back to gauge Uncle Joe's reaction.

Joe takes a sip of water, then asks, "He gets them to look into the godly part of themselves, you mean?"

"Yes," I answer.

"He was serious about this?"

"From the way Plato describes him, Socrates was dedicated to his mission. And from Kierkegaard's point of view, deeply humorous because he knew no one could actually achieve this intellectual challenge. Some scholars think of Socrates as a master of irony—kind of above it all. But Kierkegaard saw him as a witness to human fallibility. Like a great stand-up comic the caliber of Bill Cosby or Lenny Bruce."

"Meshuga," Joe shakes his head. "I don't mean this Socrates, I mean your Kierkegaard. He's serious about humor before faith?"

"He writes about it. Invents the names of fictional authors who claim to be humorists because they can only speculate about faith but claim they stand on the platform of humor."

"Aha!" Joe exclaims. "Exactly my point. He writes about it under an alias. I knew there was a trick. So how do you know that he's not joking, not trying to put one over on you?" I frown. "Sure," says Joe. "Look, I'll tell you. It's a thing about the gentiles. Original sin, fallen man. They took the story from us, twisted it a little, and made such a big deal about it, it's made them sickly. They go around beating themselves over the head because they're not perfect. There's your Kierkegaard. He's obsessed by sin, only God can heal his wounds. Only Jesus. Fine. So he'll never be happy until he's saved. Like that. Meanwhile, he doesn't play golf. He doesn't go bowling," Joe was counting on his fingers. "He was married? There was a girlfriend, maybe?"

"There was a girl when he was young. They were engaged, but he broke it off because he felt he wasn't cut out for marriage."

"Fey?" he asks.

I shake my head. "More that he felt incapable of leading an ordinary life, of sharing the intimacy of marriage. He felt chosen for a special kind of solitude."

"I knew it," Joe says and bangs his fist on the table. "He's in love with God, he's let God come between him and everyone else. That's his mistake." Suzie turns to see who's making all the fuss. She looks at Joe, laughs, waves, and turns back to her cousin. "And that's why," Joe continues, "he puts humor before faith. It's just one more hurdle. One more rest stop on the turnpike to eternity. But, Mr. Theologian"—Joe points at me with the butt of his cigar—"unfortunately—or fortunately, as the case may be—he's wrong. Why? Because faith comes before humor. I know. How do I know?" Joe lifts his palms. "Because of Abraham and Sarah." He folds his hands and sits back.

"I don't think I understand," I say.

"No?" He looks at me earnestly. I shake my head. Joe scratches his ear, pulls at his nose. "Humor, you may have noticed, is with people. Someone to laugh with you, at you, about yourself, about God, whatever. Faith is a thing you do alone. Sure, you pray in *shul*. But what did Abraham have? He was alone. God spoke to him; nobody else heard a whisper. He believed what he heard, he had faith. Only later, when the news about the kid, the mama-to-be, comes from the nomads, then he laughs, then she laughs. First faith, then humor. Only by being serious can you really appreciate what's funny. And I'll tell you something more." I sit awaiting the next pronouncement. "I'd be willing to bet that your Kierkegaard knew this."

"You think so?" I ask in surprise. "Why?"

"Simple," he replies. "Have you ever asked yourself, How does this Danish gentleman know that humor comes before faith? Alias or not, how could he write such a book, just pretending? Wouldn't he have to reach faith to see how the pieces fall together? Otherwise, he's just guessing. Unless"—Joe looks at me quizzically—"he stole the idea from somebody else."

"As far as I know, Kierkegaard is the only one to think of humor as an advanced stage of life."

"Hmm," mutters Joe. "So then he switches them around—first humor, then faith, because to him the ultimate destination makes you completely alone. Just you and God, you and Jesus. Maybe that's the way of the gentiles. I dunno. With Jews, it's different. Maybe because we're a people, a tribe. We got a different ladder to climb."

A Christian theory of life stages, different from a Jewish one? Gender differences, I knew about, but I had not considered ethnic or religious variations. True, for Kierkegaard, standing alone before God was the ultimate destination. When Jews atone, ask for salvation, pray for redemption, they do it standing together in synagogue before the open arc of the Torah. Still, did it matter whether humor came before faith or vice versa? To Kierkegaard, yes, because humor would always be an imperfect way of sooth-ing the feeling that you were separated from God and, therefore, alienated from what was most divine in yourself.

Uncle Joe's interpretation was different. For him, Sarah's laugh was the joy of faith fulfilled; Abraham's laugh, the joy of a promise kept. Faith was an individual act, but humor a communal one. A person didn't traverse the stages of life all alone, but in the com-pany of others—parents, family, maybe a dog or cat. The whole idea of chronological stages suddenly seemed to me an inadequate way of describing the interplay of vulnerability and security, hope and doubt, self-unity and collective destiny. Perhaps certain qual-ities and outlooks you had all along simply become more pro-nounced, more influential at certain times in life.

THE ODD COUPLE

"Ronnie," Joe says and puts his hand on my arm, "you'll excuse me for a few minutes. I want to say hello to a few people." He saun-ters away on his mission.

His bringing up Abraham and Sarah again takes me back to Singer's couple in "The Spinoza of Market Street." His Fischelson, too, is yearning for God, albeit in a highly intellectual way. But his approach hasn't borne much fruit. Black Dobbe has led such an unfortunate life that she is devoid of spiritual expectations. Both are barren in every way. So when she starts cooking and cleaning for Fischelson, and eventually proposes marriage, Fischelson agrees, more from motives of practical convenience than from love. Theirs is, indeed, the conjoining of an unlikely pair. But Dobbe's caring for Fischelson does improve his health. Unlike Aristotle's classic dramatic comedy, this story puts the wedding celebration in the penultimate, not the final, scene. Their guests are amused by the humorous situation—two forlorn oldsters getting married! When people wish the groom a *mazel tov*, he replies, "I don't look forward to any luck." Again, they laugh. Even as readers we laugh at the couple, though we feel sorry for them. Then comes the surprise.

When Black Dobbe shows up on their wedding night wearing a silk nightgown, her hair hanging loosely over her shoulders, Fischelson feels faint. He's certain he will fail at performing his husbandly duties. As he lies there on the bed trembling, his precious copy of Spinoza's *Ethics* drops from his hands and a power long dormant awakens in him. Miraculously, he's recovered his lost youth. He kisses Dobbe and speaks to her of love, recalling long-forgotten verses from the poets of his youth.

Likewise, Black Dobbe is moved. Faint with delight, she cries and murmurs things to him in a Warsaw slang that Fischelson doesn't quite understand. The couple lie together; the rest we can imagine. Later, Fischelson slips out of bed and looks from his window at the rooftops of Warsaw on this moonlit night. And he utters a prayer: "Divine Spinoza, forgive me. I have become a fool."

A fantasy tale, some would say. Perhaps, but, like the story of Abraham and Sarah, also a parable. Fischelson and Black Dobbe experience the miracle of communion. The walls of seriousness dissolve. They are the odd couple, unlikely paramours, whose intimacy entwines opposite gods: Spinoza's *Amor Dei Intellectualis*, the impersonal deity Fischelson adored through intellect; and the absent god of the uneducated, superstitious, forlorn, agnostic Black Dobbe.

In the Genesis story, as Uncle Joe helped me to see, it is Abraham's unwavering faith in the words of a divine voice that, despite countless stumbling blocks to the promise of a happy ending, drives the tale to its conclusion, a double miracle—Sarah's pregnancy, Isaac's birth. Therein lies its deep humor, linking faith and divine creativity. In Isaac Singer's story, the humorous conjugality of two opposite types, both at the far reaches of their lives, hopes, and dreams, produces another miracle—the renewal of life, even of romantic intimacy, through simple acts of caring. Both stories can make us laugh, if only silently. Each speaks of a letting go—Sarah, of doubt, Fischelson, of seriousness.

THE SPIRITUALITY OF HUMOR

Sitting with Uncle Joe at the bar mitzvah party also made me think about connections between humor, aging, and the Jewish spiritual tradition. While they were not born old men, I always pictured the zaddikim, masters of the eighteenth- and nineteenth-century Hasidic movements, as white-bearded sages. The stories the Hasidim tell are anything but straightforward. Rather, they represent another species of the humorous: communicating wisdom through enigmatic, paradoxical, and parabolic stories. Like the Kierkegaardian humorist, the Hasidim attempt to bridge the gap between the finite and the infinite, the human and the divine. Unlike Kierkegaard's highly individualistic humorist, they are communal in orientation, linking the redemption of the individual with that of the community of fellow seekers.

I remembered reading one of the tales ascribed to the sage Dov Baer of Mezhirech, in which he tells of a certain Rabbi Leib who purportedly wandered over the earth, following the course of rivers, in order to redeem souls of the living and the dead. Rabbi Leib once explained to his followers his own earlier spiritual mission when he set out to visit a famous sage. "I did not go to the Maggid in order to hear Torah from him," he said, "but to see how he unlaces his felt shoes and laces them up again."

The teachings of the Hasidic sages often took this form of indirect communication, shifting back and forth between the sacred, the words of Torah, and the mundane, shoelaces. The tales stretch the mind, requiring tolerance for ambiguity and incongruity in order for the listener to grasp the point with a smile of understanding. To spiritualize the mundane, "to hallow this life," is one goal of Jewish spirituality. Putting on and taking off clothing becomes the parable of a way of living, evoking the likeness to tying and untying, covering and uncovering, the Torah.

LAST DANCE

Uncle Joe has just returned from table hopping. He is humming and tapping his foot as the band starts playing another piece of traditional Jewish dance music. He turns to me and says, "Well, boychick, I got one last item that might interest you."

"Yes," I reply.

"You know, Philo?" he asks.

I nod. Philo was the famous first-century Jewish historian.

"You also know what Philo has to say about humor." I shake my head, no. "You see," he admonishes, "this you should spend time on." I nod, he shrugs. "Anyway, Philo says that if you hear the wisdom that comes from right here in your *kishkas*"—Joe thumps his stomach—"you are learning from yourself. You'll feel a laugh one day so strong, it turns you, body and soul, into laughter." Joe sees I don't get it. "Yes, Mr. Philosopher. You've been wanting to know, what is this humor that gets the *zaydes*," he says, pointing to himself, "and the *bubbes*," glancing at Suzie, "through the troubles of old age." He shakes his head. "Now you see. It's not ideas or things. It's how you live, how you lead your life. If you're too serious, you'll never figure it out." With that pronouncement, Uncle Joe gets to his feet and puts out a hand.

"*Nu*, philosopher, you can do a hora?"

"Dance the hora?" I reply, a little startled. "I'm a little tired," I demur.

"Tired?" he laughs. "Then this will revive you." He grabs my hand, pulls me from my chair, the napkin falling from my lap, and drags me toward the center of the room, where the circle of hora dancers has already started to kick their heels, jump, turn, kick, as they link hands, holding them aloft, shouting and whirling to the music. The pace grows faster and faster. Now I'm holding the hand of a young woman whose black hair flies across her bare shoulders, and Uncle Joe's, his soft paw sticking out from white cuffs fastened with gold links. Our arms are raised, each dancer bound to the others through a chain of arcs that hold together the whirling circle.

CHAPTER SIX

SLICING EGGPLANT

The philosophical tradition has long extolled intellectual contemplation (what the ancient Greek philosophers called *nous*) as the loftiest human attainment. Not mysticism's union with God, but *sophia*, contemplation of universal truths, is the philosopher's goal. Another strand of the great tradition that sometimes complements, sometimes competes with wisdom about the grand order of things is what Aristotle, in his *Ethics*, calls *phronesis*, "wisdom in action." This applied or "practical" wisdom involves our ability to exercise good judgment in matters of commerce, profession, friendship, family, and civic life. Underscoring the difference between the two types of wisdom, Aristotle observes that while "young people can become mathematicians and geometers and attain theoretical wisdom in such matters," they still do not possess practical wisdom, because it is knowledge gleaned through concrete experience that requires "a quantity of time." We should listen to older people, says Aristotle, "for since experience has given them an eye, they see correctly."

"Seeing correctly" is no easy matter. A quantity of time is important but does not guarantee our ability to wrest a guiding insight from the particulars of concrete experience. The ability to act with deliberateness—a word implying liberation, freedom, and *libra*, the constellation of the scales, justice—must be refined over time. Without refinement, we simply repeat our errors or hold fast to principles that may have been applicable in one context or period of our life, but have since become, as the poet William Carlos Williams puts it, "like the memory of success that has stopped succeeding." How, then, do we develop the art of deliberateness, how acquire a discerning eye?

To choose well and wisely how you want to conduct your life, to act from a compelling sense of what is yours to do, is at the heart of what it means to live deliberately. Deliberateness, when woven into the actions of everyday life, is an attribute that may be closer to the capability of the ordinary person than is contemplation. Not always understanding but acting with calm is an ideal many will acknowledge. Is deliberateness a necessary attribute of aging? No more than humor is a predictable stage of maturation. Aging, like the ripening of a fruit, may bring out a special capacity for reflective humor—a condition of intense awareness of finitude that, combined with acceptance of life's paradoxes, helps us to achieve a reconciliation with time. A similar case could be made for deliberateness. That is what I surmised from older friends who told me about how they faced each new day.

"To me, life is a precious commodity," said one friend. "I don't want to squander it. I'm careful about what I do and when I do it. There are rhythms that I want to follow. Balance to achieve."

Another commented, "I used to volunteer for all kinds of causes. Now I'm more careful about my choices. Where am I most effective? How can I make a difference in someone's life? I have to ask myself these questions."

To me, these statements reflected getting control over one's life. And when I observed some of my older friends making thoughtful choices about how they spent their time, saw the customary and efficient way they might use a shovel, a needle, a spatula, or tell a story, I interpreted these characteristics as being the result of self-control. But as in the case of humor, I would learn that deliberateness has more than one aspect and that as an attribute it challenged assumptions I did not even know I held. What first opened my eyes was the slicing of an eggplant.

HUNGRY IN SEATTLE

We had left the children with a sitter and driven to a suburb of Seattle where we were to have lunch at the home of Art and Ruth Farber. We had met the Farbers some ten years earlier in Denmark, when I was working as a teacher and administrator at a small innovative international school. They were on a tour of counterculture communities around the world—a sabbatical research project of Art's. "I'm looking at the ways people try to turn their visions of happiness and liberation into social arrangements," Art told me at the time.

A tall, thin, bespectacled man in his late fifties, with a light, slightly airy voice, Art was a much beloved professor of social work at the University of Washington. Ruth, cheerful and outgoing, was small in figure, but you could feel her physical strength when she hugged you. She was a well-respected social worker specializing in helping families and older people who were facing difficulties. Both were active in social justice causes and community improvement projects. Their attractive suburban home was filled with Danish modern furniture, abstract prints, wooden sculpture—which Art himself had crafted—and a profusion of house plants and flowers from their garden.

We chatted with Ruth and Art in their sunny kitchen. Knife in hand, Art stood before the cutting board eyeing the deep purple eggplants, bright yellow squash, long green zucchini, and lustrous tomatoes. Then he went to work. I marveled at the precision with which he sliced each vegetable, as if calculating just the right angle to expose each surface to the air and then to the olive oil bubbling in the skillet. We were having ratatouille—to us, a strange new dish. Not so for the vegetarians Art and Ruth.

As we stood around sipping wine, I assessed the differences between us. Everything about the Farber's life seemed balanced. Their movements, like good choreography, exhibited economy of motion, clarity of intention, gracefulness of line. In their lives, beauty and integrity fit together harmoniously.

Our own lives, by contrast, were discordant, unbalanced, and impulsive. If we made a decision one day, we were sure to undo it the next. We were swept forward by the surging growth of our children and by economic forces that had recently ushered in a recession, turning the dense foliage of my career path into a veritable jungle. Besides volunteering at the senior center, I was working a hodgepodge of jobs: Tuesday night, teaching a course called "Philosophies of the Helping Professions" at the local community college, Wednesday, sailing past pods of whales on Puget Sound as a luxurious motor yacht, once the toy of a wealthy family during the heyday of the 1920s and now belonging to the government, drew closer to McNeil Island Federal Penitentiary and its inmates—my students.

Friends our own age worried about our financial insecurity. My older friends, taking the long view, encouraged me, saying, "Don't worry, you're still young, you have a lifetime to work things out." A lifetime? I couldn't wait. I needed to know, right away, how I could get more control over my life and better provide for my family without giving up the kind of work I valued. The intensity of the question focused my attention on other people's lives and the lessons I might learn from them—lives of people like the Farbers, who exhibited a life of calm, thoughtfulness, intentionality. Art's hand and wrist moved like a violinist's bowing. The lucid, melodic sounds of a Mozart concerto seemed to emanate not from the stereo speakers in the living room but from the slices of eggplant, zucchini, and tomato that fell free of the sharp blade. How had he achieved this Zen-like mastery?

We talked about my part-time jobs, a new grant I had received to put together a public lecture series, and my uncertainty as to what lay beyond. I felt like curling up on the couch and having the two social workers perform their therapeutic magic. Instead, I feigned confidence about the future.

Ruth said I reminded her of Art's father. "Yes," said Art, "Dad was both a realist and a creative spirit. Forged his own path— that's for sure. You know, maybe that is your calling in life. Takes a lot of guts and determination." Art looked up from the skillet. "Do you feel ready for that?"

I wanted to say, no, I would never be ready. If only someone would offer me a regular teaching job, I would gladly spend time with my students investigating the great ideas and grappling with abstract philosophical problems, instead of cooking up projects and courses that yielded only enough income to scrape by. But full-time teaching opportunities were scarce. I was lucky to teach part-time. A creative spirit? I vaguely nodded my assent to the idea. Meanwhile, I listened, watched, tried enviously to figure out how people could be so deliberate about their lives.

THE CHOICE

Just a year after eating ratatouille with the Farbers, we received word of a memorial service at the University of Washington. Professor Arthur Farber, the note said, had died of a massive heart attack while walking through a museum near Tel Aviv with his wife, Ruth. I learned that unbeknownst to most of us, Art's doctor had several years earlier detected a heart valve problem, but Art decided against surgery. The odds of prolonging life by means of the surgery were, at that time, not much greater than not having it. It was a gamble. Apparently, Art chose to let nature take its course.

Several obligations made it difficult for me to attend the memorial service, but in all honesty, I could not force myself to go. I felt angry that Art had allowed this to happen without taking defensive action, even if the surgery had proven futile. His deliberate, possibly heroic, choice to forgo the operation made me feel both cowardly and disappointed. Though I knew it was irrational, I felt he owed it to me to stay alive. I needed him as a role model and was not going to accept his dying. By avoiding the memorial service, I could pretend that Art was still alive. Later I recognized my foolishness.

Over the months following the memorial service, I occasionally reflected on Art Farber's way of life and his choice about the surgery. Our relationship felt incomplete, without my ever having said good-bye to him or accepting his death. I had so much more to learn about the meaning of deliberateness, but now I wouldn't be able to talk with Art or observe his graceful movements.

In the Jewish tradition, we are dissuaded from speculating on the soul's afterlife and our own prospects for immortality, matters largely beyond our control. Instead, we are encouraged to focus on the here and now, and to preserve and honor the memory of the departed by seeking to live up to their best qualities. So, on the basis of my memories and consistent with the tradition, it was appropriate for me to sit down and hold a quiet conversation with Art.

I leafed through an album to find a photograph of Art and Ruth taken in Denmark. I studied his small, regular features, the silver-rimmed glasses, his long, narrow lips pursed in a wry smile, light eyebrow, mild gaze, thinning hair. It was a Saturday afternoon; Caroline was on duty at her job in the public library. I was sitting in our kitchen nook at a table with books, papers, bills, and a little toy car. While the children were taking their nap, I put my head down on the table, closed my eyes, and let the memory of Art flood back into my mind.

Self-Possession and the Gift

I pictured him wearing a short-sleeve plaid shirt and dark blue trousers, sitting across from me on a dark green leather, Chester-field-style couch in a living room with french doors through whose window panes I could just glimpse a small garden and patio. I could hear the sounds of birds and inhaled a delicate odor. Was it lavender? I was transported to another place.

"Exactly where are we, Art? I see you're not wearing glasses." It is an odd remark, but I am unsettled by the strange, yet somehow familiar, setting. I am not expecting a room, a home. Just a face, a voice, something in a cloud.

"I no longer need glasses, but I'm glad you noticed. That shows you're paying attention. As to the room, consider it a space furnished by memory. Actually, I think you'll begin to recognize the various pieces of furniture, the decor, the general ambience. I suppose I could take you around, tell you all about the furnishings.

But I don't think that's why you summoned me." He tilts his head and gives me one of those wry smiles.

"No," I reply, "it's just that, well, this is sort of eerie. It's not every day I pay a visit to . . ." I look around. "Is this someone's house? Is it yours?"

"Mine?" he says, looking amused. "Yes, in a way I suppose it is. But it's just as much yours. Anyway, relax. Here there is nothing to fear." His reassurance seems to have the opposite effect. "Actually, Ron," he continues, "though you may not realize it, you do visit such places quite frequently. Don't be distracted by the room. You have some question? Something you wanted to talk about?" He folds his hands and sits back on the couch looking straight ahead.

"Art," I hear myself asking, "how do you know when to push against an obstacle or give in to it?"

That isn't how I intended to start the conversation. But Art smiles, knowingly, and responds. "I believe we are given a life, a self, a body; mortal and immortal aspects entwined. As we grow up, we learn to preserve and protect ourselves, seek happiness, and serve others. We grow an identity, fashion an existence, choose who and what to love, who and what to hate. In youth, we put a high value on what belongs to us—our possessions. In our middle years, on that to which we belong. If we live long enough, we may arrive at the realization that the sheer experience of being is more important than either possessing or belonging, because, in truth, we never own anything. We are caretakers of imperfect or perishable gifts—like my damaged heart valve, like the flaws in my personality. Our duty is to honor these gifts as best we can.

"At the first diagnosis of my heart problem, the doctor told me I should take it easy, not get my heart rate up too high. I considered his advice, sought other experts' opinions, read everything I could find, and chose my course of action. I changed to a low-fat diet, lost weight, took up meditation, increased my community involvement, and began to follow a regime of moderately vigorous exercise. Until that time, I thought having a body was like owning a car. You drove around, had thoughts, read books, made love with it. Gradually, it dawned on me—my body possessed me because I was dependent on how well it functioned. That thought marked the shift from possessing to belonging. Likewise, my family possessed me, depended on me for financial and emotional support, for love and affection. I owed it to them to look after myself, and I owed it to that which made my life possible to take responsibility for myself. That's when I realized my body was an extension of my family, of generations—a great molecular chain of being, stretching from eternity to eternity."

I picture bodies, hands linked, stretching into the remote past. If Art was so concerned about his responsibility to look after himself, why did he forgo the surgery?

"Art, you chose not to have surgery to repair your heart valve, but it could have postponed your death by a few years. Maybe longer. Yet you chose not to do it. I've never understood that. I thought of you as a more deliberate person."

"And, to you, Ron, a deliberate person would leap at the chance to defer death. Correct?"

"Yes," I reply, suddenly sensing that someone else is moving about in an adjacent room.

"Ron," Art says, "I will try to explain this to you as best I can." He pauses, strokes his chin as if figuring out what to say. "I considered the option of surgery very carefully. My doctor explained that my prospects for postsurgical survival were not much greater than letting matters be. The odds, I understand, are better now. I'm glad for those who can take advantage of them. But I didn't like the idea of having my chest cracked open. If I were reaching the limits of the time I was allotted, I thought, I should concentrate on making the most of what remained, rather than waging a war to stave off death."

I ask, "You mean you chose quality of life over quantity?"

"I chose quality and only that quantity which I could gain by the means I deemed most appropriate. Ruth and I seized the opportunity to travel. We went to India, Japan, China, and, finally, to Israel. I made sure our finances were in order, brought Ruth up to date on all the details, got rid of useless papers and things I'd stored. In short, put my house in order. And I am eternally grateful because these were some of the best years of my life, ones I'm glad I could share with Ruth." He closes his eyes.

I've been squirming in my seat. Where have I seen this chair before? It's unusual. Shaped to fit into a corner, the point of the rectangular seat is in the front so that I must fold my legs to one side or the other. Moreover, it is covered with an embroidered fabric depicting—what? climbing roses or grape vines?

"You're still wondering about the furniture?"

"Sorry. Guess I am."

"I'm not surprised. You put this room together, yourself. Didn't you once say, memory is like a palace? Well, the rooms of the palace come furnished." He shrugs his shoulders. "You'll just have to accept that."

"I was quoting Augustine," I reply, though I can't imagine when he'd heard me use this analogy.

"Yes, I know, the saint."

I nod. He sounds personally acquainted with Augustine. Had they met, I wonder? I shake my head. "Art," I continue, "some of what you say makes sense. But I'm troubled by the words 'own' and 'owe.' Maybe even by the word 'gift.' If someone gives you a gift, you don't owe him anything. Otherwise, it's not a real gift. I understand the part about taking care of yourself; you owe it to yourself and to your loved ones."

Art stops me with his raised hand. "The language bothers you, isn't that it? I understand. The way you listen to my words is like the way you keep studying the furniture. Familiar, yet strange."

I see his point.

"The problem for you is that everything I say is a metaphor, and each metaphor triggers another metaphor in turn. Everything becomes a likeness, an association. But where are the real things from which the likenesses derive? What if there are only likenesses?" He laughs, closes his eyes, and lays his head back.

I smile, but, in truth, the humor eludes me.

"You'll have to excuse me," says Art. "I'm so easily amused these days." He sits up straight again. Folds his hands.

"I suppose, from your vantage point, a good deal of what I'm asking must seem absurd," I say.

"Yes, but not unpleasantly."

"Then please try to tell me this," I continue; "isn't there a contradiction that needs to be cleared up?"

Art looks delighted at my mention of the word "contradiction." He blinks a few times and raises his eyebrows as if motioning me to continue.

"Isn't it contradictory to believe that life is a gift for which we are the caretakers, while holding that we owe it to others to stay alive and well? Suppose we become terminally ill or severely handicapped to the extent that we no longer want to live. Do we have the right to take our own lives? Surely, we should be free to do what we will with a gift, even deciding when it's worn out and no longer worth keeping. Yet you say we do not own our lives in a way that would allow us to have complete decision-making power over it. That's where I'm confused. Because if we lead deliberate lives, then shouldn't we always do what we think is best? Isn't that what you did by deciding against the surgery—resign yourself to your mortality?"

"Resigned? No, reconciled. I did take my own life. Took it seriously. Lovingly. Not to foreshorten, not to avoid dependency. I
chose my mortality, accepted my limitations, surrendered, if you
will, to the inevitable. You see, Ron, even a person's deliberateness
is limited. It's when you forget the limitations that trouble starts.
The temptation to power. The desire for complete independence.
To be one's own master. You equate deliberateness with control—
that's understandable. From your point of view, taking charge of
your life seems all-important. You don't want to be carried along
by forces outside your control. You want more power. But without
understanding the inner meaning of dependency, a person could
confuse having use of power with becoming identical to it."

"Wait," I say, "not so fast. Becoming identical to power?
Meaning?"

"There are many forms of dependency," he replies, as if answering a question I didn't know to ask. "You are cradled in your
mother's arms. Being cradled is a form of dependency. Think of
your weight in her arms, the curve of your infant body, the space
you occupy. Are you the strength of those arms, the heat of that
body, its nurturance, the encircling? But you want to be both the
encircled and the encircler. And why? Because you worry: What
if this mother were suddenly to let go, to abandon you? From dis-
trust springs doubt, uncertainty. To compensate you find ways to
protect yourself. Food, smoking, alcohol, possessions, status, your
image. Momentarily, these fill the emptiness. Then you discover
power—to strengthen your body, to dominate others through
haughtiness or through weakness, to amass money and honors,
through feelings of superiority, through knowledge, even through
acts of kindness and sympathy."

I seem to have triggered some kind of memory switch. My
head is swimming. I hold up my hand to make Art stop his monologue. He ignores me.

"The shape of dependency has many other forms," he says, beaming with enthusiasm. "Think of surfaces meeting. Lips upon lips, breasts upon breasts, water against a hull, the eyelid over the eyeball, a path pushing against the sole of your foot, the air surrounding a tall tree. Everything depends on everything else." Art looks at me, smiles, and says, "I could go on. Should I?" I shake my head. He frowns. "Very well, I won't." Then, in a deep prophetic voice, he admonishes, "But this I say unto you, O man of memory. Just as you are dependent upon me as your inner voice, do not forget that what comes to you comes from a source that is not you. Therefore, you cannot forget that the gift is a gift. If you overlook or deny the hand that reaches out to you, you break the tie of memory. You can make the remnant into a whole, but it is still a fragment." Then, suddenly, his head falls forward, his chin resting on his chest.

I hear a cough behind me and feel a breeze on my neck. A face looms from out of the periphery of my vision.

"Immobilized him, have you?"

A pair of beady blue eyes appear inches from my nose. "Virgil," I shout, "what a surprise!"

"You were expecting someone else, perhaps?" says Virgil, raising his white eyebrows. Virgil, the former member of our senior center discussion group, dressed just as I remembered him, in a well-preserved double-breasted brown suit and light brown shirt, and now sporting one of those garish Tabasco sauce ties, typically incongruous with the rest of his outfit. But how has he intruded himself into my meeting with Art?

"But you . . . ," I begin.

"I know," he stops me, "since I am not one of the tribe of Judah, am I permitted to enter this memorial ceremony? You'll have to take it up with the rabbis. Anyway, kosher or not, summon me you did. And it looks like you'll be needing me since, with all your distractions, you've managed to put our friend here"—he points to the slumped figure on the couch—"into a state of suspended animation."

"I was just trying to understand what Art meant. He says since life is a gift, we do not have complete authority to determine our own end of life—but, in other ways, we have great powers of living deliberately," I blurt out. "That's what I always admired about him. His deliberateness." Do I really need to defend myself to Virgil?

"No need to explain, my boy. I overheard the whole conversation from the antechamber. And since I am, as you well know, not one to blame others, I will make no disclaimer that when it comes to your ability to remember, you are a hall of famer." With that bit of rhyme, he plunks himself down in a chair that has suddenly appeared. It's one of those recliners, I realize, since a moment later he pulls on a lever that drops him into a prone position, his moon-like face appearing just above the tips of his worn soles.

"At your disposal, I am," he announces. "But don't treat me like scraps." The two blue craters of his moon face widen.

Disposal? Like scraps? So, the old punster is still at it. He hasn't changed much. In fact, he's more himself than ever.

"Yes," confirms Virgil, who apparently is a mind reader, "in fact, I've gotten better." He dangles his tie before his face. "Elegant, don't you think?"

"Oh, most certainly," I reply, and receive a kindly smile.

"Virgil," I begin once more, "Art and I were discussing deliberateness."

"Yes," says Virgil. "You want to know how to live a rational life. And Professor Farber, bless his soul, was giving you the party line. All that nonsense about self-control, moderation, temperance, going back to the source. Sounds pretty good, *n'est-ce pas?*"

Since when has Virgil learned French? And what does he mean by "party line"?

"Party line," replies the mind reader, "you know, like the telephones of yore. Pick up the phone and find out Mrs. Jones has had another fight with Mr. Jones and that little Sally is going on a visit to see her grandmother. Mostly gossip, not gospel. Still, it could be entertaining. That's Art. He's been listening in. You hear all sorts of things. Weird voices." He shakes his head. "I don't think that's going to get you very far."

"Really?" I respond. "I thought he was going to tell me something about eternal knowledge, about the laws of the universe and how I fit into the big picture. Did you know that when Art sliced eggplant . . ." Virgil begins to shake his feet and bob his head.

"I know, I know. When Professor Farber slices *les aubergines*, a chorus of angels sings out. No. A zillion Zen masters bow down, or a million quorums of Hasidic masters dance on tables. Projections, my boy, projections. Your mind is a movie theater, and you're the projectionist. You want to know about deliberateness? Turn off the projector and just ask"—he raises his arm and points down at his large bald head—"*moi*."

I do not really want to ask him. This is not my idea of a sage from the other side of the light. As I remember him, Virgil was more of a pack rat, his house filled ceiling-high with piles of old newspapers and magazines. He was ever the prankster, now a jester in suit and tie.

"You're right, *mon frère*, mine was a distorted deliberateness," comes his reply. "I held on to every printed thing that came into my hand. Stacked them in nice neat piles. Couldn't throw anything away. Buried my life under orderly bundles. No matter, no patter, that was long ago. And I mean long. Like eons, eras, epics, light-years. Still. Forgiven, you are. Now, shall we get on with this matter? Let's take it apart, to get to the heart. Follow me, carefully, as I deliberate."

Virgil ticks off on his fingers: "One. *De*, meaning 'of.' Two.

Libra, the constellation, as in 'scale,' balance, justice. Three. *Ate*, as in 'fulfilled.' Four. *Ness*, as in the 'loch' where the monster dwells. Now, five, put them all together." Virgil pulls on the handle of the recliner. His body shoots forward to a vertical position, his feet dropping to the floor with a thud. He holds up his hand. "Voilà!"

"Voilà?" I exclaim in response to Virgil's wacky etymology. "Just what is this voilà?"

"Oh, come now, don't tell me you, of all people, with your love of words and nonsense syllables, of phrases and pages and foreign wages, cannot fathom this expansion. Of mind, that is."

What he said is complete nonsense; associations mixed up with the etymology of the word "deliberate." "No, I'm blank," I respond.

"Eh? The old tabula rasa routine? Okay, have it your way. A giver I am, said the man from Siam. Deliberateness means you're no longer afraid of going hungry, no longer afraid of the creature lurking in the depths of your mind. The scale is balanced. The constellations hum. That's what Professor F. was saying to you. He wasn't afraid to die, because he was full; he had seen the monster, been to the loch. Light as the stars. He was free, he was ready. That's *la différence*. Not the straitjacket of self-control, statically clinging to guard the soul. The art of Farber, if you'll pardon the expression, is of death-fear free, don't you see. Of himself and family, he did care. In the pulse of life, he did share. That's why he could let go. Mastery, his discipline."

"It's not completely clear to me yet. Overcoming a fear of death. It's a nice slogan, a cliché. But an abstraction."

Virgil concedes with a wink. "Should we get less abstract? Can you handle it?" he asks, deviously.

"I believe so," I answer, uncertainly.

"Then questions I'll ask, you'll answer?"

"Okay."

"When you his home first did visit, what other nice Jewish man were you reminded of?"

I think about this for a moment. Art did bear a slight resemblance to my father. Perhaps it was his mildness that I sometimes took for passivity in my father.

"Yes, your papa, exactly!" exclaims Virgil.

"And besides your own rudderless drift, whose life did you regard with anxiety?"

Again, I think of my father's lack of resistance to the onslaught of Parkinson's disease. He died a few years before our visit to the Farbers.

"Righto, your papa. So, you see, in your mind's eye you link your destiny to your father. You are powerless, passive, a vanishing specter. Then you set Professor F. as an opposite, the epitome of a deliberately led life. Unfortunately, he ups and vanishes, in a museum in the Promised Land, no less. So fear redoubles. Dr. Deliberate becomes a bubble. Determination is kindled. You vow to be unlike your father. As you so willfully act, you flee. Now you see?"

I do see. Virgil was right in many ways. My fascination with deliberateness was the product of my fear of being like my father, of my own passive tendencies, my unfocused energies, and my fear of invisibility. I defined myself negatively as if denial of weakness were the same as strength. When Caroline and I visited the Farbers, our son was two years old, my father two years deceased, my career, our family's future, unsure. There were issues about what it meant to be a man. A man did not fear death.

In the same moment, I recognize the elements of the room. The green leather couch is the one from my friend Jerry's New York apartment. He was a practicing psychiatrist who saw patients at home, taught at Columbia Medical School, and wrote books on psychotherapy, drugs, and health. Jerry suffered from Crohn's disease. His life was cut short. So, more death, more disappearances. I have conjured up a room of fears, death, and disappearance, in which to seek knowledge of deliberateness. It contains more information than I expect.

"Too much concreteness, my friend?" Virgil snickers.

"Yes," I answer, feeling teary but not wanting to show my emotions. I recover my composure and ask, "Virgil, what would it take for me to be free of acting from fear? How can I learn to lead a deliberate life? What stands in my way?"

"Ah, the mystery of the way. So simple is it to say. Would you ask a gnome?"

Virgil does look a little like a benign gnome. "Are you a gnome?" I ask.

Virgil laughs, "I am what I do not have."

"And what is that?" I ask.

"Forgiven."

"You do not have forgiveness? From whom? From me?"

"From you, from them"—he waves his hand—"from all that's human." Virgil strokes his chin, tilts his head roguishly. "In Aristotle, you'll find a Greek word sublime. A key to open every door. 'Good sense' is what you're looking for."

"Good sense?"

"Sense good, you should."

I know Aristotle recommends listening to older people who have accumulated a stock of practical wisdom over the course of their lives. But what would he have made of Virgil, who answers every question with a jest?

"And unto you," Virgil begins to sing a melody that sounds like Handel's *Messiah* while waving his arms like a conductor. "And unto you, a truth is given. And unto you, a tale is told. And en-light-en-ment shall rest upon your shou, ho, ho, ho, houl, ho-uld-ers."

"A musical talent as well? Virgil, when did you acquire all these abilities?"

"In eternity, of course." Again his blue eyes widen. He reaches down and grasps the recliner lever. "Let me know when next again on a guru you depend. For now, vanished I am." He pulls the lever and vanishes, as does Art and the room. All that remains is the chirping of birds and the scent of lavender.

Good Sense

The kettle on the stove was whistling. Had I set it on only minutes earlier? I raised my head, rubbed my eyes. Picking up an empty mug on the table, I gazed into the small dry nest of tea leaves. Earl Grey. Lavender scent. I got up, removed the kettle, poured the boiling water, and watched the leaves unfold, their color infusing through the liquid.

The children would soon awaken. Softly, I tiptoed into the living room to get my copy of Aristotle's *Ethics*. I flipped through the pages, finding many underlined passages but not the message Virgil had given me. Another wild-goose chase? But then, there it was, "good sense." This passage had apparently never made an impression on me. I read that good sense, the Greek word *gnome*— so there was my gnomic Virgil!—is the quality "which makes us say of a person that he has the sense to forgive others." Aristotle, like my friend Virgil, seems to be doing some free-associating. He connects *gnome* with *syngnome*, literally, "judgment on the side of another person." Had I read this before, forgotten it, or lacked the eye to see correctly? Was that what I had to do, forgive Art for his choice to live well rather than to live a bit longer, forgive my father for the illness he could not surmount, for a life he could live only in his way? Had I judged both unfairly, lacked sympathy? As long as I continued to struggle with them, resisted recognizing that they were the weakness in myself, I would fail at deliberateness. But forgiveness wasn't some single, momentary act that you could carry out and be finished with it. It was a process, a direction. It would take time.

I heard the children stirring. I had my task, another journey through the arch of experience.

CHAPTER SEVEN

PHILOSOPHY IN AUTOBIOGRAPHY

A few years after I started volunteering at the senior center, I was hired by a large county library system in Washington State to direct a program in which local citizens would examine and write about the relationship between their personal lives and public history. A team of writers and historians would help them explore the interplay between their views of the world and how events, big or small, might have altered the course of their lives. How had they responded? we would ask hundreds of fledgling autobiographers, most of whom were over fifty and lived in library districts stretching from suburban Gig Harbor, through inner-city Tacoma neighborhoods, to small logging towns in the foothills of the Cascade Mountains. I knew that, like those of my group at the senior center, their stories would contain useful material for understanding the human scale of history. Should I also expect general truths—the philosopher's goal—to emerge from particular lives and personalities?

There is an age-old controversy about the relationship between philosophy and autobiography. In general, philosophers are ambivalent toward the autobiographical. Their quest is to find what the German philosopher Immanuel Kant established as the twin criteria of truth, "necessity and universality"—that which must always and everywhere be the case. So what happened to a particular philosopher on a particular day would be at most something of interest to biographers, not to those in pursuit of permanent truths. Ideas in the form of logical propositions, not personal circumstances, were philosophers' meat and potatoes.

Still, as usual, there is a counterposition. We have only to think of the great tradition of philosophical autobiographies that extend at least from fourth-century C.E. North Africa and Saint Augustine, bishop of Hippo, to modern times. Augustine's *Confessions* takes commonplace events like nursing at his mother's breast, learning to speak, stealing pears from a neighbor's tree, and finding disappointment in worldly success, and discovers connections to the momentous spiritual and philosophical issues of his time. Fourteen hundred years later, the not-so-saintly, Geneva-born Jean-Jacques Rousseau, in his *Confessions*, finds the origins of his most influential ideas about education, freedom, and the modern state in experiences of childhood injustice, sadomasochism, exile, and unrequited passions for aristocratic women.

The debate over perennial and existential truths is summed up in a remarkable autobiography by the contemporary American philosopher Stanley Cavell, who defends the first-person narrative against criticism that such works are merely subjective. He argues that while each person is unique, "each life is exemplary of all, a parable of each." Going a step further, he speculates that for philosophy and autobiography, "each is a dimension of the other." And pulling out all the stops, he quotes Emerson to the effect that "the deeper the scholar dives into his privatest, secretest presentiment, to his wonder he finds this is the most acceptable, most public, and universally true."

I considered this matter as I read several thousand pages of first-person narrative toward the end of the library-sponsored project. The members of the small groups read and discussed short stories, poems, essays, and selections from published diaries and letters, to help them recall public events that influenced their lives: the Great Depression, the battlefields and homefronts of World War II, migration from rural fields to town factories to suburbs, and attitude changes brought on by the civil rights and women's movements.

Many participants wrote chronological accounts covering circumstances of their birth, personalities of their parents and siblings, what growing up was like, their experiences with schooling, marriage, having children, careers, and personal losses (such as the death of a parent or child). In many instances, the writing was informative but detached; failing to convey what these life events meant to the author. Other authors seemed to be floundering in a sea of turbulent emotion. They expressed feeling, but a reader might have a hard time grasping the situation or framework in which the experience occurred. But at least some passages of the autobiographies succeeded in connecting feelings with facts, bringing to light the issues and ideals that shaped the person's life, revealing the search for a framework by which to understand his or her personal past.

Like Cavell's Emerson, I wondered how the subjective thread of personal insight might lead to that which is "most public, most universal." I drew certain conclusions then, but another ten years had to pass before I found my way back into these small life histories and recognized ways in which philosophy and autobiography could be understood as dimensions of one another. By this time, I was living in Asheville, North Carolina, my children were teenagers, and I was working at a university directing an educational program for older adults. The occasion that led to reviewing the philosophical dimensions of the remembered past was an ordinary, yet provocative, conversation. My oldest daughter, Esther, now a high school senior, was complaining about having to write a brief autobiographical statement for a college application.

fIREfLIES

Esther came stomping out on the front porch, the screen door banging shut behind her. I was sitting in a wooden rocker, watching the fireflies wink their phosphorescent mating signs. Every eight seconds, a scientist friend told me, they send their glowing message: "Here I am."

"It's stupid," said Esther, who flung herself into the other rocking chair. She was in cutoff jeans, a white T-shirt with a picture of Jerry Garcia on it, torn-up sneakers, no socks. Esther would start university in the fall, and her college had sent her a special application asking for more personal information, including a short autobiography.

"What do they want from me?" she implored. "I already sent the admissions people that thing, that Personal Statement of Goals." She turned to me, her sun-bleached bangs falling across her eyes. "Dad, that whole thing was a joke. Admit it."

"Well, you did lay it on a bit thick." She had badgered me to tell her what to write, but, ever the good teacher, I resisted, asking her instead what I thought were helpful questions. Finally, annoyed by her resistance, I said, "Just tell the truth, how you want to be a lawyer because you like to get your way." And where they asked about initiative and ambition, I suggested she mention her escapades sneaking out the second-story window, climbing down from the roof on the drain pipe, and partying all night with Carleton, the jerk who had her twisted around his finger.

Esther looked sullen. Then she laughed. No, she thought she'd leave all that out. Instead, she'd write about the importance of civil liberties, the anti-apartheid demonstration she'd been in (mostly, she went to socialize with friends), and how moved she'd been on visiting the Supreme Court in D.C. (mostly, I remember refusing to buy her a Sex Pistols T-shirt from a nearby street vendor).

"They want me to tell about my life," Esther moaned. "What can I tell them? I'm eighteen. I don't have a life story yet. I'm just living it. Dad, can you help me write this autobiography? You did such a great job on my Statement of Goals. You're so smart about what I should say. Pu-lease."

Esther was highly skilled at imploring. "But, honey," I replied, "you need to learn to write your own story. You've done lots of interesting things, you have a good mind, a good memory, a way with words, and a feeling about the story you want to tell. Those are the essential ingredients. What the college people want, I suspect, is to get you to start reflecting on the purpose of your life so you can make the most of college. Writing it down helps to define your direction. It's like your life story is your philosophy of life."

"Dad!" she burst out. "Give me a break. I'm just a kid. I don't have a philosophy of anything; that's your department. Anyway, you say most people don't have philosophies; they just have opinions." Esther dropped her voice to a baritone and mimicked, "Only people who have reasoned out their opinions have philosophies. The rest are possessed by ignorance of which they are entirely unaware. End quote." She laughed.

"Do I really sound like that?" Esther nodded, affirmative. She folded her arms, raised her chin, and turned toward the dogwood in our front yard.

"You know, Esther, it's interesting when you decide you're just a kid and when you claim to be, as you have sometimes put it"—and here I deepened my voice—"a fully formed female adult person. End quote." I folded my arms and stared into the dogwood branches. "How come you're not a fully formed adult now when it comes to writing a few pages about your life?"

Esther looked at me sideways from the narrow slits of her eyes. She was silent. "Besides, I suspect you do have a life story and that all kinds of philosophical ideas influence the way you look at your experiences." I held up my hand, counting my fingers to make the point. "First, you have certain ideas of right and wrong actions. That's ethics. Second, you have definite preferences in music and art. That's aesthetics. And, third, you have some wonderful ideas about real people and fake ones, or about when a novel or a movie seems phony, and about the difference between love and lust. Now, how and what you know, that's epistemology. So, see." I held out the three fingers, "You're well on your way, philosopher Esther Manheimer."

Esther squeezed her eyes tight. "Oh, God," she groaned, "give me a break. Maybe I should write about how I've suffered to have a philosopher for a dad."

This was an old theme. When we'd argue about money for clothes or vacations, Esther would blame my choice to pursue a degree in philosophy for our family's limited means. The arguments were painful. Like a parent, she'd chastise me, "How could you choose something so impractical?"

Then, abruptly, Esther brightened up. "Hey," she exclaimed, "you've done all kinds of work with people's life stories. Were the stories philosophical or just a bunch of opinions? Give me some tips about what they wrote. Maybe I'll get inspired."

Was she serious, or was this a new strategy? "Well," I started slowly, unsure what exactly to tell her. "I guess I could describe some of the stories people wrote in the project I did in Tacoma before we moved east. The stories helped me see the place of philosophy in everyday life. Let me get a few of the books to help me remember. What do you say?"

"Okay, I guess," she sighed. "I just hope they're not too long and boring."

I went inside and scanned a living room bookshelf, packed from end to end with slender, paperbound booklets, in various shades of off-white. These were the products of "All My Somedays—A Living History Project." I pulled out a handful that had scraps of paper sticking out of them—my favorites.

As I had listened to people in the groups read aloud from these manuscripts, I had imagined a dance of ideas. Here was a dreamy Platonist holding in her outstretched, cupped hands the crystal ball of childhood in which she sought the deep inner truth of first experiences. And there was the hard-nosed, Humean empiricist, bent from the waist, rushing around systematically collecting facts like scattered piles of straw to be bound into bundles of perception with associative twine. Even a gesture used in the telling could express a stance toward the world, as if body language was the physical correlate of a person's metaphysical views. I observed the angular antics of skeptics, the slow, deliberate movements of doubters, the pirouette of optimists, and the rapid, freeze-frame gyrations of pessimists. Some dancers were mesmerized by surface reflections—a memory of sunlight on water, a face in a mirror. Others carefully lifted each remembered object in search of its hidden side.

Easing back into my rocker, I placed the small books on my lap. Picking one up, I showed the cover to Esther. Beneath the title was a picture of a young black couple in wedding attire.

"She's beautiful," said Esther. "Who is that?"

"Lena, the woman Charlie Hill corresponded with while he was in Korea, and then came home and married."

"That title, 'Craving for Acceptance,' doesn't sound much like a love story," she said.

"Ah, but it is," I replied.

CRAVING FOR ACCEPTANCE

I told Esther that in his autobiography, *Craving for Acceptance*, Charlie Hill, a retired army sergeant, begins by recalling, when he was ten, his father's death from a respiratory disease in the basement ward of the segregated hospital in Laurel, Mississippi. "My daddy died," writes Hill, "never once in his lifetime having drunk from the same water fountain that the white man drank from." His father, always having to answer the white man with "yes, Sir," died, says Hill, "without having a chance to choose 'yes' or 'no.' "

His father's death marked the family's decline into near-poverty. Hill reports his fear of racial violence, frustration at being excluded by his peers, and a growing desire to escape from the loneliness and isolation of his youth—a desire that eventually lands him on the battlefields of Korea. Inner and outer struggles and trouble with the law during his adolescence and young adulthood fill the chapters of Hill's book. Poor, fatherless, and rebellious, the youth must contend with local lynchings, police harassment, and personal abuses at the hands of both whites and blacks.

At fifteen, Hill leaves Laurel for Illinois, where he finds a job in a warehouse. At seventeen, he joins the army and from Korea begins a fourteen-month correspondence with a pen pal he's never met, a young woman in Toomsuba, Mississippi. Returning from overseas duty, Hill arrives with nothing but "a loaf of bread and a bus ticket home." He walks the twenty miles to Toomsuba to visit his correspondent, Lena, and shortly afterward proposes to her. Several weeks later, they wed.

In literary terms, Charlie Hill's narrative belongs to the tradition of the "confessional" autobiography, a genre pioneered by Saint Augustine. Hill owns up to—"confesses"—the emotional pain, the errors of his ways, and other shortcomings of his youth and young adulthood, narrating the events and circumstances within the framework of a religious journey, a search for the love that would redeem him from a life of suffering and turmoil. Hill's account of his meeting with Lena and their marriage of more than thirty years, combines elements of the religious search for God with those of the struggle for self-acceptance and the passion and partnership of unconditional love.

Hill is not a theologian, but his characterization of the moment when he first meets his future wife evokes the idea that time is not only an extended sequence of moments but a psychological unity of past, present, and future. "When my todays reached out for tomorrow, my tomorrows filled my yesterdays," writes Hill. In the great circle of human destiny, a future we cannot know beckons to us. If we heed that calling, our arrival casts a new light on the past, changing painful or arid memories into joyful and fecund ones. A life that seemed arbitrary and fragmented suddenly becomes an illuminated whole. New meaning infuses events of the past. One senses that Hill wrote his book with the last chapter, "Acceptance at Last," already in mind. Having reached it, the reader understands that his conclusion is the redemptive moment toward which the narrative has been building all along—his new life with Lena, the family and career that now becomes possible.

Hill's narrative centers on themes of racism and social justice, guilt and forgiveness, isolation and friendship, love and anger. These themes are not treated abstractly but as encounters with people: his father and mother, siblings, childhood friends and enemies, military officers under whom he served, soldiers he commanded, and the love of his life, Lena. And they are conveyed in events, such as the sit-ins and freedom marches of the civil rights movement.

The broad theme of separation and reunion provides the dramatic framework that brings these ideas to life. The theme of separation includes Hill's loss of his father, his self-alienation, leaving home, going to war in a distant land. The theme of reunion includes Hill's return home, the journey to find Lena, marriage, the birth of their children, being part of the armed forces, and self-acceptance.

The theme "craving for acceptance" is at once about being accepted in love by another person, Lena, about accepting himself and his past, about social justice and overcoming racism, and about experiencing acceptance and forgiveness from God. Hill offers the reader the story of his transformation from loneliness and victimization to belonging and caring, emancipation from time as an empty future, to time as a movement of redemption.

"So you see," I said to Esther, who was now holding the family cat in her lap, "Charlie Hill does tell a love story."

"It's a good story," she agreed. "It has a happy ending. And his ideas about time are far out. I felt that way, for a while, about Carleton. Like time had come to a stop."

I understood, I thought, what Esther meant. Some emotional experiences are so powerful they make us feel there are no befores and afters, the present moment being the only thing that matters. I wanted to tell Esther that her experience and Charlie Hill's were not the same—his time didn't come to a stop; it came to fruition, fulfillment. But I held back.

"Dad," said Esther, "was Charlie Hill imitating this bishop who wrote confessions in North Africa?"

"I don't think Charlie Hill read Saint Augustine's book, but the way Augustine told his story, as a spiritual journey, has been imitated by thousands of other religious seekers writing about their spiritual discoveries. What is unique to Augustine is how much of the detail from his life—from the most mundane to the most sublime—he includes. That's why Hill's autobiography reminds me of Augustine—there's so much of the stuff of life in them both."

"You said Augustine lived in North Africa. Was he black, too?"

"Augustine was born to African natives, ethnically related to the Berbers of today. I don't know whether he was dark-skinned or not."

"And is there a love story in Augustine's *Confessions?*"

I hesitated to answer. "That's complicated when it comes to saints," I said.

"Well," she said, "I'm waiting for a phone call before I start writing. So go ahead. Tell me."

AUGUSTINE IN LOVE

I told Esther that Augustine was born and raised in a small town in North Africa when it was part of the Roman Empire. He was a bright student, so his mother, Monica, a convert to Christianity, and father, Patricius, a pagan, scraped up enough money to send the youth to the cosmopolitan port city of Carthage for advanced studies in classical literature. Their investment paid off because Augustine eventually rose to prominence as a teacher of rhetoric. He was offered an important position in Milan and there seemed to have everything: money, prestige, a beautiful mistress, a handsome young son, and a big villa in which his mother and several childhood friends came to live. His was the model of the beautiful life of a classical humanist.

Despite all the outward signs of success, Augustine says in his *Confessions*, he felt he carried around "a cut and bleeding soul." He

could help other people attain power, but he felt empty and powerless. He yearned for something and imagined a contemplative
state of inner peace, such as the great masters, Plato and Aristotle,
describe in their idealized intellectual understanding of the purpose of the universe—a vision of the Good. He wanted to experience this enlightened vision of timeless truth: a direct intuition
unlocking the secrets of the universe and revealing that, from
plant growth to planetary orbits, time is not only the corollary of
change and distance traveled by physical things but "the moving
image of eternity." Augustine encountered the philosopher's paradox: By what means can a mortal mind in a changeable body
experience truths that are immortal and immutable?

He knew the answer provided by classical antiquity: master
the disciplines of arithmetic, music, geometry and astronomy,
grammar, rhetoric and logic; devote yourself to intellectual ideas
and suppress your physical senses; seek moderation. But Augustine could not renounce the companionship of his mistress, the
taste of good food and drink, the comforts provided by sophisticated urban life. Augustine considered the inward path recommended by Plato and the philosophers who had revived his
thought, the Neoplatonists. "Look into memory," they advised. "In
that great palace of facts, concepts, images, and words, all time is
copresent so that memory offers a mirror of timelessness. All
experiences that were once presents and even anticipated futures
are now stored up, a vast treasure that can be unlocked at a
moment's notice. You can stroll through the palace of memory,
tracing ideas back to their earliest origins. You can remember even
before childhood, even before you were born. Ideals of justice,
equality, fairness, mathematical theorems, and the like are all to
be found there, placed in memory at birth."

But Augustine would not settle for the cool, impersonal beauty
of a perfect cosmic order, for the love of the god Eros, whom

Plato had turned into a contemplative idea. His closest earthly love, his mother, Monica, whose tranquillity and piety impressed him, beseeched him to embrace the Christian life, but Augustine found he could not make the necessary sacrifices. Still, he wanted to draw near the very source of creation, not contemplate eternity but find eternity within himself. He looked at all the things that stood in his way: his attachment to possessions, appetite for food, sexual desires, pride in his superiority over others, love of wealth and social privilege. These, he thought, kept him fixed in mortal time. His ability to conceive of a loving God was impeded because he continued to imagine a physical God who would manifest himself in the visible order of space and time. And so he speculated that an omnipotent God might be found in the cosmic forces that keep the planets in their orbits, or the invisible web that links the world of ideas, or the timeless and perfect being you came upon in the palace of memory. God had to be "somewhere."

In an almost humorous passage of the *Confessions*, Augustine, like a naturalist philosopher, pretends to interrogate plants, animals, and people, asking, "Are you God?" "No," he hears them reply, "we are not God." Over and over he put this question. Finally, he asks them, "Then, who is God?" And they reply in unison, "He made us." If this God is the maker of all things, speculates Augustine, then he is also my maker. The next instant it occurs to him that his very capacities to ask, to seek, to remember, and to speak—indeed, to contemplate the mysteries of time and eternity—are abilities empowered through this creator deity. Suddenly, Augustine understands that he is himself a manifestation of creation, a fragment of eternity. What makes it possible for him to have a vision of the Good is the inner eye of the divine self. The truth he has been seeking is this inner self, the God within, that has been awaiting his discovery. This, he believes, is the message of the Apostles. It was hidden from him because he was distracted by earthly success. And he could not find it unless he was willing to change his life. Now he was ready.

The sound of distant thunder interrupted my account of Augustine's spiritual journey. "Sounds like we may get a thunderstorm," I said to Esther.

Esther was petting the cat and staring into space. Had she been listening? Then she turned to me and asked, "Was Augustine hung up on his mother? I mean, she sounds like the kind who pushes a son to be ambitious about things he doesn't really want. Carleton's mother is like that, too. She wants him to be an engineer, but he wants to be a sports announcer."

"She did have a great influence on him."

"And," Esther continued, "what's the connection, again, between Charlie Hill and Augustine? I understand they're both big on religion and writing about their personal struggles. But Hill finds his Lena, whereas, uh, Augustine finds . . . ?"

"I know what you're going to say, finds his mother. Right?"

Esther laughed. "Dad, I don't know what he finds. He's, like, in love with himself, but he calls that God? And what about his mistress, did he ever marry her?"

"As I mentioned, he had a mistress, which was common in those days for young men. Later, when he was in his twenties, he was betrothed to a young girl from a well-to-do family. He had to wait two years before she came of marriageable age. In the meantime, he was forced to dismiss his mistress because, he says, it wasn't considered proper to be engaged and have a mistress living with you."

"Just like that? So he was just using her until he married into money," she said indignantly.

"He claims, in the *Confessions*, she was 'torn from his side,' that he felt her loss like a wound in his heart."

"Sure," she said, "that's what they all say. They suffer more than you do. But tell me, pops, what's Augustine's story got to do with me? I don't want to be a saint. I'm Jewish, for God's sake, anyway."

"Good point," I replied. "I brought Augustine into the picture because he's influenced how people think about their life stories. But the tradition of the spiritual autobiography has come down to us through the Middle Ages, when thousands of them were written, right into our own time. Somehow, Charlie Hill drew on that tradition. Gradually, a secular tradition arose and people wrote, not about their mystical experiences or conversions to Christianity, but about other transformation in their lives that they achieved on their own or with the help of friends, family, teachers, and other important people."

"Teachers, huh?" This excited her interest. "Do you have any books like that? Maybe a woman's story? Something I could identify with?"

"Would you believe?" I replied, holding up another book. On the cover was a picture of a family standing in front of a sod house, the kind pioneers built on the midwestern prairies. Behind the house you could see a vast empty plain rising to the horizon.

FROM VALDRES TO MOOSE JAW: A FAMILY'S JOURNEY

In contrast to Charlie Hill's, I told Esther, the story of the Norwegian-born immigrant Ann Theberge is clearly secular, though no less poignant and, in its own way, spiritual.

Born Anna Anderson, the author was eight years old in 1910 when her father left their remote village, Valdres, in Norway, to journey to Canada, where the government offered land for homesteading on the prairies of Saskatchewan. Theberge describes the scene of her father's departure, remembering how "he stood sober and sad-faced in the doorway, gazing at each one of us, trying to look able and brave for this venture." Seventy-three years later, she writes about the two years of dirt-poor existence before she, her mother, and two younger siblings joined their father in a sod-built house seventy miles from the nearest town, Moose Jaw, Saskatchewan.

The only survivor among the Norwegian-born Anderson children, Theberge wrote her story to share with her six American-born siblings, who she believed were not aware of the family's early struggle for survival. She called her book *From Valdres to Moose Jaw: A Family's Journey*. Theberge chose to write only about this seven-year period. She knew that her childhood story would echo that of thousands of other immigrant settlers on the Canadian prairie. But she needed to give her own account. During those seven years, the major insights and ideals of her life took shape, addressing the humiliation of poverty, pride in survival, and emancipation from oppressive beliefs in predestination.

Theberge covers the family's two-year wait in Norway while her father saved enough money to bring the family to Canada. She describes daily life: preparation of traditional Norwegian foods, clothes making, caring for animals—especially the family's only cow. She recounts how, during the appearance of Halley's comet, the villagers, who were highly superstitious, gathered and prayed for forgiveness. They were sure the comet was a sign the world was coming to an end. Of her family's existence in Norway, she says, "My father's life was mostly work, as his parents were very poor and had no land, only a small house rented to them by a landowner. The rent had to be paid in work for the landlord at any time he chose, and the landlord set the amount."

There was no chance to improve their station in life. "None of the poor could travel or learn much about the world except their own small village and country. For those who had more ambition, this was most unsatisfactory." Her account of how the poor villagers reacted to the appearance of Halley's comet reveals an apocalyptic view of history and conveys the constricted, doomed attitude of her countrymen—the result of social oppression reinforced by fatalistic beliefs. Then came the Norwegian-born visitors returning, briefly, from the United States to tell about their life in the "new country." With these tales, a dream of self-betterment was born and a pathway opened.

But the dream turned into the reality of hardship. Once the family reunited in Canada, they were struck down by a typhoid epidemic; then there were farming accidents, the travail of sod cutting, winter isolation, and Anna's embarrassment at not being able to speak English. The dry prairie lands of Saskatchewan severely tested the immigrants' hopes and determination.

Theberge goes on to tell about her three years of schooling. On her first day in school, she breathlessly takes in the visage of their North American teacher, a young Norwegian-born woman. (Finding a marked passage, I read it to Esther.)

She dressed in a heavenly rust-colored dress with a flash of green at the throat and a split in the hem on the left side! I didn't know until I saw her how starved I was for color, beauty and art. The teacher became my ideal. I wanted to be like her and become a teacher. I had my dream of the future. To that end, I attacked the English language and the meaning of every word as if it were an enemy I was dedicated to conquer.

One of her own compatriots is an emancipated woman, a model for new expectations, a beacon of light and color. Her amazingly precise recollection of the teacher's demeanor and clothing communicates the transformation of the historically possible. For Theberge, the resignation to poverty common to disenfranchised tenant farmers turns into the immigrant's vision of emancipation and a better future. In the midst of a drab, hopeless existence, a "flash of green at the throat" becomes the symbol for breaking the circle of inevitability and announces a young girl's determination to make something of herself.

"I had my dream of the future," writes Theberge, but when the fourteen-year-old was just moving into fifth-grade work, her parents informed her that she had to quit school and take employment as a mother's helper for a family living five miles away. It was not the money she would be paid to look after four children that was so important. She had to leave home because she "got bed and board, and there were too many mouths to feed at home."

Though it falls outside the seven-year historical time frame she set for herself, Theberge tells us she eventually realized her goal of becoming a teacher. Her literary work is to come to terms with the pain and humiliation of the past. There is no sense of preordained destiny in Theberge's little book—individual will, not faith in God, is the dominant quality that shines through her narrative.

Esther turned toward me. "Is that how it ends?"

"Actually, no." I flipped to the back of *From Valdres to Moose Jaw.* "Interestingly, Mrs. Theberge includes a short additional chapter. Like an epilogue."

"Good!" exclaimed Esther, hopefully. "What does she say?"

In the last chapter, Ann tells about traveling back to Saskatchewan, many years later, to visit her aged father, now a widower. Reminiscing, her father expressed his remorse at not having been able to give the children a better life. But Ann assuaged her father's guilt and sadness and told him he had done "the greatest and bravest act," that of bringing the family out of the dire circumstances of their Norwegian life into the land of opportunity. Despite the hardships of the sod house years, and the sacrifices of the parents, their children had gone on to a better life. The act of forgiving her father, himself caught in the web of forces beyond his control, is Theberge's second transformative moment in the narrative.

Theberge's story evinces a family's determination and fortitude, qualities that create in her a sense of strength and dignity. The foods, traditions, and language of Norway are combined with portraits of her parents and those first years on the prairie to provide the symbolic map of a family journey. The journey is not only from Valdres to Moose Jaw, a geographical journey; it is as much the story of a young girl's experience of separation from her father, her journey back to him, and the reconciliation of disappointments—hers at having to leave home and school because of poverty, his at not being able to provide a decent life, free of struggle and toil, for his family.

The theme of separation and reunification is a motif that runs through Theberge's and many other "All My Somedays" authors' autobiographies. It expresses movement toward becoming an individual and, over time, incorporating painful or difficult aspects of the past into the present. Though Theberge says she wrote her book for her siblings, she also needed to record how she came to terms with difficult and painful memories.

I closed the booklet and looked at Esther. "Dad," she asked, "did you pick this story because I'm about to leave home to go to college?"

I shook my head. "I hadn't thought about it that way, Esther. At least, not consciously. But leaving your family and familiar environment and, later, returning helps you to reassess what you take with you wherever you go."

"Hmm," she said. "Anyway, the story's much better with that ending. If people are going to write their life stories, they should have a happy ending."

"Why? What if they didn't have a happy life, or what if things turned out badly? Shouldn't they tell that story?"

"What good does it do?" she answered. "I mean, why write about it in the first place if all you have to say is something depressing? Is that supposed to do anybody any good?"

"What do you think is the purpose of a life story? Is it to figure out your life in as honest a way as you can, or to pretty it up so as to reassure yourself and others that everything turned out well in the end?"

"From my limited experience, I'd say it's the latter. You put the best face on things and tell people what they want to hear. Just like the life story I'm going to write for this application."

And with that, Esther got up, plunked the cat down, and walked toward the screen door. "Thanks, Dad," she called over her shoulder. "I know how I'm going to write this thing." The screen door banged shut.

Another peal of thunder. Storm approaching. A little wind kicked up, turned the leaves of the dogwood to their silvery sides. The fireflies were settling into the branches, still emitting their little lights. I watched the pavement turning wet with rain, reflecting the streetlight that had just come on.

I knew I couldn't ask what Esther would write. But had she earned the right to such cynicism?

AUTOBIOGRAPHICAL ACTS

As the first raindrops tapped on the leaves, I sat thinking about Esther's question. What good is an autobiography if it doesn't have a happy ending? Periodically, I turned to the soul-searching stories of religious and secular minds such as Saint Augustine, Rousseau, John Stuart Mill, and Simone de Beauvoir. What did I expect to find?

I hoped to understand how people who devoted themselves to

ideas might have actually lived in and through them. For someone like myself who had a tendency to live in his head, I was looking for role models of thinkers who showed engagement with life, with others, with the world. I wasn't that naive to think that in these autobiographies I would find the whole truth and nothing but the truth. Self-deception and self-justification are powerful filters of experience, and there is always a gap between the immediacy of events, what we make of them at the time, and how we come to think and write about them years later. Still, I was especially drawn to those writers who engaged the reader in what Kierkegaard called an "enabling dialectic," writers who used language imaginatively to move the reader as they were moved, instead of merely reporting or explaining the past as if in detached commentary or a set of footnotes. From each, I believed, I might find direction in purpose, gracefulness and economy in thought, and wholeness in meaning. And, in fact, I did find these things. But also something else.

I discovered in certain autobiographies how an individual might let go of hard-won and cherished beliefs and risk confusion, isolation, and uncertainty before eventually reaching a new integration of experience. The moral philosopher Alasdair MacIntyre calls this the "quest for the narrative truth," a theme that conveys encounters with difficulty and resistance. The narrative truth that attracted me was one that evoked such risk, travail, error, and turmoil—qualities that became my criteria for authenticity in autobiography.

I admired the risks Augustine took in writing about his tender, sometimes difficult relationship with his mother, his career disappointments, his struggle to embrace and be embraced by an invisible God, and the wonderful leaps he makes again and again as he connects elementary human experience to the mysteries of the soul, time, creativity, and grace. I admired Rousseau's admission of his sexual confusions and aberrations, his wanderings and exiles, his various deceptions and paranoias, and the way he shows us his pathway to discovering the natural person, the just society, the ideal education—ideas that became the rallying cry of the French Revolution. Such passionate writing exposes the author to his reader as it exposes the receptive reader to him. The autobiographers become vulnerable to their enemies and sometimes an embarrassment even to their friends and allies. Narrative that at times seems to eclipse the author's ability to make sense of it may make us similarly vulnerable and open to new thoughts, new ways of seeing and retelling our own story.

Writing in *A Pitch of Philosophy*, the philosophical autobiographer Stanley Cavell explains how he claimed his voice from his musically gifted mother and his Yiddish storyteller father to find the right tone or "perfect pitch" for his own authoritative speaking and writing. In telling us these stories, he demonstrates that authorship, a public act, is always an act of authority—a self-proclaimed right to speak for oneself that makes a story out of unformed experiences and events. Telling that story means taking a risk, a kind of putting into play, as the word "pitch" suggests, at once "music and baseball and vending." As soon as the pitch is made, it is out of one's hands.

This is fine, some might say, for well-known philosophers to find resolution to their personal life stories in particular approaches to philosophy. But what of the less famous, such as those citizens who participated in "All My Somedays"? Must they, and we, reach such resolutions? An answer to this question comes to us from Charles Taylor, the McGill University philosopher whose influential study *Sources of the Self* provides an analysis of the philosophical roots of modern ideas of identity. Taylor argues that not to have a framework within which to think, feel, and judge what actions and choices are to be preferred is to fall into a life that is "spiritually senseless." He regards such senselessness as a malaise of our time. By contrast, those who possess such a framework possess what he calls a "moral ontology," a commitment to some end, such as human dignity, love of God, the attainment of freedom, striving for social justice, or a search for personal salvation.

Discovering and articulating a moral ontology, a framework for interpreting experience, is what some people are searching for in crafting an autobiography and in reading the life stories of others. But, as Esther pointed out, are such frameworks *true*? Or are they designed to place the author in a favorable light, make a jumble of life experiences into a coherent tale, fashion a happy ending from an ambiguous collection of events, or create a myth about one's personality and role in historic events? We have to find our own criteria for what comes across to us as true speaking.

Should I, or anyone else, care about the truth of a life story? Yes, says Taylor, because we are, each of us, caught in the dilemma of our time. There are no undisturbed moral ontologies, frameworks of meaning, that we can easily embrace, free of uncertainty, hesitation, or downright disbelief. Finding the meaning in life is a task on everyone's agenda, according to Taylor. Were we living in earlier times, we might instead feel the heavy hand of moral authority, an inescapable weight that could quash the spirit of an independent mind. But the modern seeker's existential challenge is the opposite—weightlessness. In comparison with former times, little moral authority is imposed upon us. We take on our own spiritual ballast or, forgoing the quest for moral autonomy, submit ourselves to the prepackaged rules and guidelines of some dominant political or religious ideology. The great value of life history writing and storytelling, in general, is that they give us the opportunity to articulate our moral ontology through the good small stories we may fashion and refashion as we pursue our narrative quest.

PERSONAL ESSAY

The rumble of thunder had grown distant, the rain shower trailing off into a fine mist visible in the glow of the streetlight. I heard
the spring on the screen door groan as it stretched. The door
closed quietly. Esther was standing beside me.

"Gosh, Dad, don't you ever get tired of sitting out here doing
nothing?" She looked down at me, her youthful profile illuminated by the light from the living room windows behind us. I saw
she was holding a piece of paper.

"Is that your personal essay?"

"Yup. Hot off the computer. Not the whole thing, just the first
page. I've outlined the rest."

"And did you tell them what they wanted to hear?"

She shook her head. "Probably not. It's really weird. You know
what I wrote about?"

I shook my head.

"I wrote about the time Mom made me take back the sweatshirt I shoplifted from the mall. Remember that? I was so angry
Kora told on me. Then Mom called the store, and they said they
wouldn't press charges if I brought the stuff back. I couldn't
believe she'd make me do it."

I remembered. Esther must have been about fourteen. She
made the mistake of bragging about the theft to her younger sister, Kora. When I found out, I wasn't sure what we should do. I
didn't want Esther to have a police record, but I didn't want her
to think this was all right to do—just an adolescent adventure.
Saint Augustine had stolen pears at about this age. He said it was
a sign of moral depravity. He agonized over the act, but didn't
know how to atone. The pears hadn't even tasted good, he
claimed. But Esther's mom knew exactly what to do. Caroline
called the store and whisked Esther over to the mall to return

the goods and make an apology. She had a framework, a moral ontology.

"How did you happen to choose that to write about?" I craned my neck, looking up at her. She didn't seem to want to sit down.

She shrugged her shoulders. "I don't know. It was the first thing that popped into my mind when I started writing. I was thinking about those people, Charlie Hill and, um, what's-her-name."

"Theberge."

"Yeah."

"You liked what they told about their lives?"

She shook her head. "Not exactly what they wrote. More the voices. Even though they were different, they said things their own way. So, I thought, what's my way? Then it started coming. My voice, I mean. Shouldn't I be the boss of my own words? Do you think the college people will reject me when they read this?"

"I doubt it. If they do, then it's not a place you'd want to go, anyway."

She was silent. I felt enormously proud of her, but I couldn't say it. Strange. When I tried to teach her something, I often failed. When I didn't try, sometimes something happened. She would be going away soon. So much to learn; so little time. For her? for me?

CHAPTER EIGHT

THE WHITE RAINBOW

Old age offers us the possibility of seeing life whole and understanding its natural course, claimed Schopenhauer, because we can connect life's beginnings, its "entrances," to its endings, its "exits." Though we may gain a conception of life's full span, that vision is bowed by our changing perceptions of time. Schopenhauer noted that in youth life seems to stretch into an endless future, whereas from the standpoint of old age it goes back "but a little way into the past." Through the eyes of youth, objects in the picture of life seem far away, as though viewed through a reversed telescope, while in old age "everything seems microscopically close."

Despite this foreshortening of time, Schopenhauer believed, older people are uniquely equipped to grasp the truth of life's full course—which he described as the futility of pursuing hopes and desires that can never bring a permanent state of happiness. Though disillusioned, the older person may reap the benefits of humility, inner calm, and worldly wisdom.

Though the conditions of aging and later life have changed radically since Schopenhauer's time—a healthier and more vibrant "second middle age" extending life expectancy by almost three decades—we still need a concept of life's full span and of the inter-relationship of its different phases. Individuals need to plan for and chart their path through the new, later segment of the life course, just as societies have to determine the best and fairest ways of ensuring the health and well-being of their more numerous older citizens, while also balancing the needs of younger age groups.

But can we, as Schopenhauer implied, recapture the experiences of our lifetime to hold fast a vision of the whole life course? Schopenhauer himself pointed out the folly of longing to return to a place in the distant past. When we revisit, we may find it is not the place but the time of life we wish to recover. As Schopenhauer put it, "Time mocks us by wearing the mask of space." The elusiveness of former times and the changes that affect each generation remind us of Heraclitus' famous saying "You can never step into the same river twice." Maybe that is why the developmental psychologist Erik Erikson said that comprehending the whole span of life required something like a revelation.

THE REVELATION

Arthur Fleming seems to have had that revelation. Former head of the Commission on Civil Rights during the Nixon administration and, over the following two decades, an activist for improving the lives of older Americans, Fleming was outgoing president of the National Council on the Aging's board of directors when I made his acquaintance.

After my years teaching and learning with my older friends in Olympia, Washington, and the library program in Tacoma, I was offered a job in the other Washington—D.C. I became the director of an educational program for seniors called "Discovery through the Humanities," one of the programs NCOA provided to local groups across the United States. As part of the staff, I was sometimes recruited to take on all sorts of other tasks. On one occasion, I was asked to find an appropriate gift to be presented to Dr. Fleming at a national conference in recognition of his service to the field of aging.

Fleming was a liberal Republican who greatly admired Lincoln. I managed to acquire a first edition of Carl Sandburg's two-volume *Abraham Lincoln: The Prairie Years* and, at a prearranged signal, rushed to the banquet hall podium with the gift-wrapped set, just as Jack Ossofsky, then director of NCOA, finished his congratulatory speech. I stood below the dais watching the tall, trim, dignified man with large ears carefully remove the books from the wrapping. He admired the bindings, turned a few pages, and exclaimed to the audience, "This is something my family will cherish for years to come."

His family? Years to come? Though vigorous, Fleming was already in his eighties. His attention was no longer on himself, his deeds and possessions, but on the causes yet to be promoted, and on the welfare of future generations. For Fleming, seeing the whole of life did not produce disillusionment or a sense that happiness was impossible. Rather, he found ever more reason to champion social improvements and access to a better quality of life for people of all ages. He was a vigorous supporter of new political coalitions between children's advocacy groups and those lobbying for the elderly. As I watched him acknowledge the applause and turn to shake Ossofsky's hand, the Sandburg volumes tucked under his arm, I imagined the invisible baton that is passed from generation to generation.

The bioethicist Norman Daniels wants us all to be like Arthur

Fleming. We should be able, he argues, to embrace the consciousness of the whole life course—identifying with all stages
simultaneously—when we are asked to choose what is fair and
just in the distribution of social goods such as health care. But too
often we lack this encompassing vision, the political scientist
Susan MacManus writes in *Young v. Old: Generational Combat in the
21st Century*. MacManus finds in her national studies of voting patterns that we are more likely to succumb to "generational politics,"
with older adults basing their school bond and community
improvement votes on immediate worries about their limited
income and skepticism of politicians' promises, and the young
worrying about the costs of helping to finance retirement or to
keep frail older people alive while also providing for their children's education and welfare. Pressing personal and family needs
at different stages of life tend to obscure our ability to view the
life course all at once. We tend not to see the full span.

After four years at NCOA, I accepted a new job offer, to head
an educational program for people over age fifty-five based at the
University of North Carolina at Asheville. For ten years, I have
been director of the North Carolina Center for Creative Retirement, a position that has made me particularly sensitive to the
problem of fragmented perception of the life course. I am sometimes asked by colleagues why older persons should be allowed to
participate on a campus dedicated primarily to the education and
training of young people. Though the older adults pay fees and, in
our College for Seniors, volunteer to teach their own classes, they
nonetheless use the scarce resources of classrooms, parking, the
library, and the campus fitness center. Why, some colleagues ask,
should the university lavish resources on persons whose future is so
much shorter and uncertain than that of the young, and who have
partly or fully ended the wage-earning period of their lives?

I understand their concerns and their dedication to nurturing young minds. And I have many practical answers, such as that our "senior" students make financial contributions to the university that help underwrite scholarships, they volunteer to make guest appearances in classes that utilize their professional expertise, their presence on the campus helps the university fulfill one part of its mission—providing community service. The seniors can serve undergraduates as role models for lifelong learning, and they make great learning partners in certain intergenerational classes. And I can point to studies that show the health benefits (both mental and physical) of continued active intellectual participation of people in their later years, which may, in turn, translate into public monies saved on social services and health care. Usually my colleagues' concerns are placated by my pragmatic approach of listing the assets older learners bring to the campus. But my response does not address a deeper issue. In twenty years, when today's undergraduates will be middle-aged, every fifth person in the United States will be over sixty-five—most of my colleagues included. How will our students adapt to this demographic revolution? Shouldn't we all be asking, What is the relationship between an older person's quest for self-fulfillment and the overall good of society?

With these perplexing questions in mind, I boarded a plane to Regina, Saskatchewan, to attend what I thought would be a moderately interesting international conference on lifelong learning. I had been invited to share with experts from other countries my research on education and community service programs for older learners in the United States.

MORNING MIST

The first morning in Regina, I followed my habit of going for a sunrise jog. I headed out the doors of the dormitory where we were housed on the campus of the University of Regina. While a light fog still blanketed the shrubs and trees, I rushed past an elderly Chinese gentleman, one of the conference delegates, doing Tai Chi on the lawn beside the parking lot. I waved hello. Without breaking stride, he nodded back. I ran toward the path that rings Lake Wascana, a small body of water adjacent to the university and the nearby government buildings of this provincial capital.

Close to the water, a denser layer of fog cloaked the lake and trail so that, intermittently, I'd catch glimpses of a dog leashed to a hand, a bicycle wheel, another runner's shoe and leg. Gradually, the tops of white pine and hemlock on the opposite shore became visible. That is when I saw the apparition—an arch of mist hovering over the surface of the lake, as if a metaphor over which I had long puzzled had become a tangible reality. I blinked. Was it real? The arch in Tennyson's poem—could it have been something like this?

I thought it was a mirage of some sort. But as I rounded the south end of the lake and headed west, the sun rising behind me, I saw it again quite clearly through an opening in the trees. The apex of the arch was tinged bronze by the rays of sunlight that burned through the mist. It occurred to me that I might be witnessing a rare meteorological phenomenon. Not that, only. For, while a voice in my head spoke calmly and rationally about atmospheric events, another whispered excitedly, "This could be a sign, a message."

But that was silly. Here I was in a new locale, imagining that a natural phenomenon—which, for all I knew, might occur over Lake Wascana every other morning—was intended solely for my eyes. Maybe there's a term for people who think they reside at the center of a meteorological universe.

Since I was near one of the observation points that dot the

lakeside, I decided to take a closer look. I stepped onto a small viewing platform, planted a running shoe on the ledge facing the lake, and observed the broad arch of white mist. Its reflection in the lake completed the arch's circular form, and the reflection, like the arch itself, appeared to be drifting in my direction. I stood there gazing at the ethereal piece of architecture while small waves lapped hypnotically below my feet. Several minutes must have passed, because I felt moisture on my cheek and the arch was gone.

My rational voice spoke once more. "You see," it said, "just a white rainbow." Then the second voice replied, "Foolish reason, a rainbow can't be white."

I turned away and continued my run up a narrow path that led to a hilltop, where I paused. Now the white rainbow reappeared in the field below me. I could see both ends tapering into transparency as they neared the ground. I turned around and ran, zigzagging, down the hill through tall reeds, following the path that led back to the university campus.

In the college hallway, panting slightly, sweat dripping from my forehead, I saw a ruddy-faced man in a plaid shirt coming toward me. It was Myron Sebert, a local volunteer who had picked me up from the airport the preceding day. While riding into town, I learned that Myron was a retired high school biology teacher who had lived his whole life in and around Regina. Perhaps he could tell me what I had seen.

"Been out for an early run, have you, Ron?" Like other local Canadians I'd met, Myron had a penchant for asking rhetorical questions.

"Yes, just got back," I replied, though I knew it was obvious. "Myron, I've just seen something for the first time. I wonder if you'd know about it?"

"And, what would that be?"

I told Myron about the fog, the sunlight, and the arch of mist.

"Hmm," he stroked his clean-shaven chin, tugged at his salt-and-pepper mustache. "Don't believe I've ever spotted one of those, though I've seen my share of sundogs and ice fog. Quite a sight, they are. You'll have to come see us in the winter months to get a look at them. As for your white rainbow . . . well, you've seen something quite interesting, now, haven't you?"

I nodded. So it was a white rainbow after all? Myron tapped his fingernail against his front teeth. "Yes, well, I used to teach a unit on meteorology from time to time. I wager what you've come across is essentially a diffuse rainbow whose colors have remixed into a hazy white because of the morning mist." Myron smiled, obviously pleased with his command of scientific knowledge. His words brought an inner nod from my voice of reason. Yet the other voice was still unsatisfied. A look of quizzical uncertainty must have shown on my face.

"You see," he went on, "your common variety of rainbow is formed when sunlight passes through water droplets that refract light rays, breaking up white light into its component wave lengths which appear to us as the colors of the spectrum. But the mist you encountered this morning produces a different effect. The water droplets are much smaller. The way they diffract light waves makes the colors blur or partially overlap. Should they overlap fully, they cancel each other out. So, instead of your multi-hued arch, you get a whitish bow."

"Yes, I see," I responded, "you get a white rainbow."

"Exactly. Or a cloud or fog bow. There are different names. Mind you, I've never seen one except in a textbook, so count yourself lucky." Myron glanced at his watch. I suppose he had some duties to attend to. "Ron," he said, "we'll talk later. Got to help set up for this morning." He turned and hurried down the hall, leaving me with my two quarreling voices.

I thought of Jung's term "synchronicity," which he said referred to the coincidence of a physical event with some mental state that makes us feel that an important connection has been made though there is no causal relationship between the two. No causal relationship, but some other connection? I was at once skeptical and intrigued. I didn't have time to ponder my speculations. I had to shower, change, and eat breakfast in time to get to the first lecture of the day.

As I dashed upstairs, I grabbed a pamphlet, *Walks through Wascana Centre*, from the conference information table. Maybe it would tell me something more about the lake's propensity to form white rainbows. Half an hour later, sitting in the college cafeteria spooning oatmeal, I flipped through the pages describing walking routes and tours of the various government buildings, art and science museums, wildlife reserves, and gardens that surrounded the lake. There was nothing about rainbows, white or otherwise. However, the booklet did reveal something I had taken for granted—the lake's very existence.

When Regina was chosen the future provincial capital of Saskatchewan, there was little to attract people to the area. The only variation from the flat prairie was a small winding creek surrounded by thick grass and herds of buffalo. The locale was a prime hunting ground for tribes of Indians who dried buffalo meat alongside the creek. Following their belief in the sacredness of all creatures, once the Indians had taken the meat and hides, they piled the discarded buffalo bones into heaps, which they purified with ceremonial fire. To the Cree, the creek was known as Oscana, "place of the piles of burnt bones." To the early white settlers, the creek became simply Pile O'Bones and, some years later, Wascana, an anglicized version of the Indian name. During the Great Depression of the 1930s, unemployed men were put to work turning the modest creek into a stately lake. Ironically, as

Myron later told me, the lake eventually reverted to its origins and was now so shallow you couldn't paddle a canoe across without hitting bottom. Maybe the white rainbow was a bow of smoke rising from still smoldering fires, I speculated as I made my way to the campus auditorium.

Holding a Mirror

The morning program began with the very gentleman I had earlier seen practicing Tai Chi. From the conference program notes, I learned that Mr. Liu was the president of a large study center for older people in Hubei Province. He resided in Wuhan, a major industrial city located at the confluence of the Han and Yangtze rivers in Central China. Mr. Liu was a former government official in Hubei Province, whose importance for the whole country, I later learned, could be summed up by a traditional saying: "A good harvest in Hubei, a good year for China."

Awaiting his turn at the podium, Mr. Liu gazed out at an auditorium filled with teachers and administrators from around the world gathered to share information about educational programs for their older citizens. I noticed that unlike his male colleagues, who were dressed in suits and ties—the outline of a package of cigarettes showing through the thin fabric of their jackets—Mr. Liu dressed informally in a zippered faded blue windbreaker, tan chinos, and dark blue sneakers. His powerful neck and shoulders, large, mostly bald head, and face weathered smooth like ancient limestone reminded me of a seasoned college football coach.

Rumor circulating among conference participants had it that the representatives of the Chinese universities for older people were important cadre members on whom the Chinese government had bestowed special titles and other rewards as part of a retirement benefits package. The government chose to finance these educational programs, some said, to ensure the loyalty of a burgeoning population of retirees who had sacrificed their youth and middle years to the revolution and the painful modernization of China during a period of civil wars and violent political upheavals.

Now, in old age, these officials were responsible for improving the morale of their aged peers, many of whom suffered from chronic illness, loneliness, and melancholy. Their children had married and moved into separate households—a new trend that shattered the traditional multigenerational family arrangement that included treating one's aging parents with great deference and privilege. In addition, once they were pushed out of the workforce, their interest in community affairs began to decline. A life of toiling to put rice on the table, to wrap oneself in a quilted cotton jacket, to put a tin roof over one's head, had deprived them of both education and the leisure to cultivate interests and hobbies. In old age, time weighed heavily upon them.

Mr. Liu rocked on the balls of his feet as he waited for the conference chairman to finish his introduction. Then he stepped forward to the podium as we gave our polite applause. He addressed us in Mandarin, his native language. As Mr. Liu gestured prophetically with his index finger, I pictured him alternately as commissar and as sage. Waiting for the translation, I imagined Mr. Liu as a Taoist master of college football coaching.

We are in the locker room at halftime, our side losing, and Coach Liu gently admonishing us, "The harmonious movement of play requires abandonment of self. Therefore, put aside personal ambition. Become the strategy of the way. Victory is an illusion. The successful team has no opposition; it competes against itself. Do not resist the opposite players. They are to you a shadow of yourself. You cannot catch your shadow or run from it. Therefore, seek to lead your shadow into sunlight. The opponent disappears."

Now the translator, a young man attired in a smart, double-breasted black blazer, white dress shirt, striped tie, and patent leather shoes, came forward. His black hair, cut shorter on one side than the other, seemed punkish. He was small-boned and had the slightly heavy features of a college freshman gone fleshy on beer and pizza. There seemed a vast gulf between the two men, as if they had grown up in entirely different worlds. The young man bowed to Mr. Liu and to the audience, then gave his translation.

"Mr. Liu wishes you good health, prosperity and long life," said the translator. "He tells you that today China has over 110 million elderly. By elderly, he means people who, according to government policy, must retire at age of fifty-five or sixty. Though classified elderly, the majority remain able to work and contribute to society in many ways. To that end, the Chinese government, in its wisdom, has established special universities for the old, now numbering over 5,000 institutions. The old people are indebted to the profound concern of the Communist Party of China and loving care by the People's Government."

A mandatory retirement age coupled to a national educational program for older citizens? I marveled at the contrast to the United States, where we have a third the number of older people and outlawed mandatory retirement as a form of age discrimination in the 1970s. In our country, we have a variety of programs for people who wish to continue learning—some free or at little cost, others requiring heftier tuitions. In the 1970s, it was popular for state legislatures to grant older residents a tuition-free opportunity to take courses at public colleges and universities, provided space was available. Usually the schools did not widely publicize these arrangements, because there was no financial incentive. For their part, few older people took the opportunity, not wanting the restriction of lengthy course terms and preferring classrooms where they could test their views and experiences through discussion, not note-taking from lectures. Did the Chinese elder universities offer something different?

The translator turned and bowed slightly toward Mr. Liu, who then stepped forward to the microphone, unfolded some sheets of paper, and began to read a prepared speech. A few minutes later, the translator read a translated version.

"In these universities the elderly learn many practical, aesthetic, and intellectual subjects," he explained. "For example, they learn to take care for sick people, follow proper diet, practice good hygiene, do exercise, and use herbal medicines. They also receive training in painting and calligraphy, flower growing, and other traditional art forms. They keep intellectually fit by study of world history, psychology, philosophy, and principles of economic science." The translator paused, took a sip of water, then proclaimed, "It is the sacred duty of China's older citizens to preserve health, stimulate the mind, and look after others." He glanced at Mr. Liu and continued, "We take important lesson from Confucius, who said, 'If you want to satisfy your own needs, you have to consider other people's interests.' "

Mr. Liu's ideological picture of the Chinese university for older people astonished me with its striking similarities to and differences from my own program for older learners. We, too, promoted opportunities for lifelong learning, encouraged retirees to take leadership roles in the programs as volunteer teachers and committee members, and helped to channel seniors into various community service roles, many of them with children in public schools. While our program emphasized the history, literature, art, music, philosophy, and science of a liberal arts curriculum, we also offered classes in calligraphy, herbal medicine, physical wellness, and even Tai Chi.

Yet I could not imagine standing before our members telling them it was their sacred duty to society to look after their health or that they should act from a sense of collective solidarity to serve their peers and those of other generations. Rather, our program was based on the notion that these acts should be voluntary. There was no generally accepted moral imperative, no government mandate, no spirit of collective destiny to which I could appeal. Instead, our members did these things because it felt good, because these acts coincided with some inner sense of rightness, because they found personal satisfaction in them. Unlike Mr. Liu's collectivist ideology, ours was one of laissez-faire individualism. I sat on the edge of my seat, listening.

"People about age sixty are in the mature period of life because they have acquired a great fortune in knowledge and experience. If we abandon or isolate them, that is civilization's great loss. We should not think that retirement means cease contributing to the community, or that having rest means doing nothing at all." While the translator spoke, Mr. Liu stood with his hands behind his back, his gaze fixed directly in front of him.

"The old have not only a good collection of knowledge and experience to handle difficulties, they can also increase understanding of the culture, society, and philosophy. Confucius began study of *I Ching*, ancient Chinese wisdom book, at age fifty and worked very hard to learn *yi* for the rest of his life. Mao Zedong first studied English at seventy and held a book in his hand when dying at eighty-two. The old people are knowledgeable and have desire to seek more knowledge. The traditional virtue of Chinese is 'Never quit study.' " The translator paused, smiled at the audience. "Correction," he said. "Should be 'Never quit studying.' "

The educational philosophy of the Chinese universities for older people emphasized doing for oneself as simultaneously doing for others. People have a duty to take care of themselves so as to spare the state overwhelming health care costs. They are to cultivate calligraphy and painting to avoid depression—a social drain that contributes to poor health and to social unrest. The Chinese philosophy of education for the old is intended to help keep people productive while they serve as role models for younger people, inspiring them with the collective spirit that sustained the revolution, encouraging them to avoid self-pity and envy that they may never be rich like the Westerners they see in movies—people who, though materially well-off, are morally impoverished. Or so they are told.

By contrast, many of the retirees I know in the United States have led relatively comfortable lives. Some in their youth experienced bone-hard poverty, many served in wartime, worked hard, had their share of sorrows and joys, but in retirement feel relatively free of heavy social obligations. They are challenged instead by an unprecedented array of options and choices. Yet many of the retirees who participate in the program at our university are like the Chinese elderly in their specially created universities. They volunteer to work with children as reading and math tutors, assist university undergraduates with research, and advise them about their careers. In this sense, combining lifelong learning with community service is a virtuous position taken by older people in both cultures, one that bridges the gap between young and old.

Our seniors may believe helping a disadvantaged child or an undergraduate student to get ahead benefits society as a whole. But they would be unlikely to accept Mr. Liu's interpretation that their purpose in life is to work toward social unity, that in old age we experience a blurring of individual differences. It is very important to them that they feel free to act from personal motives. Otherwise they will have been coerced, their actions no longer truly voluntary. But could voluntary initiative serve as a strong enough force to replace a sense of duty? What of those who did not experience a call to service or felt tired out and wanted to rest?

I was surprised to hear Mr. Liu speak of Confucius, since I

thought the ancient sage had been in disfavor with the Communists, regarded as a prop of the old social order and bureaucratic hierarchy. Apparently, there had been a sea change.

The sound of a cough snapped me out of my reverie, and I heard the translator's dispassionate voice saying, "Mr. Liu tells about a retired worker in Shanxi Province who, together with a cadre of other old people, moved a polluting rubbish hill away from a steel plant so that the area could be reclaimed. The government wanted to reward him with 12 million yuan, but he refused. He created both physical wealth and the wealth of unselfish virtue." He went on to translate Mr. Liu's story about a certain General Sunyi, who at ninety gives lessons to teenagers by teaching them moral standards and getting them to help send books and magazines to poor children.

The translator paused, took another sip of water, glanced at Mr. Liu, and continued, "Yes, General Sunyi provides the young people with appreciation of human justice to drive away their hollowness and make them adequately clear-minded to run toward the ideal community."

The translator seemed nervous. He wiped his forehead with a handkerchief before continuing. How would a young man in modern Western dress take the words of Mr. Liu? Did he suffer from hollowness, lack clear-mindedness, was he running from the ideal community? Despite its large elderly population, China was, I knew, a country where the young far outnumbered the middle-aged and older. Huge ideological and economic changes were taking place too, in which these universities for the old were perhaps also a compensation for lost certainties.

"The character of internal indifference and stability of old people does not mean they are free from concern, but means they truly understand—history is a long river full of conflicts."

The phrase "long river full of conflicts" echoed in my mind, reminding me that China is a country of immense river valleys along which, over the millennia, its dynasties have risen and fallen. Mr. Liu was attributing to older people a stoic wisdom in the face of historical unrest. Perhaps his image of the river of history referred to Marxist dialectics, which predicts the inevitable outcome of opposing economic forces such as class struggle. Or perhaps it stemmed from an education in Taoism, which sees opposition or duality as an illusion.

In the Chinese system, at least as Mr. Liu was presenting it, there was no generation gap. Cultural norms and government authority supplied the mandate for holding the life course together and assigned each person his or her duties to self and to others. In a society like ours, lacking cultural consensus about old age or, for that matter, about childhood, how could these gaps be bridged?

I was intrigued by what it must be like for Mr. Liu to stand before this audience at a Canadian university on the Saskatchewan prairie, everyone dressed nicely, smelling pleasantly, plenty of food, no distant sound of cannons, no screams, no smoke and fire. During his lifetime, he must have seen and experienced periods of the warlords, the Japanese invasion, the protracted civil war between 1945 and 1949 that ended with the Liberation, the Agrarian Reform, and the Cultural Revolution—all the great and painful transformations that have turned China into a modern industrial society heavily dominated by government authority and prone to periodic suppression of individual and group rights.

LANTERN PARTY

That evening, the conference participants were invited to an outdoor party at the home of the university president. Colorful paper lanterns suspended from an electrified wire stretched above the long wooden deck at the back of the house to a huge tent in which student-waiters were setting tables for the dinner.

I was standing, beer in hand, with Myron, discussing the history of Lake Wascana and trying to decide whether to share my idea that its white rainbow might be the spirit of burnt bones returning to haunt provincial legislators.

"A sad story," said Myron, concerning the Cree Indians, "but not unlike your country's history, eh?" He took a swallow of beer, wiped his mustache. "We're not proud of what happened, but you can't stop progress. Anyway, we're trying to redress the wrongs of the past through education and by giving the tribes more say over their land. There's even quite a bit of buffalo ranching going on," he cheerfully explained.

I was about to challenge his idea of progress when someone tapped me on the shoulder. I turned, surprised to see Mr. Liu's translator. Smelling of tobacco and cologne, the young man wore a wide grin as he extended his hand. "Excuse me, you are Mr. Manheimer?"

"Yes," I answered, shaking his hand, "Ron Manheimer. And aren't you Mr. Liu's translator?"

"Yes, I translate for some of the Chinese gentlemen. Also, I am section chief." He handed me a business card with Chinese characters on one side and Hubei Province Foreign Affairs Office printed on the other. "I have been in your country many times on trade missions. We are very active in the States, especially your Ohio and Alabama. Yankees and the Rebels, yes?"

I smiled and nodded. American Civil War history suddenly sounded very strange. I wanted to ask about his travels in the United States and made an attempt to pronounce the name on the business card.

Clearing his throat, the translator said, "In the States, I am called Benny."

"Benny?"

"Benny. Yes. It is very nice name, don't you think?"

"Oh yes," I replied. Then I introduced Benny to Myron, to whom he also handed a card. He looked back at me.

"Ah, Mr. Manheimer," he said, a note of hesitation in his voice.

"Ron," I corrected him. "No need for the formality."

"Yes, thank you. Difficult to change long habit. My purpose, I will explain. Mr. Liu has heard some story about you." He shifted from foot to foot. "Something about rainbow. Yes? That is possible?" Benny looked puzzled, as though he was certain a mistake had been made.

"I did see an unusual rainbow. I mean, unusual to me," I replied. "But how did he know?" I glanced at Myron, who smiled sheepishly. He must have told some others. A conference is like a small town—stories travel fast.

"Ah, very good," he said, apparently relieved there was some basis for this conversation. "These gentlemen, you know, they have not traveled much outside China until recently. They are curious about many things. Sometimes strange. When Mr. Liu asked me to invite you to talk with him about rainbows. Well. You understand?"

"Yes, I guess it would seem strange." Here was my chance to talk with Mr. Liu. "Benny," I said, "I would enjoy talking with Mr. Liu about rainbows."

"Excellent," he replied, a wide smile disclosing several gold-capped teeth. "I'm certain you will find the colonel a most interesting person."

"Colonel?" I exclaimed, but he was already several steps ahead.

I followed Benny across the patio and a section of lawn to a picnic table under a huge oak tree. Mr. Liu was examining an open-pit barbecue device used for cookouts. Several other Chinese men stood around talking and puffing on cigarettes. A veil of smoke drifted skyward. Passing them, Benny said something that brought nods and smiles.

Mr. Liu bowed gracefully, and I made an effort to do the same. He studied my face for a moment, then said something to Benny. "He is happy to make your acquaintance. He wants to know if you have a few minutes for conversation."

I said I was delighted to talk with him and that after listening to his lecture about the Chinese universities for older adults, I, too, had questions. Benny translated, and the elder man nodded. Now I had a chance to examine his face close-up. There was a mole beside his right eyebrow and a small scar on his left cheek. His skin was remarkably smooth for a man in his eighties, as if his skull had expanded, stretching the skin tight. Mr. Liu radiated well-being, with a trace of guile at the corners of his eyes and mouth. He rarely smiled but had a wide, open face as if a moment of astonishment, or horror, had formed into a permanent mask.

Mr. Liu said something that he accompanied with gestures, describing arcs in the air, level planes, pointing to his head, then to his belly. Benny nodded, but his wry smile and sideways glances suggested uncertainty. Then he turned to me.

"Mr. Liu says he did not see the white rainbow, though he has on occasion seen several in different part of China. Because of prior experience, he thinks you should know about old Chinese superstitions concerning rainbows. Mr. Liu says he understands in Western countries rainbow means good luck, much fortune to ones who see it. But in China rainbows have many meanings, some signify good fortune, others, bad. Also, Chinese tradition recognizes many types. For example, red, green, gray, or white, curved or straight." Benny raised his eyebrows. "Also male and female rainbows."

The elder Mr. Liu spoke as soon as Benny paused. Benny listened without expression, then translated. "Mr. Liu wants me to explain. Rainbows also predict what will happen in political affair and in, how do you say, marriage faith?"

"Marital fidelity?"

"Ah, yes, marital fidelity."

I studied Benny's face for some reaction, but he remained expressionless. Then he continued, "Perhaps you know about double rainbows?"

"You mean when you see two rainbows, one inside the other?"

Benny put my question to the elder, who nodded vigorously.

"Yes, correct. Double. Mr. Liu says, like birds, brighter one, male; less bright, female. This is also written in ancient Chinese poetry."

The types and meanings of rainbows in Chinese traditional culture were fascinating, but it didn't seem like the kind of subject to which a lifelong party member would devote his time. I could see by the expression on Benny's face that he was wondering the same thing. Had Mr. Liu turned a bit eccentric in his old age?

Then the elder spoke again.

"Mr Liu says he began study of ancient Chinese philosophy and poetry after seventieth birthday. He is student of Chuang Tzu and Confucius, also of Tai Chi Chuan philosophy." Benny executed a few quick movements to demonstrate, and I nodded my understanding. "He wants to know, where did you obtain white rainbow?"

Obtain my rainbow? He made it sound like a scouting badge or a driver's license. "Over the lake there." I pointed in the direction of Lake Wascana, on the other side of the university from the president's house. The elder Mr. Liu understood without need of translation. He looked in the direction I pointed, then at the sky, raised his hand as if framing a picture.

I couldn't resist flaunting my new expertise. "I, too, have learned a few things about rainbows," I said. "For example, white rainbows usually occur in fog or mist. It's something about the size of the water droplets and the angle of the sun." I looked at Benny to see if this made sense to him. He was taking it all in, so I continued, "Apparently, when the light is reflected back through the droplets the usual colors of the rainbow overlap so you see only a grayish white arch. I thought it was very beautiful. My first."

Benny spoke to Mr. Liu, who, though blinking a few times, gave no response. In fact, the three of us stood there in silence. Finally, Mr. Liu turned toward me. He talked for several minutes, raising his finger in a sage-like gesture. I glanced at Benny, who alternately bit his upper lip or pursed his mouth while nodding in apparent understanding.

"Mr. Liu says white rainbow is female, very yin. You understand yin and yang?"

"Well, sort of," I replied. "These are male and female principles. Attributes of people and things. Is that it?"

Benny seemed either satisfied or indifferent to whether I had grasped the idea. He continued translating. "White rainbow is special, not many people see." This, I was learning, was true. "Also it has a special meaning for the one who sees." Mr. Liu seemed to be Myron Sebert's opposite—all poetry and symbolism where Myron was all prose and scientific explanation. "White rainbow means," Benny paused trying to find the right words, "means, uh, overcoming separation; striving with one mind. In battle, for example, all must act together, else you lose."

Benny digressed for a moment to explain that Mr. Liu was, as he put it, "a big-time soldier in the war against Japanese imperialism. Also, part of the Long March, you know, with former Chairman Mao."

"Yes," I said, "I have read about it."

"Good," he replied. "Here is something else Mr. Liu said. How to make unity, this is big question. Mr. Liu says this is question for

you, because white rainbow is, um"—he bit his lower lip—
"belongs to you."

Belongs to me? It was then I remembered something Myron
said. "There are at least as many rainbows as observers." Myron
explained that it took just the right atmospheric conditions, the
right angle of the sun's rays, and the position of the observer, for
the reflection or refraction to reach the eyes of the beholder. At
the time, Myron's scientific explanation failed to impress me, but
Mr. Liu's account helped me understand Myron's point. You do
"obtain" a rainbow since timing and position are essential qualifi-
cations. I didn't have to choose between two ways of interpreting
rainbows—empirical and emotional—they could be complemen-
tary. But how to integrate them?

"Do most other Chinese people believe these things about
rainbows?" I asked Benny.

He studied me for a moment, then replied, "I cannot explain
more about that."

Could not, or would not? I watched Mr. Liu gazing toward the
lake. He was a survivor of horrendous times and changes, yet now,
in old age, he appeared serene. Did this come from studying Chinese philosophy, or was it the quietude of old age?

Mr. Liu looked away from the lake and addressed me. Benny
listened stone-faced, glanced at me several times, but without
revealing anything. Then he spoke.

"Mr. Liu explains to you the hidden meaning of white rainbow."

The hidden meaning? Had Mr. Liu grown childish in old age,
or was he some kind of Chinese Merlin, a Red Army magician? It
didn't seem possible. I knew by now that this was not going to be
another account of physical causes.

"Youth," Benny announced, "is like colorful rainbow. Sunlight
in cloud makes many colors. This brings feeling of happiness. You
see many possibilities, much variety. Later, rainbow tinted red or

green means strong feeling." Benny shook his head. "No, more than that." He raised his eyebrows, exclaiming, "Passion. You understand, much passion?" I nodded. "This is both happiness and suffering—river of life. Then comes white rainbow. This is old age. Like white hair, white rainbow brings sadness to some, happiness to others, makes anger for some, calm to others. Colors give illusion of difference, of separation. Simplicity. This shows you that possibilities are many but necessity is one."

Mr. Liu spoke again, and Benny translated.

"He tells you that white rainbow also show unity of the people; many types working together, great beauty in"—Benny screwed up his face—"sameness? No, togetherness."

I mulled over Mr. Liu's oracular pronouncements about my white rainbow. According to him, I was supposed to grasp the social philosophy of the unity of multiplicity, to perceive both natural and social law in this physical phenomenon.

"Benny," I said, "I want to ask Mr. Liu a question." I briefly described the program I directed in the States and the importance we placed on doing good deeds more from private motives than from group solidarity. How our members made virtuous use of their leisure time, enjoying special learning opportunities and, in turn, providing benefits to the community. Some were role models for the young. Did it matter if one were motivated by a government-endorsed spirit of a collective mission or by a feeling of good will?

While I presented my question, Benny plucked a cigarette from inside his jacket and lit up, blowing a puff of smoke into the air. He watched me intently as he exhaled smoke through his nostrils. Mr. Liu was interrupted by a colleague who asked for something, which Mr. Liu was rummaging through his pockets to find.

Stepping closer to me, Benny leaned over and whispered, "Solidarity. This is big question me and my friends talk about a lot. I am married. Have one child. We would like to have more. But, you see, government policy, do what is good for China—lower birthrate. One couple, one child. No choice."

I wondered whether that child was a boy or a girl, but was reluctant to ask. Instead I said, "And if you have another?"

"Second child?" He shook his head. "Good-bye job, nice clothes, travel. You understand?"

I did. Benny turned to Mr. Liu and conveyed my comments and question. Mr. Liu, who had found the key he was searching for and handed it to his colleague, listened, squinting occasionally as though he was unsure of or disagreed with my views.

Mr. Liu rattled off a stream of words, and Benny was ready to translate.

"Mr. Liu admires the great ingenuity of the West, especially technical achievements. In capitalist society, everything can be done. Build highway through mountain, big hydropower plants, efficient machine production. Also, in capitalist society, control over life, highest virtue. Submission to destiny, lowest. You have much optimism and belief in force of will. Make great effort to find cause of social problem. If you have fever or headache, doctors find cure for symptom. In traditional Chinese medicine, symptom is not cause of problem, only a sign. You must go deeper to find cure for imbalance, disharmony. Same with older people. They are not a problem, only symptom of social ill. In the West, you shun moral imperative because you have illusion about freedom. False optimism."

I shook my head. Mr. Liu was right about our debate over the proper place of old people. Our society did have a problem balancing equitable distribution of resources among age groups. And there was a problem about figuring out the benefits and purposes of a longer lifetime. But old people and old age were not in themselves the problem. The difficulty was not having a coherent picture of the life course, a willingness to imagine oneself as a future older person, or to reimagine childhood, adolescence, and stretches of adulthood. Did Mr. Liu think that we in the United States should embrace a collective solution as had China?

I was about to ask him to explain what he meant by moral imperative when a strange sound reached my ears. We turned and saw a woman—I believe she was the university president's wife— walking toward us shaking a cowbell and singing out, "Supper time. Please come into the tent and enjoy the food and music."

Mr. Liu bowed to me and I to him. I shook hands with Benny and thanked him for serving as go-between. "My pleasure to serve you," he replied. The others dropped their cigarette butts and crushed them underfoot. We walked beneath the glowing lanterns into the big tent.

RETURN TO THE LAKE

The next morning, a little hungover from sitting with some of the Chinese men who kept insisting I drink with them, I slept in. I headed outside, knowing that I would be late for a lecture on education and older people in Ireland, but I needed time to think. Until the preceding morning, I had neither seen nor heard of a white rainbow. Now I had both the experience and two accounts: a scientific explanation of the physics of rainbows, in particular the white variety, and a mixed cultural, mythical, and political interpretation of the meaning of rainbows in China, including white ones. I could hold on to both accounts; they were not mutually exclusive. Yet I was still unsettled and couldn't resist wondering, Why had Myron never come upon a white rainbow while I, my first morning in Regina, had? Was this one of those chance encounters in which a phrase, a dream, a scent contains some special message for us?

By the time I crossed the dorm lawn, the sun was already above the tree line. There was no mist, and no Tai Chi master. I decided against jogging, which that morning seemed too jarring and ungraceful. Instead, I meandered along the path around Lake Wascana, trying to picture the Indians busily drying buffalo meat and setting fire to piles of dry bones. The water lay flat, perfectly reflecting the handsome stone bridge about a quarter of a mile away. Again I entertained contrary voices.

Wasn't the modern life course like this lake, said a voice in my head, a product of human invention? It, like the lake, was fabricated from science and technology, government policies, economic forces, and the accidents of history. Why, then, appeal to a vision of the life course to justify older people's place on a college campus? In China, there was a decisive need to build up the country. The moral imperative that each had to do his and her part for the good of the nation was the product of collectivist ideology; sacred duty, an ancient piety now used to promote social policies. Appealing to a vision of the whole life course was more a rhetorical device—like invoking laws of nature that, as everyone in our postmodern era understood, were historically and culturally influenced dogmas paraded as immutable truths. Besides, so-called natural events like earthquakes, floods, droughts, or good weather—or even old age—do not possess moral authority. We read meaning into them.

Although the lake might be a creek altered by pick and shovel, countered my other voice, the white rainbow was real. Though mathematicians and physicists had sought to explain its material properties, there was no getting around its being a spectacle of nature evoking deep psychological responses. You know it impressed me, even made me feel blessed. Birth and death, growing up and growing old, working, loving, playing, and resting take many forms. But they are not wholly invented, despite the many ways human beings re-create them in their minds and memories. The span of life, like a white rainbow, can be a sacred thing.

As the conversation went on in my head, I tried to imagine Arthur Fleming. What would he say? I knew stories about him from some of my NCOA colleagues, so it wasn't hard to imagine. Suppose, after the award banquet, Fleming and I had sat down for a few minutes at a deserted table. I pictured him carefully placing the Sandburg volumes on a clean spot and listening to my tale of perplexity. Nodding thoughtfully, he might reply:

"If rainbows inspire you, that's fine. We all look for inspiration. Some to nature, others to religion. For my part, I have been inspired by my family and the people I grew up around in our valley home."

"Your valley?"

"Yes. The Hudson Valley. You know, we used to picnic over at the Roosevelts'. Well, those are the sort of people I got to know. Some people have a jaded view of political figures. It's understandable. But I've met or learned about many a dedicated civic leader. They are my role models. Lincoln, for one. And it is from them that I've drawn encouragement in my old age. Never stop learning, acquiring new skills, and making your abilities available to society, as long as you have the energy and the health to continue on. This is my credo. And I think it's a good one."

"Yes," I replied, "an admirable point of view."

"Now, as far as your Chinese friends are concerned," he continued, "that is a long, complicated story, understanding their history, their way of looking at the world. Mind you, big changes going on there. They've come a long way since Chairman Mao wrote his famous essay 'Serve the People.' From what I hear, with capitalism coming on strong, the younger Chinese are out to serve themselves. Make money. Lots of it. Still, at least for the older generation, sacred duty has a special meaning. I'd propose

another for our country, and it, too, has ancient roots—all the
way back to Athens and Sparta. Civic duty, that's the ticket. I'm
not talking about patriotism, though I suppose patriotism is a part
of it. What I mean is that everyone, young, old, and in between,
has a duty to his or her fellow human beings. Call it the Golden
Rule, whatever you want. Just common sense tells you that if you
help others, they will be inclined to help you when you need it.
Neighborliness, that's another word. Just because people get old
doesn't mean they no longer have that duty. And what better
place to make sure the mature citizen has a chance to flourish,
grow, gain additional knowledge, and find encouragement than
our universities? They can do their part. That way"—he pointed
at me—"that way people like you can help them remain a part of
society. Stay in touch, don't you see? That's terribly important.
Once you feel cut off, you lose interest. You become resentful.
'What's anybody done for me lately?' you find yourself saying. No.
We don't want people to lose touch because they're elderly. They
still have something to give—for some, maybe more than ever,
because they have the time, you see, and the motivation. That's
why education is so important for them. It can serve as an engine
of social change and betterment. Think what unique perspectives
older people bring to learning and guiding others. Maybe it's the
first time in decades they've had an original thought—something
outside their work, their careers. I know people also want leisure.
Fine, they should take time to recreate, rejuvenate the spirit and
the body. But that is not an end in itself. Some think it is, I know.
But recreation is just that, a time to relax, get some exercise, soak
up new energy. Then you start creating all over again."

Fleming paused, wet his lips. He had a great capacity for making long speeches. "Here's my advice to you. Take it for what it's
worth. Don't worry too much about what other people think.
When it comes to thinking about the span of life, there are no

easy answers. Some will tell you that to each person is given a limited lifetime allocation of social goods. Once you have used up your quota, you have an obligation to step aside—give the next generation its due. Others will tell you it is the duty of the younger generation to look after the old because they have sacrificed for them. There's some truth in both positions. Now, here's my point." Fleming reached across to a basket on the table and lifted up a single remaining piece of bread. Breaking it in half, he gave me part and said, "This is what you must do."

Was he exhorting me to work to feed the masses, take communion, break bread with my enemies?

"If you wish to nourish yourself," Fleming continued, "think also of what will nourish others. Make your plans in accordance with this principle. Resist abstractions. Work to test reality. Think of practical measures that demonstrate what you believe. Dream but continue to doubt."

It was true, I was hoping to find some all-encompassing theory to justify the place of older people on our campus. Dr. Fleming seemed to be pointing me in another direction. "Take small, practical steps to bring young and old together in shared study and celebration," he told me. "You will need science to help you understand what it is to grow old. You will need myth to help you understand the enduring questions and expectations about what is possible in life. You can learn from the Chinese sages who view discord as the path to unity. Use your confusion to find harmony. The main thing is, stay the course. People give up too easily. Talked out of their own good sense. Just think. If a white rainbow is possible, what other miracles can be worked? If we're all part of creation, and I for one believe we are, we have the ability to make our own rainbows—metaphorically speaking, that is."

CHAPTER NINE

IN SEARCH OF CONTEMPORARIES

What does it mean to be a contemporary? A few years ago, I was leading a discussion group at a historical society museum where we were exploring life on the "home front" during World War II. I referred to articles describing the urban race riots in the United States that took place in 1944 and the internment of Japanese-Americans living on the West Coast shortly after the bombing of Pearl Harbor. I noticed some discomfort among members of the group when reviewing this material. In the middle of the discussion, a gentleman suddenly protested, "I don't remember any of this sort of thing happening. I just don't believe it." Several others nodded, saying, "We didn't know about this" or "Isn't this an exaggerated account?"

"But it's part of history," I protested; "these are the facts." My assertions didn't seem to convince them. These were good people, kind, well meaning. What was happening?

A little shaken by this rejection of the historical record, I wandered around the museum after the group broke up, looking at portraits of community leaders, etchings of streets and buildings of the town's past, the usual dusty dioramas that fill historical museums, cases of military garb and gowns from a hundred years ago, and the other memorabilia representing the past. Then it struck me. Despite thirty years of scholarship in social history and growing recognition of the many ethnic and racial groups whose lives and contributions make up the community's past, the members of the historical society still resisted the notion of inclusiveness, just as some of my group members could not accept the idea that other peoples' historical experiences, different, yet simultaneous with their own, belonged to their lifetime.

Contemporaneity, the felt experience of connectedness in time through a shared sense of history and personal destiny, is based not simply on proximity—walking the same streets, hearing the same news—but on inclusion, acceptance, and mutual recognition. Sharing ownership of the past with others whose values, background, and life experiences are distinctly different is sometimes a threat to our identity, to assumptions that provide comfort and meaning in our lives, or a source of guilt, and thus denial, over the past misdeeds and injustices of our ancestors. Inclusion and exclusions are such powerful elements of group identity that in a heterogeneous democratic society that depends to a considerable degree on consensus, voluntary loyalty, good will, and identification with certain common goods, true contemporaneity may be difficult to achieve.

A thinker who offered a profound and imaginative way to address the issue of historically connected communities was the California-born philosopher Josiah Royce, one of the first Berkeley graduates (1885) and a professor at Harvard and at Johns Hopkins University during the early decades of the twentieth century. Everyone is an interpreter of reality, searching to make meaning out of life experiences, said Royce. We do not do this in a vacuum but in the context of other interpreters. Whether over a neighbor's back fence, in scientific journals, or through literary criticism, we are busy interpreting ourselves to our selves, and interpreting our neighbors and colleagues to one another. All this interpreting depends on the symbolic discourse we call language, and because all the knowledge we obtain is passed along to others in some specific set of symbols—innuendoes and rumors, theorems, metaphors—all knowledge is social and forms a vast interconnected matrix, "a single Community of Interpretation."

For Royce, we are each intermediaries in sets of interlinked communication triangles. However different our perception of reality, we participate in the order of self-interpreting communities. "The history of the universe, the whole order of time," Royce grandly concluded, "is the history and the order and the expression of the Universal Community." This Universal Community is like a great symphony we can perceive only one musical phrase at a time because we are finite beings. We can merely guess at the plan of the entire composition. But our part, the meanings we derive, would be unintelligible unless we assumed they had a relationship to the whole. For Royce, it followed that there must be an infinite mind capable of perceiving the entire symphony simultaneously—a supreme conductor. Perhaps his theory would have convinced my discussion group members that they should listen for other musical instruments, other voices than their own.

Royce's proposal for a universal community of interpreters may strike us today as both lofty and naive. Various scholars have attacked theories of universal history and those positing a unified world community as tantamount to intellectual imperialism. Seemingly benign, they can conceal an underlying assumption that a particular metaphysical or religious view of the world will eventually encompass and subsume all the rest. Royce's conception of Christianity was one such enveloping view. Do we need theories of universal humanity?

Our society can take only so much diversity, so many group claims to special "rights," so much individualism, argue social analysts like Christopher Lasch, who proposed "moral discipline" and "conscience" as correctives to rampant individualism and narcissism. But others respond that we can no longer rally around theories that presuppose a universal "human nature" crowned by conscience and rationality. For one of the chief spokesmen of the Enlightenment, Immanuel Kant, reason is the foundation of our capacity to derive universal categories of thought—such as space, time, and number; and also of categories of morality—such as duty, obligation, and justice. Yet for the twentieth-century anthropologist Clifford Geertz, who has studied tribal cultures with radically different ways of categorizing reality, reason cannot provide the "glue" to repair a broken society, because rationality is itself an example of European "ethnocentrism." Geertz, in a provocative essay, "The Uses of Diversity," asserts that the appeal to rationality is often a guise for suppressing or trivializing difference. Influenced by the French postmodern thinkers, Geertz champions emancipation of traditional cultures, native tribes, the poor, the eccentric, and other groups that have been judged inferior because they deviate from presumed standards of universal humanity; to grant them equality, he believes, we have to throw off all claims to a collective or universal history.

Responding to both sides, the contemporary American pragmatist Richard Rorty argues for "Cosmopolitanism without Emancipation." Rorty suggests abandoning belief in "a single set of criteria which everybody in all times and places can accept," while favoring the powers of persuasion (rather than force) and "constant, experimental reformulation" of our social institutions under the banner of the liberal, democratic tradition and its history. Let's have a tolerant, fair, and humane society without having to resolve our philosophical differences, Rorty suggests. We can work out our political differences without having to settle perennial philosophical disputes.

Perhaps pragmatic solutions to threats of disunity and disorder are workable, as Rorty suggests. But does his or any other approach speak to the issue of contemporaneity—the experience of community in and through time? Or should we assume there will always be not *e pluribus unum*, "one from many," as appears on our coinage, but simply "many"—a multitude of contemporaneities, but no unity in time?

TURNING fifty

The group at the historical society museum and Josiah Royce were on my mind the morning of my fiftieth birthday. Maybe it was the realization I had reached the midcentury mark that drew me to thinking about contemporaneity. Around the time you turn fifty, you may start wondering about how you fit into a wider context of history, social change, multiple generations—Royce's symphony. I had decided to throw a "Turning Decades" party, inviting men friends ranging in age from their thirties to seventies, and from different backgrounds, to share their stories. So I had another reason for contemplating communities of interpretation—how would this diverse group of friends connect?

My wife frequently participated in all-women parties on the occasion of various friends' birthdays, and her friends seemed to have a great time celebrating one another in this period of feminist consciousness and solidarity. Perhaps I wanted to comfort myself through the sympathy and companionship of other males, while looking for a way to put my personal history and aging process in the perspective of the generations.

On the invitation, I asked the birthday participants to come prepared to talk about how they remembered the beginning of some decade—whether it was becoming ten or seventy. The only gift I asked each person to bring was a snapshot of himself taken around the time of the birthday he would commemorate. The picture would function to jog the memory and serve as a prop for the story.

The turning-decades theme party posed several challenges. I had certain things in common with some of these individuals—profession, religion, generation, and some harder to define feelings of kinship—but this would be the first time the group had assembled. Some knew others, but I alone knew everyone. Moreover, a good forty years separated the youngest from the oldest. Would my friends have enough in common to make the occasion interesting—one person's story making a connection with another's? Enfolding the personal past into the living present—"becoming historical to oneself"—was difficult and problematic enough. What were the prospects of linking lifetimes in becoming historical to one another?

I remember the day was typical for late March in our southern mountain town. The wind blew low scattered clouds, creating a succession of shadow and sunlight across the living room floor. An hour earlier, there had been rain, even a threat of snow or sleet. Black, shiny branches of the side yard tree tapped against the windowpane. I carried in a tray of glasses and a bottle of good scotch that someone provided for the group to share. There was also iced tea, a beverage for all seasons in the South.

The guests were already seated around the living room. Earl was in the canvas director's chair. The side arms made it easier for him to hoist himself up. An avid tennis player, he started having trouble with his knees around the time he turned seventy. Norm preferred the leather lounge chair with ottoman. I could see his once stylish white loafers propped up. Rick, Peter, and Dwight occupied the couch with its green slipcover that Caroline had tie-dyed. Alan, my health-minded, weight-lifting doctor and friend, had chosen to sit on the rug near the fireplace. Shmuel, my rabbi, closing the circle alongside me, had pulled in one of the chrome-and-wicker dining room chairs. He was trying to decide between scotch and iced tea. I can still hear him muttering.

THE BIRTHDAY PARTY

"Oh, what the hell," Shmuel said as he splashed two fingers of scotch into a glass. "How often do you turn fifty?"

Rabbi Shmuel, born "Scott," was in his midthirties. Athletic looking with wiry red hair and a dense red beard, he looked more like a Scott than a Shmuel, the Hebrew name he took when, at age twenty-seven, he decided to become a rabbi. Shmuel handed me a picture. It was the beardless Scott, standing in front of a tent, against the background of forest and distant mountain peaks.

"Very nice," I said. "I think I like you better with the beard."

"That's just because *you* have a beard, Ron. You know, there's a saying in the Talmud." Shmuel rattled off something in Hebrew.

"Which means?" I asked.

"Which means"—Shmuel looked around at the others— "which means, a person who sees his likeness in the face of his neighbor also sees the face of God." He raised his eyebrows and stroked his beard.

"Well," I said, "that's why I invited both those with and without beards. To explore our commonalities and differences."

"Good," said Shmuel, "and because I am one of the youngest here, Ron said I should go first." Shmuel winked at me. I didn't recall having said this, but I was glad he was willing to break the ice.

"I am going to read a couple pages from my vast collection of diaries. I've been keeping them for years." He glanced at some of the gray and bald heads, and added, "Well, to me it feels like many years. Are some of you finding your memory capacity declining?" he grinned. "I never had one to begin with." We all laughed. "Which is why I wrote everything down as it was happening."

Shmuel had been known for lapses in memory. In the middle of a sermon, he might suddenly ask the congregation's indulgence. "I've lost track of what I was going to say," he'd complain, "who can help me out?" Then he'd get the congregants to figure out where he was going with his interpretation of a passage in the Torah. Some people suspected this was a trick to get them involved. It seemed to work.

"This is taken from a diary. Let's see," he continued, flipping to the first page. "Yes, it would be just after I turned twenty. A long time ago. Or so it seems."

Shmuel raised his glass to the others. *"L'chaim,"* he exclaimed, "to your health." The others raised their glasses of scotch or tea. He opened his diary and read.

"Today I covered twelve miles of the Appalachian Trail. Everyone who hikes it just calls it the AT. At first the AT was a dotted line on a map. How far could I go? Then it was a series of uphills and downhills, going through rhododendron groves to tall oaks, spruce, and pine, then back through the dark groves. Like life's ups and downs. Sunny periods. Dark ones. Gradually, I begin to notice birds, squirrels, signs of deer and bear, temperature differences, and differences in myself. The trail is my path. Even though I share it with others. We pass each other and stop briefly to talk about where we started from and how far we hope to go. Yesterday I met Bob, somebody who said he was doing the whole AT by segments. While he was talking, I looked at his face and almost broke out laughing. He looked like a hedgehog. Maybe it was because of his teeth (an overbite) or the way he kept looking up and down and from side to side. We become animals on the trail. We are part of nature. The challenge of hiking helps us to find ourselves. How could I explain this to my parents? They raised me to be a rational city boy; not to believe in what they regarded as magic or superstitions. And now I'm a red fox trotting along the AT. I'm not Scotty. I'm a bushy-tailed red fox. Part of nature. A creature. Part of the creation."

Shmuel closed his diary, and we applauded.

"Can we see your tail?" laughed Norm, an agile bald man with a neatly trimmed white mustache who, in his early seventies, was still doing some consulting work as a petroleum geologist.

Shmuel fluffed up his red beard, in reply.

"What I really want to know," Norm continued, "is what actually happened to you."

"What happened?" Shmuel swayed back and forth in his chair. "What happened was that my experience of the outdoors opened an awareness. Of what? Nature? Yes. But also of my spiritual side. At first this was not a problem. I just kept it separate from my other pursuits. I was studying to become a chemical engineer. I had a close relationship with my parents, but we were a strictly secular family, culturally Jewish but completely emancipated from what my parents believed were the backward superstitions of religion. Yet I had this growing sense of belonging to a larger, sacred order of being. It was encroaching on my motivation to be a scientist in a primarily secular world. The AT and other trails were leading me on a collision course that would result in old Scott"— Shmuel held up the photograph—"coming face to face with Shmuel."

Shmuel scratched his beard, looked again at the photograph.

"After hearing Shmuel," Norm laughed, "I should probably go next because my story is just the other way around."

"Take it away, Norm," said Shmuel.

"Well," began Norm, "you see, Dad was a Methodist minister; Mom, his assistant and commander of the household. Unlike the rabbi, here, as kids, we were raised on sermons about sin and God, Calvary and the Apocalypse. Everything in our home was religion or, to be more accurate, Christian. I found it stifling, couldn't wait to get out on my own. My chance came when I went off to college at Washington and Lee. That's where I discovered geology. I distinctly remember turning twenty. Boy, I was an adult, I thought. It was then I discovered rocks."

Norm extracted two pictures from a manila folder and passed them around. One was of a jaunty young man in a college uniform walking with a group of similarly dressed students on a campus sidewalk overshadowed by tall trees. The other showed a sturdy-looking young man in shorts, wearing a campaign hat, a cigarette dangling from his mouth. He was holding what appeared to be a small pickax and standing beside an outcropping of rock.

Norm took a sip of iced tea. "Geological time, by golly. Now that made the Bible seem like a modern-day novel. Think about the eons of time. Time measured by eras. The Paleozoic and Neolithic. Measured in thousands and even millions of years. Religions are just recent inventions. The truly great mystery is far older. How our planet was formed, which, I might add, to the trained eye, is apparent from the stuff just under our feet or when you drive through one of the mountain passes that have been cut for road building. There you can read about heat, pressure, fracturing, upheaval; what we call"—Norm made a tent with his fingers—"mountain building. You can read the story of evolution from the mineral and fossil record right in front of you. You can measure it, subject it to tests, have your analyses and theories confirmed by other people thousands of miles away. That's science. That's my idea of faith. A firm belief in hard facts."

Norm shifted in his chair, recrossed his legs, as he warmed to the subject. "We didn't even know about plate tectonics or continental drift, when I was a student. Talk about revelations. This was the stuff I was looking for—it explained so many things we never understood. Hot damn! I wanted to celebrate the material world, not as something lower than the spiritual but truly worthy of awe. It had all the spirituality you could ever want right in it. Science was my way out of the dark ages of religion. The way of progress; human betterment. Of course, it didn't all turn out that way, partly because people can't help clinging to certain beliefs that are sometimes, well, sometimes downright irrational. But I don't mind, if it gives them comfort."

Norm looked over at Shmuel. "I'm not trying to denigrate religion, mind you. Religion can be beneficial. It helps guide people to do good things and not bad—at least it's supposed to." Norm winked at Shmuel, who nodded back.

"But, for me, religion has always seemed too negative. A good geological field trip can be like spending time in an elaborate and beautiful cathedral, many of which, I hasten to point out, are themselves made of—what? That's right. Of rocks. I didn't figure all this out when I turned twenty, or even thirty. It sort of grew in me over time. Yet, in some way, I knew this is where I was headed. Maybe it's just that one generation always wants to do the opposite of the previous one."

The photographs made their way back to Norm. He replaced them in the folder and leaned back in the recliner, signaling the end of his story.

"And did your father ever understand your position? Did you have arguments?" asked Shmuel.

Norm pulled himself forward. "Oh, I suppose you could say we had an amicable relationship. My wife helped. Dad adored Phyllis. I guess she sort of made up for what he found missing in me." Norm sat quietly looking at his outstretched feet. No one spoke.

We had agreed not to scrutinize each other's stories; to ask questions but otherwise to focus on the telling.

"It's interesting that several of us chose twenty for our decade," said Peter, breaking the silence. In his midforties, his full beard showing streaks of gray, Peter taught literature at the local university. Originally from a small town in Michigan, he grew up in a working-class family. His thoughtful, ironic, yet earnest temperament was reinforced by the way a small gap between his front teeth showed when he smiled.

"This is me in Vietnam," said Peter as he handed around a photo of a group of soldiers standing in a dusty street. "Let's see. Uh, huh. I must have been all of twenty-one then. Unlike some of you in your forties now, I did not try to avoid Vietnam. I was a choirboy in the Catholic church. A good working-class kid. You just accepted the war. Military service was a given. I didn't question it. My number came up. Right, the lottery. You all remember that. And I was called for a physical. Passed it, went to basic; a few months later I was in Vietnam." Peter snapped his finger. "Just like that.

"I hadn't ever been far from home, and suddenly I was in this tropical climate in an Asian country. The war changed my whole way of looking at things. I was shocked when I saw how other GIs treated the Vietnamese. I couldn't believe the brutality, the indifference. And we were supposed to be Christians. Well, most of us. These weren't strategic killings to protect the security of the troops. Once guys were over there for a while, they turned into beasts. I could feel it in myself. Fortunately, or unfortunately, one day I was riding on an armored personnel carrier when it hit a mine. I got thrown to the ground. Next thing I knew I was on a stretcher. Leg broken. They sent me back home. By the time I mended, my duty was over. After what I'd seen, I decided to become a draft counselor to help other guys avoid Vietnam. The whole experience had an amazing effect on me, like I'd woken from some kind of sleep. Most of what I did after that, go to college, study literature, and become a lit teacher, was completely different from what I had anticipated before I went in the service. Even now, I can't quite believe it."

Peter smiled and looked at us. Then he added, "I feel like there are two Peters separated by a stint in Vietnam." He finished the scotch in his glass.

"Separated or connected?" asked Earl. Everyone looked at Earl, a handsome, tanned man in his late sixties with a head of well-groomed, carefully parted white hair. "Don't you think, Peter, from what you've said, that you could connect your two Peters because of what happened to you in Vietnam? There must have been something of the college teacher in you, just waiting to happen. But it took a war to bring it out."

Peter cocked his head sideways and pondered this idea. "Well, it's true, I did enjoy English literature in high school. But I never took it seriously. I'll have to think about that."

Earl turned toward me. "Oh, I guess I forgot the ground rules, Ron. We're supposed to ask questions, not offer opinions. But I couldn't resist responding to Peter's story, because my stint in the service during World War II helped me figure out I didn't want to be an engineer, like my father." Earl rubbed his jaw, ran his hand down his sinewy neck. "But that's another story. Not the one I planned for your party."

"Go ahead, Earl," I said. "Seems like it's your turn."

"Well, I guess it's my turn next because my story is also related to Vietnam and my sons, who did manage to avoid going."

Earl showed the picture of a neat and tidy-looking business-man with his arms around two scraggly-looking young men with shoulder-length hair and psychedelic T-shirts.

"My sons," explained Earl. "That's Richard, and that's Tom."

"I had hair like that," exclaimed Alan, my physician friend in his early forties. Alan lightly touched the bald spot on the crown of his head.

"There's something to be said for moderation," Earl replied. "Now, where was I. Oh yes, the boys. It's hard to believe that was twenty-five years ago. I was, let's see, forty-two or -three because the boys were nineteen and twenty-one then. Even though it wasn't exactly turning a decade, that time of my early forties was difficult, very difficult. I think everyone has a tough time with some decade. It could be twenty, or thirty, and so on. But in my experience most people have one particular Waterloo decade transition. I think, for me, the situation of my boys and the war in Vietnam made my early forties especially tumultuous." Earl looked up at the ceiling.

"Like some of you old-timers, if you'll excuse the expression, I was a World War II veteran. Navy. I would have gone to the Pacific theater, but because I spoke German and French they sent me to Europe to translate. We interviewed German scientists about their technology. Mind you, I'm patriotic through and through; I just couldn't support our role in Vietnam. I didn't want the boys going there, and I supported their draft resistance. But I was scared for them. And I thought, Is it just because I want to protect them, don't want to lose them, that I feel this way? Because, for most of us back then, there was no question about fighting. This was a just war. The enemy was evil. They'd started it. We were on the side of good. And, besides," Earl added, with a laugh, "everyone said you looked great in a uniform."

Earl looked at Norm for confirmation. Norm nodded and gave Earl a salute. "Had I changed this much because I was no longer a fearless kid of nineteen or twenty, but a dad of forty? I had seen enough pain and agony during my duty, so I had no illusions about the heroics of war. I'm thrilled about the way the boys went on, after they managed to get rejected by their draft board. They're good husbands, fathers, responsible and creative in their professions. Still, I know that others, like Peter here, were not so fortunate. They didn't have any way out. Many never came back. They never had a chance to figure out whether it was right or wrong for us to be over there. That was a distressing time. I'm glad it's over."

No one spoke. Rick handed the photographs back to Earl. He looked at the pictures, then put them back into an envelope.

"Well, I'm not going to talk about how I became a literature teacher, or about war or rocks," said Rick. He took a photograph from a file folder and showed it to the group. "I turned thirty in Israel in 1983. This is me standing at the *Kotel*, the Wailing Wall in Jerusalem." He handed the photograph to Norm.

Rick was balding and bearded with wrinkles radiating from the outer corners of his eyes. He had small hands and feet but a barrel chest and muscular forearms.

"I went to Israel as a *Sherut La'am*—someone who commits to doing volunteer service for a year. After that, I stayed two more years. How did it happen?" He shrugged his shoulders. "I was walking on the plaza that slopes down to the Wall when a man, about my age, came alongside me and put his arm over my shoulder. 'Do you know what time it is, my friend?' he asked me. I started to look at my watch, but he shook his head and laughed. 'Not that kind of time, my friend. Time to feast at the Queen's table, set with palatial silver and bread and wine. You know?' and he laughed again. Right, I got it, he meant Shabbat, the Sabbath. 'How will you feast with the Queen? How will you dance with her?' he asked me. I put my hand on my back pocket to make sure my passport was there." Rick went through the motion of checking his pocket. "It was," he laughed.

"The guy introduced himself—Jacob Katz. Originally from

Milwaukee, he now lived permanently in Israel. Then he stood in front of me. Looked me up and down and started to tell me things about myself. Like that I was searching to fill the emptiness I felt inside me. That I was adrift spiritually and looking for a teacher. That I felt disappointed by the Judaism I grew up with. That I had tried other religions, maybe Buddhism, maybe I had been a Moonie or a follower of the Maharishi. And now that I had come to Israel, I felt even more confused, because the boundaries of my secular American identity had begun to dissolve and I was in fear and pain.

"I just looked at him in amazement. How could he know all this about me? I was a complete stranger. I felt I was going to start crying. Then he asked me if I wanted to meet his teacher, a rabbi who ran a yeshiva, a small community of religious students, to join them in welcoming the Sabbath. I was hungry and didn't have anything else to do. I'd come to the Wall, not to pray, just to watch the spectacle. So I went with him. The meal was simple but delicious. We began singing and praying with the first benediction over wine and didn't stop until two in the morning. I stayed the night, and the next day."

Rick pushed himself up from the chair and stood in the middle of my living room. We looked at him, wondering what he was doing.

"I have to move around to talk about this. I can't sit still. You'll understand." Rick started to make a circuit around the room.

"They gave me books to read—some in English, some in Hebrew. I began to immerse myself in the study of Kabbalah, Jewish mysticism. I began to study the mystical teachings of the Four Worlds and the *Sefirot*, the ten manifestations of God's unknowable infinitude. Even my dreams, now, were in Hebrew. I was entering a spiritual Eden. What did New Jersey, where I grew up, have to do with my new life in Jerusalem? Chanting the prayers

three times a day. Studying the sacred books. Singing, endless
singing, pounding on the desks and study tables as we chanted. I
lacked nothing. I was completely fulfilled. I couldn't imagine
doing anything other than this. No other language would do.
What most fascinated me was a strange and wonderful book that
was handed to me; written by one of the great sixteenth-century
mystics, Elijah de Vidas, a man of Spanish descent who lived in
Safed, the wonderful city of whitewashed stone houses with blue
doors and narrow winding streets. How I grappled with the *Beginning of Wisdom!* I learned about the Five Gates—of fear, love, repen-
tance, holiness, and humility. Learned I should surrender to the
commandments. The habits, urges, confusions of my prior life
would fall off as I passed through each gate.

"When I went out of the study house, it was like I turned inside
out. Meeting people, even those I had known before, was painful.
The sunlight was too strong, even with sunglasses. I couldn't
cover myself enough; I was raw flesh. I'd walk through the narrow
winding streets of the ultraorthodox neighborhood where, they
say, there are a hundred gates and archways. I would go out of my
way to walk through them. I knew this was ridiculous, because the
Five Gates was a metaphor. But I was obsessed with seeking spiritual ecstasy, of shedding the skins of my past, of purification."

Rick paced up and down and then began walking in a small circle before us. The others looked uncomfortable. How much
longer would he go on like this? He stopped at the center of the
circle and spun around. "Yah!" he shouted.

"Yah?" repeated the incredulous Norm.

Rick stood in front of Norm. "Did you know the road that
leads to Eden has a flaming gate?" Norm looked at the others for
a clue about how he was supposed to answer. Rick shook his head,
"I never saw it. And why?" he asked Norm, who shook his head.
"Because one day, one eternity later, I happened to walk into a

bookstore on Ben Yehuda Street, and there I met a woman in front of the travel books section. I don't know what drew me there. Maybe there was a book in the window about gates. She was dark-skinned, dark-eyed, a soldier on leave. She saw me standing there, like in a trance. She asked me in English if I was okay. I was startled. I couldn't answer. Then she asked in Hebrew whether I had ever been to the U.S. 'Yes,' I answered in English. Then she understood. 'Tell me, you are studying mysticism? Am I right, yes?' I nodded. 'You are studying with the Black Hats, yes?' She was referring to the sect of Chassids that wore black, full-brimmed hats like those popular in the 1940s.

"She told me I had forgotten my family, my place of birth, my secular name. That I had been captivated by magicians who could perform wonders. That I was living in a dream, wandering without a body, dancing around in the world of eternity. I just stared at her. The bookstore had a small couch, and she invited me to sit down, which I did. Even though I didn't ask, she started telling me about her life. She spoke very slowly and carefully, as if it were terribly important I understood each word. Her father, she said, was from Romania and her mother, who was French, from Algeria. They'd met in Israel on a kibbutz. She had two brothers, both older, and a younger sister, still in high school. She told me her name was Rivka, that after the army she was to begin studying to become a radiologist's assistant. She explained she had met others like me. Recognized the look. Had I learned about mystical gates, or was it rooms of a palace, or the pillars of the temple? I just nodded. When had I last eaten a steak or drunk a beer? I found the idea repugnant. When had I last slept with a woman? 'A nice-looking guy like you?' A shiver went down my spine.

"We left the bookstore together. I was mesmerized by her eyes, her smell, like the sea, her eyebrows, like arches, her soft lips and glistening teeth, like gates. On the street, I bought her a bright scarf from a Yemenite woman. She tied it around her waist. She led me to her room in a large apartment building on Tchernichowski Street. And that's where she taught me the dance."

The dance? We looked at one another. That was not what we were expecting.

Rick stretched out his arms and swept one foot in a semicircle across the wood floor. He turned slowly, then swept the other foot. He turned his head from side to side, drew in his arms, one at a time, with his palms outward. Then he gestured for us to get up and join him. He stepped back and pulled Shmuel up first. Shmuel reached and pulled up Norm, who pulled up Peter. And so it happened until we were all standing in a circle, our palms raised above our shoulders, just touching. Then Rick showed us the sweeping step, the turn, the sideways movement. As he did this, he began to chant. "Ya, na-na, na, na; na, na. Ya, na-na, na, na; na, na." Rising and falling. Soft at first, then louder. We were an awkward bunch, stumbling, stepping on one another's feet, trying to catch the rhythm of the dance and the chant.

As we got the hang of it, Rick showed us how to stamp our feet on the last two beats. "Na, na," we shouted as we stamped. He swept once, twice, turned, moved from side to side, swept again, turned again, stamped one foot, then the other, all the while moving in a circle, our chanting getting louder. Stamp, stamp—"na, na," we chanted. The dance went faster, the chant louder, the stamping heavier. I knew this was hard on Earl's knees, but he joined in, grimacing occasionally. We were panting when Rick, his head bent down, his right foot raised and held, signaled that we should bring the dance to an end. We stamped once "na," twice "na," and fell back into our chairs with a concluding "na, na."

More scotch and ice tea were passed around. Then it was my turn.

"Earl said that he thought everyone had trouble turning at least one decade," I began. I handed Norm three photographs. In one, I am standing on a narrow gravel road holding an infant wrapped in a plaid woolen blanket, the deep blue-green band of color, what looks like a river but is actually a fjord, crossing behind my shoulders. A second photograph shows a hedgerow beside a paved highway. In the third, Caroline and I are walking toward sand dunes and have turned our heads in the direction of the camera so that our profiles are nose to nose.

"My difficulty was in turning thirty," I continued. "But I have to explain something about what led up to it.

"In my late twenties, what I call a wave of biology swept over me. That's how I thought about it at the time. Before that I strolled the highways and byways of intellectual life as a graduate student and a single person. I adored the world of possibility, worshiping process over any particular outcome. But then came the wave, or some kind of developmental time-release capsule. I started to get an urgent feeling that time was passing and that I hadn't much to show for it. Suddenly, I wanted to make things that would last, would endure.

"My adviser said he thought I was ready to tackle my preliminary thesis, a long essay required to qualify for doing the big dissertation. In a matter of a few months, I produced a hundred-page manuscript. Part of the thesis dealt with one of Kierkegaard's essays in *Either/Or*, "The Aesthetic Validity of Marriage," an argument for transcending romantic love in favor of a deeper, enduring intimacy, part of a larger justification for living an ethically responsible life. As I read the essay, I felt I was reading with new eyes. Right then I decided. I wanted to marry Caroline. The exciting uncertainty of repeatedly reexamining whether to live together had worn off. Within the next three years, this generative urge led to a doctorate, marriage, two children, and various jobs teaching philosophy.

"I have to admit, the path of endless possibilities had narrowed. Diapers and student papers replaced late-night conversations about matters such as the 'teleological suspension of the ethical' or the status of the transcendental ego. But, in Kierkegaardian terms, I was learning to infinitize the finite, to discover the enduring and universal—marriage, family life, a profession—in what, before, had seemed time-bound and option-limited. I experienced a euphoria of delight over my productivity and wondered why I had needed to delay these actions so long. I loved being a father, enjoyed the long hours of thinking and writing, the nurturing of students, the intensity of commitment in marriage. When I looked back on the years of my life just before the wave, I saw someone unwilling to commit himself wholeheartedly to anything or anyone. A tentative person. Now I had eclipsed that former self." I paused for a moment and looked around to make sure the group was still with me.

"I understand the connection with the two pictures of the baby, you, and Caroline," chimed in Shmuel, "but what's with the row of bushes? Are you hiding behind it?"

"I'm coming to that."

Shmuel turned the photo over and showed everyone the blank backside.

"Okay, I'll explain about the hedgerow." I thought I could tell my story chronologically, but I realized that would take too long. Anyway, did anyone else need all the details?

"I keep this picture because it reminds me of turning thirty. You see, a few years earlier I had read a short story by C. S. Lewis called "The Other Side of the Hedge." It was about a guy who spends a lot of time taking long country walks and carrying a pedometer to check his time and distance. He wasn't going anywhere, he had no purpose, other than this kind of meaningless discipline. Well, one day this absurd fellow stops to tie his shoe.

As he bends down, he notices an opening under the hedge runs beside the road, and he hears beautiful music coming from below. He puts his head through, leans forward, and slips, rolling down a slope. As you might guess, he's in a different reality, an enchanted world where people indulge themselves in singing, dancing, being creative, taking care of one another—a utopia, quite unlike the world from which the country walker has just fallen. Maybe Lewis is reversing the biblical story of the fall. This fellow falls down into a place that is higher, spiritually, than his upper but dreary walking road."

"So you're under the hedge, not behind it?" Shmuel teased.

"Not exactly," I answered. "Like every wave, the one that carried me to generativity also crested, crashed, and withdrew. And I crashed and withdrew too. I knew there was no way back to my earlier, more carefree life, but staying committed and involved with my family and work, day after day, became a burden. I started to feel worn out, that my youth was over, that I was on the wrong side of the hedge, like the man with his pedometer. Even though I knew I had chosen this life, I couldn't have known all the implications. An irreversible momentum is set up. You can't stop caring for the children, working out disagreements with your mate, trying to succeed with your work, making enough money to keep the whole enterprise going. The initial choice leads to a perpetual motion machine. I felt my life, as I had known it, was over. I felt prematurely old at thirty."

"Ron," Earl said. "You're not unique in what you've described. I'm sure we've all had moments like that. But you get over it. Haven't you?"

"What about the picture of you and Caroline," insisted Shmuel, who was growing impatient with my wandering narrative.

I looked over at Rick and wished that I had a dance I could lead the group through instead of this convoluted tale.

"All right, the third photograph. This is from when we were still in Denmark, from a day when we were visiting our friend Sara at her farm near the North Sea. I must have spent six months to a year moaning and groaning over turning thirty.

"I was explaining to Caroline that I found it difficult to feel enthusiastic each day when life had become so predictable. Naturally, she felt I was being critical of her and that I was unhappy with our marriage. We had been walking for close to an hour on this dirt road, a right-of-way between fields where, on one side, ewes and lambs were grazing and, on the other, horses were nibbling grass or galloping across the heather. It was April, still chilly and windy, especially walking against the wind off the sea. Several of our friends were a short distance behind. That's how the picture happened to be taken.

"At some point in this awkward conversation, I said something really annoying like this: When we get to the sea, we'll just have to turn around and walk back on this same road; that's how my life feels—a repeating pattern. Caroline turned toward me, then turned back to look at the road and our friends. I looked back too. There"—I pointed to Rick, who held it—"is the picture."

"Caroline then said something like the following: 'When you look back, all you see is this simple road. But what I see is a path that people have been walking on for hundreds, maybe thousands, of years. We could be in the Middle Ages or the Bronze Age. We don't know what other people were thinking as they walked on this road, but we could imagine how they enjoyed the wind, the big sky, the lambs bleating, hearing the distant waves breaking on the beach. Maybe they were Vikings about to sail off to conquer and pillage. What fun! Maybe they were peasants hoping to catch a fish for dinner. Sure, they walked to the sea and back. But look at what's going on at the same time. Don't you see, Ron, this road is one strand of a whole cable of roads that are braided together.

We're walking simultaneously through separate channels of the same cable. Try to imagine the other people. Use your mind to slice open the cable to see all the channels, to experience all of us walking together. We're not just getting to the end, the beach, the sea, but being part of all the other people in history who are hearing the lambs, seeing the horses, inhaling the salty air, worrying about their animals, or crops, the next big spring storm, God, the devil, whether they had evil or good in their hearts, all of this. It's all in how you look at it. If you want to look at it in a boring way, that's your business. Because, yes, you're right, in a way it is repetitious. But even more repetitious than you were thinking. It's like walking through a biblical story, an eighteenth-century landscape painting, one of Dickens' novels, all of this.'"

I stopped, unsure of where to take this next.

"Very Jungian," said Peter. "Caroline pulled you out of mundane time by invoking the eternal repetition of the life cycle."

"Or maybe," asserted Norm, "she was telling him to smell the roses, or the heather, I guess."

"Did Caroline's version help you deal with your feeling trapped?" asked Rick.

"Did you discover the other side of the hedge?" asked Shmuel.

I was trying to formulate an answer when Alan spoke up. "I don't know if Ron has an answer for us right now, but his story makes a perfect segue to the time I turned ten." Everyone laughed. The doctor was coming to my aid. He took out a photograph of a young boy in a sailor suit.

TIME AND COMMUNITY

The stories told at my birthday party illustrated Royce's idea that we often make sense of our lives in the context of important relationships: Shmuel trying to interpret nature, and God, to his parents; Norm interpreting geological time to his minister father; Peter interpreting his war experience to his family and to draft resisters; and so on. Our stories are both related and relatable because they touch upon widely shared experiences and themes: turning away from religion to science or from science to religion, accepting the call to arms or resisting it, feeling that your life has come to a dead end or reimagining the pathway. Even if we haven't had the other person's experience, we can imagine its plausibility as one of our own roads not taken. As we become historical to ourselves, seeing our personal experiences in the context of public events, changes, situations, and conflicts, we join the fellowship of interpreters—not a static universal order, but an expanding one.

But how far does this take us in binding one person to another?

Many people are connected through shared observance of religious and secular calendars. The cycles of holidays of the Christian, Moslem, Jewish, Hindu, Islamic, and other faith traditions invite adherents to personally reexperience the trials and tribulations, sufferings and joys of the central figures, the matriarchs, patriarchs, gods, and goddesses whose lives and attributes become aspects of individual memory, values, and behavior. Practitioners of the great religious traditions may find their Scriptures echoed in their lives: an annual cycle of spiritual wanderings, searchings, betrayals, victories, defeats, heroism, sacrifice, and other acts and attributes contained in the sequence of sacred stories.

Upon this we overlay the secular calendar of national holidays, reminding us of the people and events that forged our national institutions and contributed to our character traits. To the extent that we know much about or identify with the nation's heritage, the people and events of our nation's past form another time-structured history, set of role models, and reenactable conflicts and resolutions.

Then there are birthdays, anniversaries, memorials, and other family remembrances. On another level, there are the years of gathering around the electronic campfire, the TV set, on whose flickering screen we observed, in weekly ritual order, the rhythmic tension and release presented in episodes of *I Love Lucy, The Twilight Zone,* or *Star Trek.* As a recent commentator pointed out, some members of the younger generation can cite episode, plot, and character of *Star Trek* the way some of an earlier generation could cite chapter and verse from Scripture.

Our affinities through shared time are multilayered, ranging from close identification through religious fellowship to generational cohort affinities through shared social and cultural experiences. The simultaneity of temporal frameworks can lead to conflicts—for example, when we are torn between religious observations and secular duties. Our wristwatches and clocks (within time zones) show the same hour and minute. But the ties that bind us to traditions of sacred time unite us with some groups and separate us from others. There are many time traditions, but no universally shared, braided-together time.

Efforts to find unifying time concepts often fail because they are contrived and have little compelling power or because they give the appearance of covert acts of domination. For example, in my hometown, a local community leader formed a committee to identify shared values as a way to promote community cohesiveness. During the discussion, he alluded to the virtues of the Puritans. The historical reference failed to impress the African American, Jewish, Moslem, Native American, and other members of the committee. Instead, it made them wary. We are quick to identify such historical traditions with attempts by more powerful groups to impose their own ways of life on the less powerful. One can no longer innocently invoke their name and expect cheerful assent.

The contemporary critique of individualism in the West, that everything has become privatized and commodified, is directly related to the problem of contemporaneity. We can live isolated in time even while existing in closely shared spaces such as neighborhoods, classrooms, sanctuaries, homes. Each person has become a self-involved isolated timekeeper, no longer connected to a public, a community, or even a neighborhood. According to the critique, a misdirected version of liberty makes each person free to invent and reinvent his or her self, to fashion a persona or discard one at will. Many of the attempted correctives—ethnic and religious group identity—also produce group hatred, prejudice, fear, paranoia, the perpetuation of intergroup violence, oppression, and endless suspicion.

Social withdrawal and self-preoccupation, loss of historical continuity, fear of aging and a perception that death is meaningless, and lack of interest in the future and in posterity—these problems are all interrelated. Proposed solutions range from promotion of the Judeo-Christian tradition to inculcating a common set of values among schoolchildren. Right-wing and left-wing solutions mix with feminist, libertarian, socialist, liberal, and other Band-aids from the various ideological repair kits. Unfortunately, these fail to solve the problems, because each promotes among one group what other groups perceive as an imposition—an artificial form of contemporaneity.

There does not seem to be enough "glue," whether the holding power of conventional liberalism, faith in the democratic process, belief in a unitary deity, belief in technology, trust in the cosmic forces of historical change, or other integrative powers to establish broad common experiences of time and meaning. Instead, we have parochial enclaves of absolutism for some and socially detached, free-floating relativism for others.

Perhaps widespread contemporaneity has never really existed

except among homogeneous populations or faith communities, and it is an impossibility in our multi-everything world. But there is another possibility, one that arose at my birthday party, that contemporaneity can be understood as more than a state of mind, or something that happens to you: it can be seen as an active, will-ful process. In fact, contemporaneity is an action or practice dis-coverable just where we might least think to find it—in differences between ourselves and others, and through encounters with our "incommensurable" past selves.

CONTEMPORANEITY THROUGH DIFFERENCE

Recently, I participated in a program entitled "Building Bridges," sponsored by a black Baptist church in Asheville. The program was designed to acquaint the white community with forms of institutionalized racism against African Americans and other minorities; its leaders hoped to build communication between blacks and whites. First, they would show the radically different historical perspectives of African Americans and Caucasians that produced our lack of mutual understanding. Then, in face-to-face conversation, they hoped to "build bridges," that is, to establish a link between histories and a shared sense of the present and future—what I've called contemporaneity. Each of the sessions began with a lecture for the whole group (about 150), after which we divided into small discussion groups.

In the smaller groups, it became clear that there were other candidates present who felt victimized by prejudice. Gay and les-bian individuals spoke up, as did feminists, Jews, Hispanics, and Asians. Almost everyone had a claim on the need for liberation from institutionalized forms of repression and discrimination. While this complexity of liberation themes diluted the issue that the organizers had hoped to make the central focus—namely, subtle ways in which white racism against blacks becomes institutionalized and almost invisible—the multiple "coming out" created a remarkable sense of sympathy and interest. The Building Bridges program provided an entirely new experience for many people by providing face-to-face contact with people who were different and who talked about their differentness. It was like Caroline's vision of the braided cable. We walked separate paths with different perceptions of history. We might just as well have lived in different historical periods.

There might be connections if we understood one another's stories, but obstacles would remain. One event in particular stands out. At the beginning of each small discussion group, we were instructed to offer a prayer. The program was, after all, held in a church and organized largely by Protestant clergy. At one of the first meetings, since no one else offered to lead the prayer, our discussion leader, a black minister from a nearby church, folded his hands, bent his head, and recited a prayer of hope that ended, "In the name of Jesus Christ, amen." Having had to put up on numerous occasions with Christian invocations at "public" events such as civic meetings where I had been invited to speak, a luncheon of the Asheville Board of Realty, for example, and even at conferences sponsored by state agencies, I spoke to the man after the session.

He listened patiently and nodded his head. Then he replied, "But if I don't use those words, the prayer is not a prayer, for me. I have to speak out of my tradition." Couldn't he have just made it an ecumenical prayer and left out Jesus? "No," he said. Granted, this was not a public event sponsored by the city or county. Granted, we each had the opportunity to lead or offer a prayer, if only one of silence. Could I, for just that moment, participate in a Christian prayer, without feeling excluded or entrapped in someone else's time-faith tradition?

What if for the moment I imagined myself a Christian and prayed, earnestly, with hope for the group and in the name of Jesus? In the next moment, I would still be a Jew. I would not have been converted. I would have joined that community of believers, whose tenets are, after all, not all that alien from my own, for a moment of contemporaneity. I would not lose myself in order to find the other. I could be the other only through an act of imagination and only for a moment, despite the accidents of history or destiny that make me who I am and them who they are. But that moment might serve as a touchstone, a reminder that "nothing human is alien."

Yet I could accomplish this moment of interchangeability of self only through a corresponding act of forgetfulness. I had to forget the centuries of religious persecution of Jews at the hands of Christians. I had to forget the pogroms, the Crusades, the Holocaust, defacement of our local synagogue, hate literature thrown on the lawn outside the Jewish Community Center. Could one remember all this and still be a contemporary, or would the act of remembering one's group, people, roots, culture, tradition, or credo pull one back from moments of universal oneness? If forgetfulness is the price of contemporaneity, is it too great? If one can make the leap across the paradox, *imagining* oneself as the other and *remembering* oneself as not the other, while holding both truths in tension without breaking the link, then uncompromised unity is possible. Rational understanding of the events and experiences that have shaped our different realities is valuable, but a leap is still required. A leap of imagination, a forgetting and remembering of self—a bridge that connects while it affirms separateness. The Building Bridges program pointed the way. It confirmed something I had discovered in my World War II discussion group at the historical society museum.

Reinterpreting the Past

A few weeks after my discussion group at the historical society museum expressed consternation about altering their remembrances of the war years, I invited an African American friend who had served in the submarine corps during World War II. He told the group a little about his life in the segregated South before the war and about how he had chosen the submarine corps because he figured his opportunities would be less demeaning there than in other branches of the service. "After all," he explained, "it's pretty hard to uphold segregation in tight quarters while floating a hundred fathoms under the surface." His stories were funny, yet poignant. At one point he had to pause, choking back the painful tears of a humiliating encounter.

The following week, I invited a woman who had taught in one of the California compounds where Japanese-Americans were interned. She spoke about how much she had learned to appreciate Japanese culture and family life. Years later, she had made a trip to Japan to further her education.

These individuals' personal stories began to change the tenor of the group. In response to the woman's story about the camps, one member said, "Yes, I believe I do recall hearing about that." She continued, defensively, "You have to understand, we were so frightened at the time." Almost in a whisper, she added, "I suppose, looking at it now, dragging those people off to camps in the desert was unfair."

CHAPTER TEN

TIMES INCOMPLETE

Since I arrived in Asheville to take on the leadership of the Center for Creative Retirement, I have taught periodically in one of its programs, the College for Seniors. The college reminds me of my early days at the senior center, but it is also very different. For one, classes are conducted in regular campus classrooms and the participants pay modest fees to enroll. There are almost equal numbers of men and women, and most are retired professionals, well educated, relatively financially secure, and active in community affairs. In retirement, the majority have moved to Asheville from other parts of the country. Attitudes toward aging and expectations people bring to retirement have changed dramatically. Still, this new generation of seniors struggle with making sense of their lives just as did my friends from the senior center. And many believe they will benefit from understanding something about philosophy.

I believe it, too. But where should we start? Contemporary

moral problems? The history of ethics? A review of the world's great philosophies? Sometimes I think the best starting place is with reading Plato. One of my favorite entry points is the dialogue about love.

THE SYMPOSIUM

The after-theater party is in full swing. The host, a thirty-one-year-old playwright and already crowned with laurel, has invited poets, artists, a doctor, a politician, and an itinerant philosopher to the banquet. Gracefully reclining on couches pulled into a circle, the men dine on spiced meats and dainty fruits, taking their food with a heady wine, which they sip from clay cups. The members of the party have spent the whole day at the amphitheater, where, among some seventeen thousand fellow citizens, they wept and laughed at the chanting choruses and masked actors.

The banquet room fills with the sounds of gossip, teasing, and flirtation, especially between the distinguished middle-aged men and the young, handsome ones just coming into their manhood. Then one of the revelers calls for their attention. "Friends," he declares, "I wish to be excused from our customary rounds of toasts." The citizen explains that he's still recovering from a previous night's debauch.

"Agreed," another chimes in, adding he too had a "good soaking yesterday" and would like to avoid a headache. The physician concurs, moralizing, "Drunkenness is a dangerous thing."

Instead of wine, the good doctor prescribes another elixir. Let the members of the party intoxicate themselves with words. They agree that each will deliver an impromptu speech on a subject the group deems worthy, and what better topic for a gathering of friends who adore drama than to praise Eros, the god of love?

The *Symposium*, Plato's famous dialogue on the meaning of love, is recounted as a conversation at a banquet that took place at the playwright Agathon's house in 416 B.C.E. following the prizewinning performance of his first play at an Athenian drama festival. Among those who hold forth is the comic playwright Aristophanes, whose plays, such as *Lysistrata* and *The Clouds*, are performed to this day. When his turn comes, none of the guests can be sure whether they are in store for biting truths, ironic jests, or some combination. Propped on one elbow, the reclining toga-clad figure begins his tale.

The primeval state of human gender, Aristophanes explains, was not as it is now. Eons ago, besides the two sexes, male and female, there was also a third, "a male-female sex," the name of which, hermaphrodite, survives to this day, though the dual-gender beings described by Aristophanes have long since vanished. Anatomically, these creatures were round, had four arms, four legs, and two faces on either side of a round neck. The androgynous beings had special powers. They were marvelously swift of foot since, by extending their four legs, they could roll over and over the way acrobats tumble. Exceedingly strong and ambitious, they threatened to storm the heavens and even do battle with the gods.

Naturally, explains Aristophanes, the gods were worried and sought one another's council. Zeus decided the hermaphrodites should be spared, but only if they could be weakened. To do that, he sliced each of them in half, says the playwright, "as you slice hard-boiled eggs with a hair." Their skin was pulled around and sewn closed to form the navel. The single face and half the neck were turned toward the cut to ensure the creatures' mindfulness of their previously errant ways. Unfortunately, Aristophanes continues, Zeus' solution failed. The new half-beings immediately sought their severed counterparts. Finding and throwing their arms around each other, they strove to reunite. Because they refused to do anything while separated from each other, they began to die of starvation and idleness.

Zeus arrived at another solution. He moved their sexual organs in front so that now male and female halves might gratify their desire for union and procreation. Other, same-sex halves, who may have lost their counterparts, could also find satisfaction in a mutual embrace. Having satisfied their desire for union, the new creatures could return to their jobs and look after other practical matters of life.

Given these origins, explains the crafty Aristophanes, we may better understand the various forms desire takes. Whether between different gender or same gender, the urge "to make one out of two, and to heal the wound of human nature," is the desire we call love.

Aristophanes' mythic account expresses an age-old belief. Desire for another person is the longing to find that significant other who can fill the deficiency in one's very being. Whether in same-sex or opposite-sex unions, the way to happiness, says the playwright, is to attain perfection by finding the right beloved. In this manner, each comes as near as possible to his or her greatest hope, to be restored to an original state of oneness. The *Symposium* presents a series of what would today seem remarkably candid speeches. Homoerotic love was widely accepted among the well-born, well-educated elite of Athenian society. Friendship between men, especially a sort of "mentor" relationship between mature men and young boys, whether openly sexual or "Platonic," was lauded as loftier than heterosexual relationships. Aristophanes' discourse on love comes midway in the order of speeches in the dialogue between depictions emphasizing the emotional and physical aspects of love and those promoting love as an intellectual pursuit, such as fellowship among truth seekers. Not surprisingly, Socrates gives the penultimate speech—the intoxicated politician Alcibiades, who arrives late, makes the last.

True to character, Socrates shifts the focus of the conversation from examining the individual's state of desire to considering instead the nature of the object of desire—that class of entities he calls the Beautiful. Most things of beauty—human bodies, works of art, attractive personalities—are impermanent. They change, decay, and, eventually, perish, Socrates reminds his friends. So our attempts to permanently possess these beautiful bodies and personalities leads, as it must, to frustration because their beauty is temporary and ephemeral. Socrates depiction brings embarrassed laughter from several of the guests, while others wink knowingly. Together, they wonder whether fulfillment, the goal of desire, is always unattainable.

No, says the philosopher, continuing his speech. A true seeker after beauty, if he is persistent, is like someone who ascends a stairway from a lower plateau (desire for a single beautiful body) to a higher one (the quality many beautiful bodies have in common). Eventually, the stair climber arrives at the realization that perfect beauty can be experienced only through a contemplative ideal, one that never perishes, because it is timeless and universal. It is that in which all particular beautiful things participate and without which they would not be beautiful. That the concept and ideal of a quality should have greater reality than appearances or sensations is the hallmark of Plato's philosophical idealism.

Physical instances of beauty will fade. Emotional states of perceived beauty will prove transitory. But lovers who rationally ascend the stairway, experiencing and transcending particular moments of love and desire for beautiful bodies or objects, will complete their ascent—achieving direct intuition of the Beautiful as "the love of love itself." Arriving at this destination, the lover of beauty will have stepped beyond subjective states of desire to discover an objective and independent realm in which love's true motive is finally realized.

Socrates denies authorship of this stairway-to-love theory. He claims to have heard it from Diotima, a priestess from the city of Mantineia. A look of skepticism appears on several faces in the room. How can they be sure Socrates is more a truth teller than Aristophanes? And what of Socrates' mental instability, his periodic trances, such as the one that overtook him as he was about to enter Agathon's home, leaving him staring into space? Various messengers, sent to find him, could not rouse him from his trance, though he eventually snapped out of it and joined the party.

The *Symposium's* sequence of discourses presents a hierarchy of stages, moving from passionate or carnal desire to a form of transcendent contemplation that permits the mortal mind entry to a realm beyond the limits of human finitude. The unreflective, according to Socrates/Diotima, identify love with sexual desire and the bonding of kindred souls. Upon reflection, they will learn that love's deeper motive is to "give birth in Beauty," to achieve a semblance of immortality through reproducing physical offspring, acts of glory, or good deeds.

What humans most desire, implies Socrates, is to outlive death. This analysis of the human soul links back to Aristophanes' androgynous beings who sought the power of the immortal gods. But Diotima claims that the final and highest mystery of love, untainted by the distorting lens of human finitude, is different. Beauty itself is divine and subsists in a realm that does not depend on human intelligence. Diotima purportedly has told Socrates that he, like most mortals, will catch glimmerings of this knowledge of love, but never truly grasp it. Nevertheless, he who pursues love pursues wisdom and, because he seeks true immortality, is most beloved by the gods.

If the idea that love is based on some primeval severance seems familiar, it is because it parallels another story of origins, the Book of Genesis in the Hebrew Bible. In one version of the creation of human beings, Eve is generated from a part, a rib, that has been removed from Adam. The story of the fall conveys the theme of separation, alienation, and yearning to return to a state of completeness by recovering a lost oneness. The Genesis story also accounts for the dawning of sexual passion and the birth of the first generations of human beings. Only through the incomplete is the ideal of completeness born.

METAPHYSICAL HOGWASH

I pause to survey what effect my words are having on the class members. This is the fifth week of my College for Seniors seminar on a few of Plato's dialogues. I stand, leaning against a low table at the front of the classroom, and survey the rows of gray, white, and colored hair, and the numerous bald heads. For some, taking a noncredit course in philosophy was a first-time experience. They had been educated as engineers, doctors, lawyers, nurses, teachers, businesspersons. "We didn't have time for philosophy," was a frequent comment, "it was the Depression, and we had to sign up for courses that would help us earn a living." For many who attended college on the GI Bill after World War II, the emphasis was on immediately practical knowledge, and that seemed to exclude studying philosophy. Now, in their later years, a latent desire to reconsider their life experience through the various frameworks of the philosophical tradition found fulfillment in the opportunity to continue learning among peers in a college setting.

A hand goes up, a throat clears. I shift my gaze. Dressed in a handsome blue blazer and white turtleneck sweater, a former international banker, the eloquent Parker Padgett, wants to offer a comment on my lecture.

"Not to sound disrespectful," he begins, "but I rather suspect that Plato is trying to palm off on us a variety of what I, uh, would have to call, uh, metaphysical hogwash."

I hear giggles, see heads shaking. Some are shocked at Parker's boldness. Other enjoy his candidness. Anyone who chooses to teach worldly, well-educated retirees invites challenges. Not disrespect, but older students' eagerness to test their opinions and convictions. Few are as direct as Parker Padgett, and many guard their cherished beliefs, preferring to consider competing ideas in the privacy of silent listening. For some, the class is intellectual entertainment; for others, a chance to satisfy a great hunger for knowledge. But the Parker Padgetts in the class have put their finger on a crucial question: What possible difference could studying philosophy make at this stage of life?

The laughter ends, and Parker continues, "I went to a Catholic high school, and this is the sort of mysticism the Jesuits fed us. But I always thought it was the ploy of an elitist sect, making us believe in something the ordinary person could neither see nor touch, which only certain privileged intellectuals, the priests, could understand. That's one of the ways they exercised their authority over us. From my experience, I think Aristophanes' fanciful little tale about the psychology of love comes closer to the mark. Plato, I suspect, was probably a mystic. Wouldn't you agree?" The wide eyes that were fixed on Parker now turn toward me.

"Was Plato a mystic?" I repeat, so that everyone can hear the question. I pace back and forth, considering how to answer. Is seeking intellectual union with ideas the same as seeking direct experience of the divine? The thought triggers a spontaneous memory. One evening in a bar in Detroit near the university a group of us students were teasing each other and laughing about a book we were reading for a seminar; it was Pascal's *Pensées*. We amused each other making sexual puns on Pascal's famous phrase "man is a bending reed." Suddenly, out of the haze of the smoke-filled room, a hulking form loomed over us. It was our teacher, Professor Marshall. For some reason, he fixed his gaze on me, knelt down, and whispered in my ear to make himself heard: "Someday you will fall in love with an idea. Then you'll see." Drops of perspiration stood out on his forehead. Was he drunk, I wondered? He stood up, turned on his heels, and disappeared into the gloom of the bar. What did it mean, fall in love with an idea?

True to his prophecy, I had fallen in love with certain ideas. I was enamored with Plato's idea that "all knowledge is a form of recollection," that by examining the past and tracing our beliefs and opinions to their sources, we can uncover primary truths. Is that mysticism?

"To answer your very important question, Parker," I begin, "remember, in Plato's time there was no sharp division between philosophy and religion. So it's not surprising that Socrates would claim he's learned about love and beauty from an authority on what we might call spiritual matters. In several of Plato's other dialogues, Socrates recounts beliefs held by religious sects and then uses them as analogies or to make a bridge to rational parallels. In the *Symposium*, he turns Aristophanes' tongue-in-cheek legend into a logical hypothesis, insisting that often the things we desire, once possessed, may disappoint us. They turn out to be unsatisfactory or ephemeral, illusions that collapse when we get close to their reality. As a result, we feel bitter or become skeptical about ever satisfying our quest. But, as Plato suggests, we can turn toward the intangible, invisible something that maybe exists only as an idea. Is this mysticism? Well, if mysticism means striving for a direct experience of the divine, then the love of love itself might qualify as mystical. But if the means to achieving this knowledge is reasoned discourse, then we might think otherwise." I watch to see if Parker is with me. He tilts his head, thoughtfully. Does he picture me clad in black shirt and white collar?

A hand goes up two rows to his left. I look at Betty Kimberly, a stunning woman in a pale lemon-colored sweater that accentuates the fullness of her breasts. Her tanned skin and swept-back white hair are dazzling refutations that people become sexless in later life.

"Ron, ah may be missin' the point here," says the native southerner, "but Plato seems to be speakin' di-rectly to me?" Betty has a way of sounding the syllables to emphasize certain words, and her sentences often end as if each were a question. She turns toward Parker and fixes him with her gaze. He looks a little uneasy. Then, swiveling her head, she surveys the classmates on her other side. Betty is a former psychotherapist.

"Ah do not claim that I fully undah-stand Socrates' ultimate destination in his climb up the stairway of love," says Betty. She gives me a wink. "I'll come back to that." She flutters her eyelids, teasingly. "On the other hand, the amusing story about the herm-aphro-dites belies the old sayin' 'Many a truth is uttered in jest.' From my experience as a therapist, I cannot tell you how often people would come to me about their desperate need for something that would make them feel whole. For some, it was a matter of getting a mother or father to affirm their worth, to approve of them as a genuine human bein'. Oh, if only there was something they could do to have that loving recognition of worth. For others, unfortunately, alcohol or drugs or food became the way to lessen the pain of feelin' incomplete. And others, well, it was one bad relationship, one failed marriage, after the other. They just never could figure out that the other person would never, could never, be what we, uh, in our profession, call the 'completing object.' And *that* is the problem Socrates seems to be addressing. How-evah," she says slowly, shaking her head. "Ah do not think that intellectual contemplation would have worked for most of my clients. Do you understand what I am sayin', Ron?"

I nod and am about to answer when a loud cough distracts me.

"So, what did you tell them to do?" the voice pipes up. The new player in the debate is Charlie Duggan, a former Episcopal priest. Betty has to turn completely around to see the balding, heavyset Duggan.

"Tell them, Charlie?" exclaims Betty. "We don't *tell* them anything. Advice giving doesn't help people." She turns back toward me. Another wink. I hear Charlie mumble something and poke Hank Schwartz, seated beside him. Hank laughs, then covers his mouth like a misbehaved fourth-grader. Betty has more to say.

"We don't tell them what to do, because then it wouldn't work. You know, *act*-ually, a good therapist is rather like ole Socrates. We ask questions. We ask them to remember how they first fell in love or how something a parent said or did made them feel. As they tell their story, we point out little things along the way. You see, *they* have to see the pattern. Only *then* will they get it, that it's them, they're producing the problems, don't you know, in the very way they set about solving them."

Betty swivels around again facing the back of the classroom. "Charlie, I don't know how it was in your line of work, but as mental health professionals we try to help our clients realize that the feelin' of being incomplete does not make them a bad person. It's not their or anyone else's fault. And it can't be fixed by possessing things or other people. That's what they have to understand. They have to let go of this compulsion. To see that, after all, there really is not a thing that can fill the void. *That's* the truth that sets them free." She turns back toward me, smiles, and folds her hands in her lap.

Charlie Duggan leans forward, supporting his large, round head on his elbows. His face is as ruddy as his red plaid shirt.

From previous classroom discussions, we know that Charlie is quite an outdoorsman, a hiker, fisherman, canoeist. After he retired from the pulpit, he did volunteer work with the police department as a chaplain. He lifts his head, raises his hand from the elbow to signal he wants to respond.

"Betty, after these people you spoke about left your office, you know where they went? They came to my study in the parsonage. They were looking for answers, for hope, not for more questions. What you say about the Socratic method in therapy I'm sure has its truth. But"—here Charlie puts his hands on the table and pushes himself back to an upright position—"but, it's only one aspect of the truth. The way I see it, people are looking for what, in my line of work, we call redemption."

Betty rolls her eyes disapprovingly. Charlie cannot see the expression on her face, but others, aware of Betty's secular leanings, chuckle. I look from one to the other. He has a pretty good idea of her reaction and prods Hank Schwartz again, who laughs and shakes his head. Then Charlie continues.

"Maybe I'm getting back to what this gentleman, ah, Padgett here, said earlier about the mysticism stuff. For my part, I regard Plato as a pre-Christian spiritual seeker. And Socrates' formulation of love as virtuous action comes close to how I view it. But then Plato takes it into a strictly mental orbit, whereas in my theology, loving compassion is the highest form. That's something you don't just contemplate; it's something you do." Duggan's voice grew reverent. "You do it with others, the way Jesus showed his care for all the creatures of God."

I was getting fidgety. Charlie had a tendency to sermonize in class, and that could irritate some folks and make them defensive.

"Ah, Charlie," I reply, "without too much elaboration, could you tell us what you mean by the term 'redemption'? Connecting it up with our discussion of the dialogue?"

"Doc, I don't mean to preach," Charlie replies. "Well, I guess I do have that inclination," he adds. Betty's eyebrows go up. "But let me just clarify what I mean. It'll just take a second, here. That all right?"

"Yeah," I say, "if you can be brief, give it a shot."

"Okay." Charlie spreads his fingers out on the desk, palms down. "Redemption, as we all know, just means getting something back you gave up or lost. Remember back in the fifties when we had all those green-stamp redemption centers where you could turn in the booklets of stamps you got when you bought stuff? Some of the money you paid out for those goods you'd get back by exchanging the stamps for toasters or lamps or TVs, whatever. You'd redeem them. Well, in the spiritual tradition from which I come, your faith is like those green stamps. You use it to ask for release from spiritual bondage. That's the same as this feeling we've been talking about—incompleteness. The Greeks didn't invent it, but Plato took a good look at what it might mean. Now, I won't go into the sin stuff, because I know that rankles some people. What I guess I'm saying is that I agree with Betty, here. You can never really get over incompleteness. It's part of what you might call the human condition."

Betty cocks her head, opens her eyes wide, and nods her approval. I sit down on the desktop behind me. I notice that Parker is furiously writing in his notebook.

"What's more," Charlie continues, "I agree that almost nothing will be able to, as she says, fill the void. Understanding that is part of growing up, of maturity. It's a damn, if you'll excuse the expression, damn hard lesson to learn. No matter what you do, or how hard you try, that feeling of not being whole or not being a finished person just lingers on and on. You come to the realization, maybe, that you can't complete yourself and no one else can either. When you can admit that, you are ready to exercise faith.

Maybe there's a being who can help you find completeness. I'm not going to go into that more. I'm just kind of bringing us up to that point in the discussion."

Betty half turns and speaks. "But, Charlie, you're sayin' it *has* to be a religious thing. And that's where I must disagree. I think there can be a"—Betty pauses, purses her lips—"well, maybe a sec-u-lar equivalent of redemption. From my way of seeing it, people have to discover they have the capacity to save themselves. It's their own responsibility."

"Redemption?" cries out Murray Klein. "What is this redemption?" The former businessman, in his college sweatshirt and red baseball cap, could no longer contain himself. "I didn't sign up for this class to hear about redemption," he complains. "I could have gone to my rabbi for that. Although, it's true, I haven't seen him for a while. Anyway. This is, or is supposed to be, a philosophy course. First, we're talking about a bunch of gays sitting around getting soused and talking about their boyfriends. Then we're on the therapist's couch; next, in church. What happened to philosophy, to the great ideas?" Murray looks at me, his eyes fiercely black.

"We've digressed a bit," I reply, to calm him down. "But let's just see where our discussion leads. Maybe it will all fit together," I say, trying to sound encouraging.

Murray looks dubious. "Fit together? Tell me, Doctor Manheimer, how might it fit together?" He folds his arms, waiting for an answer. But before I attempt mine, the eager, fast-talking Carl Struer, a former ship's engineer, blurts out, "Don Ameche." Carl is shaking his head excitedly. He's a great movie fan and frequently brings in examples from movies he's seen to tether our flights of abstraction.

"Did any of you see the movie *Cocoon?*" Carl asks. Several people nod. "Oh, I just loved Don Ameche in the white suit singing

'Some Enchanted Evening.' That was great; just great. Well, anyway, the movie, ladies and gentlemen, you may recall, unless you didn't see it, is about a bunch of old folks in a Florida retirement community. Three elderly chums—what great actors, you know, Cronyn, Brimley, and Ameche—go swimming in a pool at an abandoned estate next to where they're living. What they don't know is that a crew of space travelers from another galaxy have energized the water to bring some of their people back to life. See, they pulled them up from the bottom of the ocean, preserved in these pods."

Struer pauses to catch his breath, and I'm on the verge of interrupting him—I'm worried this is taking us even farther afield. I don't dare look at Murray. "And so, the point is?" I say.

"You mean, what happens? Well, nothing short of a miracle. You see, each man has a different ailment, like a bum ticker, the big C, problems in bed, maybe a prostate condition." Carl looks directly at Murray, who's mentioned in class his bouts with an enlarged prostate. Murray grimaces and shakes his head.

"The point is," Carl continues, "well, see, they're rejuvenated: healthy, sexy, full of life. Whatever weakness they had, they become strong in the reverse way. That's the metamorphosis. The cocooning. Get it? First, you think, right, cocoon, it's about the pods. But later, you see it's a metaphor about the old guys. Like they're turning into butterflies. And, oh, remember the ending? I loved it. They all go off in a spaceship to live forever with the aliens back on their planet. It's like perpetual retirement. Where do I sign up? Right?" Carl has everyone in stitches, except Murray.

"Carl," says Murray in a dead serious voice, "I fail to see the connection."

"Oh, Murray, come on," insists Carl, "it's Hollywood's version of finding eternal life. It's redemption!" he exclaims. "See, they get back exactly what they lost. Just like Chaplain Duggan says. It's a great plot. They find the power to overcome their ailments. In fact, everything that was a disability turns into an ability. Then, given the choice, they go back with the friendly aliens to their home among the stars where people live almost forever. Now, that's what I call eternal life. Literally. So, from this point of view, Plato was right. Immortality is the answer, though, granted, the movie is only a fantasy, and kind of escapist at that. Still, what can you expect?"

"So they redeemed themselves," interjects Betty.

"Or maybe it's like modern medicine, extending your life," chimes in Hank Schwartz, who is still hobbling after recent hip replacement surgery.

"But notice," says Charlie, "they need the water, the baptismal water symbolizing God's sanctification of the flesh."

"This is supposed to be fitting things together?" exclaims Murray, looking around for others to rally to his cause.

A hand is waving from the back of the room. Virginia Mitchell, former nurse, former stockbroker, attired in sensible outdoor clothes adorned with L. L. Bean and Lands' End labels, looks for a chance to come in.

"I hope I'm not just adding more confusion. Sorry, Murray," she waves at Murray, who closes his eyes and shakes his head. "But, getting back to life as incomplete, I don't agree. I've had lots of complete experiences. Take, for example, getting my nursing degree. I completed a course of study and my practicum. Then there's having children. Out they came, complete, ready to grow up into fine young men and women. I can think of countless numbers of completions. I don't feel the least bit incomplete. So I don't know where this is going or even why we're talking about this. The Greeks had a lot of problems. Look at Oedipus or—what's his name?—Sisyphus, the guy who has to push the rock up the hill. Am I missing something?" Virginia scans the group for confirmation.

Betty swivels around toward Virginia. "Ginnie, those are *little* completions, hon. I mean, they're important; don't get me wrong. Life is full of little completions. But it's the overall sense of wholeness I think we're talkin' about. Finishing a degree, having kids, even a great orgasm, are momentary ways we experience completeness. But life goes on, you can't linger too long. You gotta roll out of bed, so to speak. The *big* feeling of incompleteness still gnaws at us."

The ever-candid Betty has produced a blush on the face of Virginia Mitchell. I hear her mumble in defense, "They didn't seem so little at the time."

"You know what I would call the big feeling of completeness?" interjects Murray. "I would call it death. Am I right? Tell me, am I right? Death." Klein looks around for agreement, hears laughter behind him. The next moment, seven different conversations spring up around the classroom.

"Wait a minute. Hold on," the voice of Parker Padgett cuts in. Parker holds up the spiral notebook in which he has been writing. A systematic thinker and great synthesizer, he often pulls things together for us.

"Let me see if I understand, because I think I am beginning to get the gist of this." All eyes are on Parker.

"Let's suppose that not one but several levels of truth are involved here. First, Aristophanes. Despite his unlikely tale about slicing the dual-sex people in half, he gets at an important"— Parker makes quotation marks in the air with his finger—" 'psychological' truth. He equates love with an emotional need for a beloved, male or female, who offers qualities or attributes missing in the lover. This isn't too hard to follow, right?" He pauses. No one replies; we're all waiting.

"The psychological truth here is that many people are drawn to an opposite personality type. An introvert, say, teams up with an extrovert. An impulsive person with a someone cautious, deliberate."

"In other words," teases Murray, "it takes two to tango."

"Exactly," says Parker. "Everyone has some degree of all these attributes, but developed differently. And some of this, we now know, is a matter of individual chemistry or how the circuits in your brain are wired. So, psychological truth. Okay?"

"Keep going, Parker" says Betty.

"Right," says Parker. "Now, the next level is the"—he makes quotation marks again—" 'philosophical.' Socrates tells us that what we love is beauty, and it comes in different guises, like beautiful bodies and art. But we're not to pay too much attention to things that are beautiful, because they change. Instead, we should think about what beauty is in itself, as an ideal. He invites us to climb up the staircase of love and visit with Diotima, who tells us what we really desire most of all is what would make us immune to death. So now love is the pursuit of fame, progeny, and beautiful thoughts of beauty. Something, once you attain it, you can never lose. Apparently, Plato believes this ideal never changes. Although why he believes this is beyond me. Because, well, if we each said what we thought was beautiful, we'd have as many definitions as there are people in the classroom. Some would overlap. Sure. But we'd still have many different, even opposite, ideas of beauty. In addition, these change over time. Different eras have their own ideals of beauty. What appeals to us at one time in our lives may not in another. So I don't at all agree with this formulation.

"That objection aside, his real aim might be to frame a generalization about beauty; make it an abstract idea. At least then we would be able to state our criteria for beauty and test our ideal against particular examples to see whether they really matched up."

Parker takes a deep breath, looks around at the admiring gaze of his classmates, pokes his finger in his notebook, and continues.

"Now, next, and here I had a lot of trouble, next is the"—he makes the quotation with two fingers—" 'theological.' " That's where our good friend Father Duggan came in with *redemption.* That really threw me, for a while. Then, thanks to Carl's account of the movie *Cocoon,* I realized we had made an important shift. The redemption factor, that's getting back or making an exchange for something you lost. Could be your youth, health, love of life, innocence, even integrity. Getting back what feels like a missing part of yourself is a little like Aristophanes' myth of desire. Plato exchanges Aristophanes' desire for beautiful others with the idea of having beautiful thoughts. Desire, though, is still a search for something missing. However, and correct me if I'm wrong here, Ron, but from reading some of the other dialogues we learned Plato thinks these timeless ideas are already imprinted in our minds, only, somehow, with all the distractions of mundane existence, we've forgotten about them. These ideas, they're, um—"

"Innate ideas?" I respond.

"Yes, that's it, innate ideas. The ones supposedly implanted in our brains like on a computer chip. At least, that's what Plato would have us believe. We have them, but we aren't exactly aware of them. At the same time, he says we didn't invent them, either, because they are not derived from experience. Is that right?"

"Yes," I respond, "Plato wants to establish these ideas or forms as independent of human cognition, as part of the very order of the universe, not a projection or derivation of the human mind. If they are only concepts reached through generalizing from particulars, then they might just be true to human consciousness and, therefore, subject to revision, variation, special conditions. So, innate ideas are both logically prior to experience and independent of reason, even if it's only through reason, and contemplation, that we can know them."

"Reminds me of the gold standard in banking," says Parker.

"Some kind of hard currency. Very conservative. Plato must have wanted maximum stability."

"At the time, it was quite a radical idea," I reply. "And, yes, he did want to stabilize the metaphysical truths on which Athenian society was based. That's why he believed only philosopher-kings could ensure wise leadership."

"Humph," snorts Parker, "not very likely. Now, let me try to round out my little summary."

"Wait," interjects Murray, "I still want to know why everyone thinks we need redemption."

"Because," laughs Betty, "we've committed a great sin."

"Which is what?" asks Murray.

"Which is that we've grown old. Younger people can't see any good in it," she replies.

"Oh, that," he sighs.

"I was talking about redemption and theology," says the tenacious Parker, determined to finish his train of thought. "Plato's innate ideas would be an example of getting something back you lost or didn't know you had deep inside your brain. As I recall from our discussion a few weeks ago, he called that the theory of recollection. If someone asks us the right questions, we find we can remember all kinds of deep truths. Really, I think it's just deductive reasoning. In any case, it's not the same as redemption, because redemption introduces a new element besides forgetting. There's an active element of resistance or denial, and the need for penitence. Something keeps us from completing ourselves, some obstacle we can't overcome. Like the frailty issue in *Cocoon*, we have to go through something painful to get redeemed. Betty, I surmise, would describe it as resistance to change. Charlie would describe it as despair. Betty's solution is self-knowledge—seeing the patterns of your life and changing them. Charlie's is faith. Recognizing that you can go only so far and then you've got to call, well, I guess, pray for the help of a higher power.

"So that, my friends, is as far as I've gotten." Parker puts down his pen, adjusts the fold of his turtleneck, and smiles. Several of his classmates break into applause.

Noticing Murray Klein squirming uncomfortably in his chair, I announce, "This is a good time for us to take a break."

THE VISIT

A few days after the discussion of Plato's *Symposium*, Murray Klein shows up at my office. This isn't an unusual occurrence. Murray likes to come by to chat about his favorite social causes, talk about his beloved dog, tell stories about his career in the women's apparel business in Manhattan, or complain about our local minor league team, the Asheville Tourists. Below the visor of his Yankees baseball cap are a tanned face, mischievous brown eyes, and a wide smile. But today he looks a little anxious, uncertain, as if unsure why he has come.

"Hi, how're ya doin'? This an okay time to come by? You don't look too busy." Murray doesn't wait for an answer. He plunks down in a chair, removes his ball cap, and drags his fingers through his thinning hair. In his other hand, he holds some papers bound in a clear plastic folder.

I swivel away from my computer screen and extend a hand. Then I wait.

"Ron," he begins, "I want to talk about the last class meeting when I got all excited about that Plato stuff and the crazy talk about redemption. You remember?"

Murray watches me carefully, looking for a reaction. "You seemed confused about some of Parker's ideas," I say.

"No, that wasn't it," he insists. "Parker's a great guy, a very smart man. And what he said was helpful. He always tries to be helpful, Parker does. It wasn't that. And as far as Plato is concerned, I admire the guy. He could have been a great playwright but, unfortunately, he got mixed up in the philosophy business. Don't misunderstand. Philosophy's great. We've all got to try our hand. That's what life's all about. You have to have some sense of meaning, of purpose. We need to examine our lives. I believe that. I do."

Murray is getting fidgety. He's scrolling the plastic binder. "So what else is on your mind?" I ask.

"I have something I want you to read." He holds up the binder. "It's a screenplay I wrote. Something I've wanted to do for years. Finally did it. But it wasn't easy. Wasn't easy. You have to be patient. I had some help from another of the students in the class. You know, Jody Finch? She has a background in literature. She helped me. I knew the plot, the characters, how they'd talk, knew exactly what I wanted to write about, but she helped me get it down on paper."

"Great," I say. "I'd love to read it. But what's this got to do with the class and Plato?"

"Nothing and everything," he replies, puts his cap on, tugs down on the visor. "See, it was the talk about redemption. Funny. Usually I don't much go for words like that. Rabbis and ministers talk about stuff like that. I don't take it seriously. Anyway, I figure, what's done is done. Best to move on. You know, that tomorrow is another day. But afterwards I got to thinking. What I'm doing. It's redemption."

"You mean writing this screenplay?"

"Not the screenplay. What it's about. It's about my work as a Big Brother, about my Little Brother Jesse, how I got to know him, gained his trust after he'd had so many disappointing relationships with adults. Well, when we got talking about the movie *Cocoon*, about getting something back you lost, it hit me. What I've been doing? It's the same. Years ago, with my own kids, I was out of town a lot because I had to call on customers all over the East Coast. I worked hard, had to be number one. And I did it thinking, for them, I'm doing this for my family, to give them a good life. But things didn't turn out that way. I should have spent more time with the kids, should have been more even-tempered, instead of jumping on them about small things when they needed attention, needed to know I loved them." He removes the cap, sits back in the armchair, places the cap on his knee. "Now I'm trying to do it right, be the father I would like to have been." Murray leafs through the pages of his screenplay.

"That's what you wrote about?" I ask.

He nods. "I think my story could inspire others to become Big Brothers or Big Sisters, too. I'm sending it off to my niece. She's a big-time casting director in Hollywood. Maybe, if she thinks it's good enough, one of the studios will want to make it into a picture. Wouldn't that be something?"

"Yes, it would be something."

Then neither of us seems to know what to say. Watching Murray sitting there clutching his manuscript and his Yankees cap, I think about the many new books exhorting readers to experience the completion of being, discover the ageless self within, achieve mind/body ecstasy, find new meaning in the second half of life, and all the "you're never too old" books about ecstatic sex, renewed creativity, and challenging outdoor activities. It seemed we hardly lived until we grew old. The keys included positive attitude, personal prayer, megavitamins, exercise, low-calorie diets.

Yet one very thoughtful book on reminiscence in old age, by Edmund Sherman, identifies a philosophical dimension in the work of reviewing the past. Reminiscing can involve reminding ourselves of the "profound division" that occurs early in life between the sheer joy of being and the need to meet the obligations of becoming a grown-up. We forget our deep spiritual nature, which Sherman calls "the primal, original impulse toward being," because we are preoccupied with doing—our need to labor in the fields of the material world. But in old age, says Sherman, the impulse to recollect may help us correct this imbalance so that it is "tipped toward being." We become more contemplative, more aware of our true nature. Though trained as a social worker, Sherman seems to have felt the tug of ancient philosophy.

Now, I'm wondering whether Murray Klein, the hard-driving businessman who strove to be number one until he discovered what he had forgotten, was finding the key to completion through addressing mistakes of the past and making things right in the present.

"Murray," I break the silence, "do your kids know about your work as a Big Brother? Do they have any sense about what you're trying to do?"

Murray smiles. "They know a little about Jesse, my Little Brother. But, you know what? I think they're a little jealous. Really, I think they're jealous. They probably think, 'why didn't the old man show us that kind of attention, help us with our homework, take us to ball games, and ooh and ah over our wood carvings or home runs?' And you know what, they're right. Oh, we get along better now, but somehow I still fall back into the past, get angry about some stupid thing they do or say. You just can't escape the past; it comes running after you. I don't have any illusion about that. You have to live with your mistakes, have to accept that what's incomplete stays incomplete. That's life. Maybe a Plato can contemplate love and reach some kind of oneness of being. I can't. All I can do are simple obvious things, like teach Jesse to read and help him bring his grades up from an F to a D minus." Murray laughs, slaps his cap on his knee. "D minus. Not much better, but it's an improvement. Next year, maybe C minus. Call me an optimist."

"You have hope," I say. "That's important."

"Ya gotta have hope. Otherwise you're finished," he responds. "And I'd rather have small hopes than big ones. Little hopes I can hold on to. Like Jesse, he's a little hope for me. Of course, I want him to be a big hope for himself. But right now he'd settle for little hopes, too. You see, Professor, if you've had a few setbacks in life, had your big hopes dashed, either you give up or you replace the big hopes with little ones and you stick with them. The way I figure it, I've learned a few things, picked up a few skills along the way. I shouldn't hoard my small riches. I need to invest them in the future. My future? Tomorrow. That's my future. But Jesse's future? That's a long, long future. At least I hope it is."

"Making the past present," I say.

"You got it. Except, I'd add, if you don't mind my being a little philosophical, making the past present by remembering the future."

We look at each other, and I think maybe the past cannot be fully redeemed in old age or the self completed, but maybe, like Murray, you can become a redeemer of others.

I hear the phone ringing in another office. Shadows of the trees outside my window flicker along the wall and across the carpet. A door shuts to one of the classrooms on the corridor.

"Hey," Murray exclaims, "wanna go to a ball game with me and Jesse? The Asheville Tourists are playing tonight." He rubs his hands together like a pitcher working sweat into the ball. "Against Greensboro. I'll buy you a hot dog."

I haven't been to a game in a couple of years. There's so much waiting around for something to happen. But I like our small new baseball stadium and the homey atmosphere of the minor leagues. With Murray and Jesse, I'm sure, there will be no dull moments.

"Okay," I reply, "you're on. A hot dog with lots of mustard."

"You'll love it," says Murray. "We always have a good time."

CHAPTER ELEVEN

POSTCARDS FROM PARADISE

My Danish friend Augie Nielsen says eternity is happening right now—you can taste it in a piece of bread, feel it in an embrace, hear it in a very good hymn, smell it in the vapors of a glass of cognac. I suppose he means that when the fullness of a present moment permeates your whole being, you experience a kind of timelessness.

To philosophers and theologians the word "eternity" can mean that which neither begins nor ends, an immutable truth, or the infinite awareness we might attribute to a divine being. Augie's awareness is finite, but he has his moments, his intimations of the timeless. "We're all following some path to fulfillment," Augie once told me, "and what we seek bears the stamp of eternity."

"A stamp? Like on a postcard?" I teased him.

"Ja, just such a one," he teased back. "A postcard you send home every day, with a picture of your paradise on it."

Augie has an odd way of putting things, but he's the kind of person you can talk to about an enthralling idea or a haunting question. That's why I went to see him, why a cemetery in Denmark seemed a good place for a conversation.

WOODEN SHOES

Augie Nielsen is short and stocky with white hair he has allowed to lengthen like a mane falling over his collar. He wears the traditional Danish *træsko*, wooden shoes with leather uppers, and has pairs for everyday wear and for dressier occasions. The shoes also make him look taller.

Raised among the small farms, crossroads towns, and fishing villages that dot the region of Denmark north of the Lim Fjord, Augie is one of a proud and stubbornly independent stock of people from the west Jutland district known as Thy (pronounced "two"). He is a "Thyboer," an inhabitant (*boer*, lives) of an area that is, as locals will pridefully tell you, "north of law and order." Historically, they have resisted the authority of crown, clergy, and, more recently, national government.

Born to a pietistic farm family, Augie was the black sheep who insisted on moving to the sin-ridden city of Copenhagen to study and have adventures. His wayward spirit led him to New York, India, and many other places. A brilliant and eccentric educational innovator, Augie had a history of starting maverick organizations that, as they achieved success and respectability, became increasingly conservative. More than once, he was fired by an executive board he had originally picked during the organization's formative years.

I took some years off after college to work with Augie Nielsen when he was rector of New Experimental College, an adult-learning community for soul-searching types inspired by Augie's vision of a global approach to education. His energy was contagious; students and teachers sometimes even unconsciously emulated his stutter. The school was first located in a Copenhagen suburb, then relocated to a rural setting where farm buildings were converted to classrooms and dorms on a piece of land not many kilometers from Augie's birthplace. Twenty years after my apprenticeship with Augie, I returned to Denmark to visit him.

Augie is what the Danes call a *pensionist*, a retiree drawing the Danish government's equivalent of our Social Security. At age seventy-two, in a small apartment packed with filing cabinets and shelves holding old papers and letters from his various past enterprises, Augie is occupied as usual with ambitious, far-flung projects for the future. People continue to be drawn by his undiminished charisma, and there are frequent visitors, correspondence, and phone calls. But now Augie complains of the disturbances. He is an old man, he says, who needs his midday nap. He's had enough of other people's dreams, fantasies, and problems. Still, he won't turn them, or me, away.

Augie lives just outside Ringkøbing, a charming west Jutland town where tradition and modernity intermix. The town's center is a cobblestone square on which an eighteenth-century town hall crowned with clock tower rises. Inside the tower, a satellite dish receives signals from remote places. A seagull perched on its weather vane inspects the labyrinth of orange-tiled roofs winding away from the square. Below, local citizens gaze through plate glass windows at fine cuts of beef, ropes of hanging sausages, warm breads and rich cakes, cigars and pipes, the latest Copenhagen fashions, Danish modern furniture, and ultramodern electronic devices. Usually, the gull finds more interesting fare in the fjord harbor where wooden flats of iced cod and flounder are stacked beside the fishing boats. But not on this day of rest.

My conversation with Augie takes place in the cemetery surrounding a whitewashed stone church at the edge of town. I've accompanied him to a traditional Sunday morning Lutheran service. He had at one time trained for the ministry, but his unconventional views cut short his prospects for ordination. After we sing the last hymn, we stroll the gravel paths of the beautifully maintained cemetery with its rock walls, climbing roses, close-clipped grass borders, and boxwood hedges. The rows of gravestones form a solemn, well-ordered version of the town.

I am trying to figure out how to ask my aging mentor the big question: Is there a universal purpose to life, or is each of us responsible for making one up? In old age, does the aim of life become clearer, or does the inevitability of frailty unravel the fabric of meaning we've worked so hard to weave? Maybe Augie's unconventional mind and his own recent close encounter with death will give him a unique perspective.

fINDING fULfILLMENT

Augie is busy greeting local farmers and shopkeepers and chatting with them in a local dialect almost unintelligible to a Copenhagen Dane. I wander off to study the names and inscriptions on the stones. I notice a phrase chiseled into several of the monuments and wonder which of two interpretations might be correct. Augie waves *farvel* to a woman in a flowered hat, as she closes the wrought-iron gate leading out to the roadway.

"Augie," I call to him, "tell me about these inscriptions." I stand in front of one of the stones and run my fingers over the letters that read *Det Er Fuldbragt*. Does it mean "It Is Ended" or "It Is Accomplished"? The verb form, *fuldbringe*, is commonly used to mean bring to an end, or complete. I point to the inscription as Augie's wooden shoes crunch to a halt beside me.

"Fuldbragt," he nods, fingering a small scar above his lip from a childhood accident, "this is, ja, these are the words about Jesus and the resurrection. You know the story. Jesus disappears from the cave where he was put after he died on the cross. He pushes a giant boulder away from the entrance to the cave and goes up to see his father, our Lord. Then, after a fantastic conversation with the Maker of us all, he comes back to earth to tell his disciples what an amazing experience this dying thing is, that they shouldn't be afraid. If they have faith, they can conquer death and live in eternity. Then he leaves them to figure out what he meant." Augie winks at me. "It's quite a story."

I nod. I found the Jesus story as challenging to interpret as the dividing of the Red Sea, or God staying the hand of Abraham.

"So the inscription means that just like Jesus these people have fulfilled the journey of life and returned to God in eternity. Is that it? Because," I add teasingly, "it could also mean their lives are simply over, their worn-out bodies and minds finished with their travail."

"Ja," Augie nods, "it could mean this, if you want it to." That was one of his tricks, getting you to avow a truth when you intended only to cast doubt. Still, I persist.

"But don't you think these inscriptions are put here for our sake, to make us less fearful of death, to make us feel that the lives of the living make sense, at least as part of a series of stepping stones?"

I gesture toward the Reformation-style architecture of the church façade. Like every traditional Danish Lutheran church, it rises through a series of staircase-like steps to a flattened apex silhouetted against the tall trees and sky.

Augie looks up at the church façade and squints. "Th, th, that's possible, Ron," he stutters. He pauses and looks back at me. "Of course, this is typically the way you humanists and most of the young Danes think. We from the older generation take it literally. We are hanging around for eternity." Augie tugs at his ear. "Take our minister. Every Sunday, he makes a competent and boring sermon for the handful of people who show up. Wha, why not?" he shrugs. "There's no need for excitement. He's just waiting, too."

I know Augie is baiting me. Whenever he talks about something as acceptably boring, it's to lure you into expounding on some cherished ideal or belief you didn't mean to reveal. Next thing you know, you're on the defensive. I'm not going to fall for it.

"But," I go on, "you really believe in the story of Jesus. For you, the meaning of *Det Er Fuldbragt* must point to a higher completeness than simply the termination of a long struggle to put bread on the table, enjoy a beer and a pork roast, have a decent home, a nice car, and be a respectable citizen."

Augie laughs. "Now, Ron, you know it depends on the type of car. If a person were to drive a red sports car like my 280Z—or enjoy a glass of good red wine or a Flora Danica cigar—well, then that's different."

In a way, Augie is not joking. He's become quite a hedonist in his old age. He loves speeding down the small country roads in his now classic sports car, good cigars, and not only red wine but scotch and brandy as well. And his predilection for younger women, usually exceptionally bright and capable, has not diminished, despite several relationships that ended in disappointment. Usually the woman, but also Augie, was apparently genuinely surprised that things had not worked out. In a way, he is living testimony of the incompleteness of the quest for wisdom or happiness. I cannot imagine *Det Er Fuldbragt* inscribed on his stone.

A few years back, he had a serious illness and underwent a series of critical operations. Augie was in a coma for two weeks. He claims to have had out-of-body experiences and even several conversations with God. Having looked through the tunnel of death toward the light at the other end, and returned to the land of the living, he discovered no fewer than five women prepared to mourn their lover's departure. Unchastened by this brush with death, Augie embraces a life of pleasure with even greater zeal. Hasn't he learned anything?

Still, we are here at the church, not the pub. Perhaps Augie is trying to have it both ways.

Augie begins walking down one of the gravel paths toward a group of stones surrounded by a low iron railing.

"Ron, see here." Augie points to the inscription on a polished granite stone, *Til Evighed*," He repeats the Danish slowly, til a-ve-heth, "to eternity."

"It's like a house address or a sign in a store window, Out to Lunch."

"Yes," says Augie, amused with this notion, "gone to eternity. Won't be back soon."

"I just don't understand this vocabulary," I respond. "The words are abstract. They impose a meaning, but there's no experience. Here's Mr. Lauritsen, who died five years ago. It says he was a baker. And now he's followed Jesus' path to eternity. I see two story lines, the baker and the savior, but I don't see their intersection."

"The baker and the savior," laughs Augie. "Ja, that's good. Maybe we should make a film about it. Which role would you like to play, Ron?"

"I'm serious, Augie."

"Yes," says Augie, "I hear that. Maybe too serious. You're never certain about anything unless you can see for yourself how the whole thing will turn out."

"It's mysterious," I say, defending myself, "and I want to clear up the meaning."

"Or disturbing," sighs Augie; " 'eternity' can be a scary word."

"Because of death," I reply.

He shakes his head. "No, because of life." He looks at me side-ways. "Do you want to hear a story about *evighed?*"

"Please."

"Ja, this was a night, maybe nine, maybe ten years ago. I was tak-ing a student to the train station in Hurup. The last train that night. You know, he was going to Copenhagen and flying home home to, uh, ja, to Omaha, I think. We hugged. He climbed aboard. The train slowly and quietly began to move. Our modern Danish trains, you know. So quiet. I was waving, as we always do, and he was wav-ing back from the window as the train moved farther and farther away. Late at night, I was the only one on the platform, I thought. But then I saw, no, there was a man in a tweed cap and a raincoat, even though it was a mild evening. No rain. We hadn't had any rain for days. Well, I was still waving although I knew that the student—Richard, I think, was his name—that Richard couldn't see me any longer and I could see only the little red light glowing on the end of the train. And this man, I don't think he put anyone on the train or was there to meet anyone. I think he is one of those lonely men who come to see the train arrive and leave. That's all. And I started to feel . . . what? How to describe it? *Uhyggelig.*"

"Strange? Eerie?" I translate.

"Ja, 'eerie,' that's the word. Even the friendly little redbrick sta-tion looked different. All shadows. Then this man, he came toward me, looked at me. Such a sad face. An old farmer. Probably never married. 'Good evening, my friend,' I greeted him cheerfully, as we do in the countryside. And he doffed his cap, gave a quick nod, and turned. As he walked away, he started whistling. Whistling to himself and walking up the platform. And I could just barely hear the whistle of the train mixing in with his whistling. And I began to feel weak, the way you get when you're coming down with the flu. Can you understand this, Ron? I don't know. I drove home very slowly, carefully. Something had gone out of me, been sucked away. How long had I stood there? A few seconds, a minute, longer?" Augie looks at me as though he expects an answer.

"No, you can't really say, can you?" He continues, rubbing his chin. "I've thought about it many times ever since. That night, the man in the tweed cap, his whistling, the train. And I feel—no, taste—in my mouth a bitterness, the word *evighed* . . . eternity." Then, as if shaking off the gloom of this tale, Augie looks up with a gleam in his eye. "So, Mr. Philosopher, can you explain this?"

"You had the experience, and now I'm supposed to supply the meaning?"

"You're much better at meanings than I am, Ron."

I have to laugh at such a remark, typical of Augie. Still, I have an idea as to the meaning of his story. "Augie," I say, "isn't this about loneliness? Here you are, sending someone off into the night, the train disappearing into the infinite distance as if it were taking part of you away. Then you meet this silent man. It's one of those moments—a hollow eternity, an emptiness of time. You feel your very soul drained of vitality. Then, there's the aspect of separation . . ."

Augie puts his hand on my shoulder. "Ron, I knew I could count on you. Yes, maybe that's what it means. Funny. You can't stop the feeling. A meaning can try to catch a feeling, like caging a wild animal. But the feeling is restless. Being there on the platform. I'm still there." Then he brightens up. "Fantastic, isn't it, just fantastic that we can have such experiences? And better, Ron, that now you're having this experience with me."

We stroll along for a few paces, and I turn to Augie and ask, "But, Augie, if eternity is such a bitter feeling, why put it on these stones?"

"Because," he replies, "this isn't the bitter *evighed*; it's a sweet one. This is the *evighed* of fullness. You see, when we seek fulfillment, we seek this sweet eternity."

"And do you have a story about this sweet eternity?"

"Another story?" he laughs. "No, I don't think so. But Kierkegaard had such a story. You remember what Kierkegaard called the fullness of time?"

"Of course," I reply. Augie knows I wrote my dissertation on Kierkegaard, the nineteenth-century Dane whose emphasis on personal freedom as the basis for a "leap of faith" led to the religious strand of the existential tradition. "Jesus, as God and man, enters world history as a pure act of divine generosity to reconnect with human beings. Kierkegaard was using an idea from Hegel about the logic of historical advancement and how Christianity appeared in human history at just the right time and that now we are becoming aware of how history is fulfilling itself, even in our being able to think it through. But Kierkegaard had a different conception, he . . ."

Augie puts his hand on my shoulder. "This is wonderful, Herr Philosopher, that you can explain the idea of the fullness in time. Too bad that you are missing the point."

"How is that?"

"Kierkegaard is telling you that you are forever on the way to fulfillment, because you can be saved from your own fear of running out of time. We have to get ready. That is the message on these stones, asking us, Are you ready for eternity? Our lives are a time to get ready. If you understand that, then you can experience how each moment is *til evighed*, 'toward eternity.' When you're younger, you try to forget about it. As you get older, things happen, little reminders like a heart attack, or a friend dies, or your hair turns gray. And each of these is a little reminder about what you've forgotten. That you're supposed to be getting ready."

I don't like being told that I missed the point about Kierkegaard.

"What's the point of being alive if we're just waiting for death?"

I shoot back. "Isn't this the life-denying theology that makes religions so depressing?"

"It becomes that way at times," says Augie, "when people misunderstand. They start thinking that eternity is something you have to promote, like car insurance or toothpaste. They want to put a *varemærke* on it."

"A trademark?"

"Ja, trademark. Like they had a patent on eternity, or a franchise. They could sell it to you in little bottles like aspirin or tonic."

"And this sweet eternity?"

"Can't be sold."

"You know, Augie, what we are saying reminds me of the Ingmar Bergman movie *Wild Strawberries*. Remember, at the beginning the old physician, Dr. Borg, is having a dream. He's standing in a deserted street of a small town. He's lost, even though it's where he lives. And he looks up at a round clock above the door to the watchmaker's shop. But this clock has no hands. Dr. Borg takes out his pocketwatch and it, too, has no hands. He's frightened. He hears his heart pounding. That's another kind of eternity, the timelessness of despair."

Augie nods. "I have had that feeling," he says. "But don't forget the strawberries, the wild strawberries the doctor remembers from his youth. What a taste. So intense. Flavorful. Isn't that a word in English?"

"A good word," I reply.

"That emptiness of time is the opposite of what Kierkegaard means by the fullness of time. It's, ah . . ." He pauses trying to find the right word.

Augie looks around the cemetery. Then his gaze falls on a pear tree alongside the farther stone wall. He begins again.

"Ja, it is the difference between ripening and rotting. When you live with readiness, you are ripening. When you live in battle with readiness, you are rotting. Do you understand this, Herr Doctor?"

I nod slowly. "So, you're saying that our lives are a process of reaching completion by drawing closer to God through following the teachings of Jesus and emulating his life. According to this spiritual path, we are pilgrims seeking the fulfillment of time. We long to transcend our finite lives, our sense of incompleteness, through a way of life 100 percent devoted to seeking salvation. Is that it?"

For several seconds, Augie just stares at me. Then he nods slowly. "It is something like that, Ron. But, Mr. Jewish Philosopher, do you suppose Jesus would have been successful if he had gone around talking like that? And when I hear you put it that way it reminds me how difficult is this pilgrim's path, as you say. That's why, in those times, we Danes didn't pay much attention to Kierkegaard. Later we turned him into an export product, like the excellent cheeses, hams, and beers we send all over the world. Now people come to Denmark to study Kierkegaard. It was the German theologians, almost fifty years after his death, who really discovered Kierkegaard and made him world famous. We in Denmark followed Grundtvig instead."

"And why was that?"

"Because Herr N.F.S, you know, Nicolai Frederik Severin Grundtvig, who was thirty years old when Kierkegaard was born and lived another seventeen years after Kierkegaard died, wrote songs about how much fun it was to be a Danish Lutheran. Søren Kierkegaard wrote big, dense books that made being a Christian about the most impossible thing a person could do. So which do you think people chose?" Augie pauses and begins to hum something under his breath. Then he breaks out in song.

"'O day full of grace, which we behold.'" He turns to me, "Ron, do you remember?"

I knew this was one of Grundtvig's most famous *salmer*—the hymns you would certainly hear in church but also at weddings, anniversaries, and birthday parties.

Augie continues. "'Now gently to view ascending, / Thou over the earth thy reign unfold, / Good cheer to all mortals lending, / That children of light of every clime / May prove that the night is ending.' You see, when Grundtvig says 'Good cheer to all mortals lending,' he means that the kingdom of heaven is here and now. Oh, he didn't give up on wanting to be saved, but he discovered that creation wasn't so bad after all. And, did you know, it was a woman who changed Grundtvig from being a Lutheran pietist with a pilgrim complex to the man who proclaimed that first we should be human, then Christian?"

"Yes, I've heard that phrase. *'Først menneskelig og saa kristelig'*? Isn't that it?"

"So you haven't forgotten everything I've taught you?"

"No, not everything. But about this woman. I don't know that part."

"Oh, she was a very elegant English woman, Mrs. Bolton. Grundtvig spent several evenings with her in London. She became his muse. She convinced him that there was something wonderful in being natural men and women, not to deny the flesh and blood but to see the real world as God's creation, not a big mistake. We don't know what they said to each other, but Grundtvig wrote something about her. Have I told you this one? *'Alt hvad der ret skal gaa os til hjerte, skal gaa gennem Kvinden til os.'*"

I struggle to translate this old-fashioned, poetic phrase.

"It means," Augie continues, "that matters of the heart come to us only through women. Today it probably doesn't sound too— what is it you say?—politically correct. But once his heart was opened, Grundtvig decided to push for a new Danish constitution that would create improvements in everyday Danish society and open what had been a very narrow, very orthodox Lutheran church to diverse beliefs. He wanted a *folkekirke*, a people's church. And for that new kind of church, Grundtvig wrote hundreds of hymns that we sing today. His vision was to separate the religious from the cultural to make way for a more humane society, free from domination from the religious authorities. Some people credit Grundtvig with starting a secular Danish society. But that wasn't his goal. It was to make the ordinary life of the poor farmer, the shopkeeper, the banker, and the schoolchildren, how do you say it in English? *Verdsliggøre?*" Augie turns toward the church building and squints into the sunlight.

"*Verdsliggøre?*" I search through my mental dictionary. "Well, literally, it means to make worldly. I suppose it means secular. Like the separation of church and state."

Augie shakes his head. "In one way, ja, it does mean that. To take away religion and put humanism in its place. But Grundtvig had another meaning. It was to turn Christianity toward the worldly problems of everyday life and try to deal with them in a Christian way. He wanted to take the spiritual ideals of the early Christian communities and revive them in the villages and farms and towns of the kingdom of Denmark. So Grundtvig brought us the cooperative movement from England, inspired the Danish folk high schools movement, and gave the Danish people a new optimism about the future of our tiny country, which had gotten even smaller after we lost Norway and Schleswig-Holstein in the wars."

"So, while Kierkegaard wrote about the fullness of time in being one with Christ, Grundtvig tried to fulfill the needs of his time by offering people a kingdom of heaven on earth."

"That's right, Ron." Augie turns back to me. "But we need both a Grundtvig and a Kierkegaard to point the way. You see . . ." He pauses, rubs the stubble on his chin, then continues,

"Kierkegaard could never be satisfied with what we Christians call the fallen man. To be imprisoned by time, by finite existence. It was like, um, how shall I tell it?" Augie looks at his hands, palms up. Then he pushes up his sleeve. "There, you see, this wristwatch," he exclaims. "It's a good one, too. And Kierkegaard had such a one. A very large and heavy wristwatch. So heavy it made his arm sore. And it was fastened in such a way that he could never take it off. He could always hear its ticking. The sound was painful to him and made him wonder that other people were not bothered by the sound of their watches. He would ask them, show them the watch, but it made no impression. He desperately wanted to find a way to take it off, because the ticking made him feel apart from everyone and everything. He had a terrible longing to overcome this deep loneliness, the feeling of estrangement from God and from his true self."

"Which was?"

"Which was to be at one with God. Now, Grundtvig, who traveled a similar path, changed course when he was about your age. Let's say, fiftyish. He became reconciled to being a finite creature, separate from God. He decided that being a person had its own special dignity. So his aim was to make the most, ja, to make the best of it. He decided to turn Denmark into a little paradise. And, for better or worse, he succeeded. Don't you think?

"Yes, Denmark's a wonderful country. But why for better or worse?"

"Because we became such a successful country that people forgot all about being finite, fallen creatures. Now we have the state to take care of us if we get sick or have a toothache or need a place to live. In our country, it is illegal to be unhealthy or homeless or unhappy. And this is a wonderful thing. Really. But it also means that we have, ah, ja, I would say, spiritually fallen asleep. We have lost the ability to long for anything besides this comfort and security. So we still need these two Danes, even if they are poles apart in understanding what makes life complete. Do you understand, Herr Philosopher?"

"Yes, I think so. Grundtvig came up with a communal solution. He wanted to make a kingdom of heaven on earth. But it turned into the social welfare state. And Kierkegaard opted for an individual solution of surrendering himself to God, but it isolated him from people. Each is a different approach to the fulfillment of our mortal lives. I guess you could say these are the dual eternities of modern Danish history."

"That's good," exclaims Augie, patting me on the shoulder, "our two eternities. Like an escalator, one stairway going up, the other down."

"We shouldn't forget the bitter and the sweet eternities, Augie."

"No, we'll keep them, too."

"But there's another thing I want to know."

"And what would that be, Ron?"

"What about Mrs. Bolton?"

Augie laughs. "Yes, well, she is important to the whole story. But, you know, Grundtvig never saw her again. Maybe that's why she was such a powerful muse for him. Which reminds me. I have a lady friend who is a little like Mrs. Bolton. I want you to meet her. In fact, if you want to come with me, we can have afternoon coffee at her place. It's not far."

"Another Mrs. Bolton?" This should be interesting. Augie always has a surprise up his sleeve. Probably another of the young women who bring rejuvenation into his life.

Augie reaches into the inside pocket of his frayed suit jacket. He extracts a cardboard box with the colorful picture of a judge in robes on it and in large black type ADVOKAT, the Danish word for attorney.

"Do you care for a cigar, Ron?"

I stare at him. "Is it proper to smoke here in the cemetery?"

"Of course not," he replies. "But since when have you become concerned with being proper?"

Augie motions me to follow him through the gate. We sit down on a wooden bench against the rock wall that encloses the cemetery and church. Now that we are on the outside, we light up. The two threads of smoke twist and turn in the still air. Then a breeze, with a tiny hint of the sea, wafts the smoke up into the trees.

———

The ends of time, Denmark's dual eternities, one solitary, the other communal, arose when quite different Christian religious perspectives collided with the forces of secularism and nationalism in nineteenth-century northern Europe. Kierkegaard rejected the culture of Christendom, because he thought spiritual growth had become too easy, too much an accepted part of middle-class culture. He wanted to restore the great difficulty posed by the faith of an Abraham, by the pathos and self-sacrifice of the God-man Jesus. The end of the process of development would find the individual standing alone before God. Taking a different stance, Grundtvig rejected the narrow reactionary position of the Lutheran church in Denmark. He sought an activist role—the church and the community would reproduce the miracle of the fishes and loaves with the help of the Danish cooperative agricultural movement. The aim of his dream was a Denmark in which fellowship and abundance would bring heaven to earth.

By contrast, my views of the goal of life were mainly secular, influenced by twentieth-century investigations into developmental psychology and, close to the time I visited Augie in Denmark, by a contemporary American philosopher, David Norton, who traced the stages of ethical development from childhood to old age. These were the perspectives I wanted to review with Augie.

We already had discovered four eternities during our stroll, and I wondered whether there would be more.

PYRAMID OF LIFE

Augie looks at his cigar with satisfaction, then turns toward me. "You know, Ron, I am practicing up for eternity."

"You can do that?"

"Oh, ja. I have been exercising my capacity for timelessness. You see, I almost died a couple of times but I couldn't quite get it right. I meditate every day, occasionally sip a good cognac, enjoy my afternoon naps. In this way I study eternity. It's useful work for an old man, wouldn't you say?" I nod, though I'm not sure what he's driving at. "But you?" he continues. "You want to know fulfillment because, maybe, you are near to completing something that you cannot yet know."

Augie has a knack for paradoxes. How could I know whether I was close to something I couldn't know? It didn't make sense. Or did it? Wasn't he asking me to take mental leaps instead of my usual plodding steps?

"Like you, Augie," I say, taking the leap, "I want to know what's at the end of time."

Augie laughs, then grows serious. "The end of time," he exclaims, "that is what I call a real question."

Encouraged, I plunge on, "Getting to know older people has made me think about this. Can we recognize life's purpose from looking closely at the last stage of life?"

"Like reading a novel and finding the key to the story at the end?"

"Sure," I say.

"Then why don't we read the end first?" he asks.

"We would miss all the drama, the suspense set up by the plot."

"Exactly," he replies. "If you already knew the ending, you would ruin the whole story. Dostoevski? Boring. Tolstoi? You would throw down the book—too long. And poor Shakespeare. You might as well stay home from the play. Anyway, maybe the ending doesn't tell us about the purpose of life. It just tells about the end."

"Okay," I say, "maybe the last chapter doesn't explain everything. But I remember a very interesting comment made by Jean Piaget."

"The man who spent a lot of time watching his children at play?"

"Yes, the Swiss psychologist. Piaget said that development could be pictured as a pyramid of steps with infancy and childhood at the base. But though the pyramid rises from its bottom, every theory of human development really depends on what is put at the top, the apex of the pyramid. Everything points in that direction."

"So," says Augie, "the pyramid actually hangs from the top."

"Yes, that's the idea, and I think it's true. Piaget was trying to trace development to the maturity of cognition in young adulthood, but many others have placed old age at the apex and found some major goal there that helps clarify the meaning of the life-long process of growth and change."

"Like writing *evighed* or *fuldbragt* on these gravestones?" Augie teases, pointing over his shoulder toward the cemetery.

"Miniature pyramids," I reply.

"It's good they keep the best for last," says Augie. "That way we have something to look forward to. What if we fulfilled our potential at twenty or even thirty? We would have nothing to live for. We would just be trying to hold on to something we were bound to lose anyway."

"The trouble is," I continue, "we tend to picture the life course as a linear process—time, an arrow, with its notched end in the past, and the tip in the future."

"The arrow of time, speeding along. And you're saying there's something wrong with this idea?"

"Not exactly wrong, just misleading. The arrow of time fails to take into account the experiences we've been talking about. Like the situation you continue to remember of the night at the railway station, or Kierkegaard's and Grundtvig's eternities, or the idea of fulfillment etched on these stones. Or take the philosopher's love affair with the timelessness of truth, or the physicist's with unending time."

"So many eternities," Augie laughs, "it makes me dizzy. But, Ron, what do you hope to do once you have climbed the pyramid and touched the words on the highest stones?"

"If I had a firm grasp of the apex, the goal of development, I could better understand the importance of studying philosophy with older people, know whether I was really helping them."

"That would help you?"

"I'd be better equipped to understand what lies ahead and to connect my time of life with my older friends. It would be like having a map."

"A map to the end of time," Augie muses, tugging at the loose skin of his neck. "I, too, would like to have such a map because, well, you see, Ron, I have a hard time giving up the pleasures of this life. I'd like to be a saintly person, but I'm very fond of my sinfulness." He looks at me sheepishly. I've rarely seen Augie act contrite. Then he brightens up, takes a puff on his cigar and, waving it in the air, asks, "Do you remember that line in my 'Morning Song' where we sing 'confusion is sweetness when taken to heart'?"

"Yes. That's a good line," I respond. Augie carried on the Grundtvigian tradition by writing lyrics for all sort of occasions that he set to traditional Danish hymns and patriotic songs. We used to sing his "Morning Song" at the college.

"Well," says Augie, "since we are both confused about the end of time, and since you have given it much thought and read many books, please accept an old man's request and tell me what you have found out. I'll just enjoy the warmth of the sun and listen." Leaning back, Augie closes his eyes and rests his head against the rock wall.

"Okay," I say. I guess it was the "old man" routine that got me. I couldn't turn him down. "What I have found out is that to deal with old age you have to acknowledge that people are running out of time."

"Ja," says Augie, "that's a good place to start."

"So you have to figure that maybe how we experience time, how we understand it, also changes."

"My *evighed*," mumbles Augie.

"Yes, or the idea," I reply, "of immortality, the feeling or belief that somehow your life goes on in others, that you can pass the torch, hand on a legacy of insight and skill, that your life is part of a cosmic chain of being. Or as the psychologist Erikson says, you achieve a sense of integration of experiences; you reach a point where you can say, 'I accept my life as the only life I could have led.' "

Augie's right eye pops open and rotates in my direction. "And God rested on the seventh day, and said of his work that it was good," he quotes. "It's nice that the psychologists can play God."

"The spiritual element does tend to creep into the language of those who write about the last stages of life. Everybody wants a resolution, some type of closure."

"But what do they expect to gain by this?"

"Eternity, Augie. Just like you."

"No, come on, Ron," he laughs, "is this true?"

"It's true for theorists who view development as a lifelong process and want to reconcile the aim and the end of life," I reply. "There's an especially interesting book by an American philosopher, David Norton, who tries to align the process of aging and the quest for ethical understanding. In *Personal Destinies*, Norton describes life development from a philosophical point of view. You'd like his book, Augie, because he talks about how, eventually, we experience the eternal past."

THE ETERNAL PAST

The right eyelid opens slightly, then flutters shut. He's interested. "What does this Mr. Norton have to tell us?" asks Augie.

"Norton says that passage from one stage of life to another is triggered by a surprise that makes us think differently. Childhood is surprised by the sexual and physical potency of adolescence, which in turn is surprised to find that adulthood means accepting weighty responsibilities. In adulthood, we strive to fulfill our potential, struggling with commitment to the choices and promises that are ours to pursue. We establish a concept of the future as that which is yet to be done, and the past as what we have done. Human temporality is not just the watch tick of chronological time for Norton; it's the tension between the having-done and the yet-to-be-done. The whole process is driven forward by our need to turn the possible into the actual."

"That's what I love about you Americans," says Augie, "your eternal optimism, your belief in the future, human perfectibility." He turns his head from side to side, stretching the muscles of his neck. "And the fourth stage," says Augie, yawning, "another surprise?"

I hesitate for a moment, suddenly aware of what I'm telling my older friend. "The surprise of old age," I say, "is recognizing we do not have a future."

"No future," Augie chuckles, "so I'm running out of time, eh?" Augie raises his arm to show the watch.

"Not chronological time, Augie, not exactly that. You see, Norton argues that the driving motive of life, fulfilling your potential, simply ceases in old age. Instead, a person gains a clear realization of the finality of his or her life. It's true, says Norton, that in some, this may produce the heady feeling that everything is permitted. That the rules of life no longer apply." A wry smile appears on Augie's face. "But," I continue, "Norton argues that special values, virtues, and obligations now assert themselves." Augie frowns.

"Now comes his version of eternity. In relation to other generations, the special task of old age, he says, consists in recovering the past and making it the foundation of present and future living. This past that old age recovers is not the past of the given present but what he calls an 'eternal past.' It's not only the individual's past but the past of many generations, of humankind," I exclaim, "the world, the past of historical being."

Augie nods. "An eternal past," he repeats. "We already have two eternities in Denmark, Ron. Do we need to import a third?"

"I've wondered."

"And you figured out?"

"I figured out that those who try to describe the stages of life need some vantage point, some privileged perspective. Otherwise, if all stages are relative to one another, there can never be a theory of the whole process, because one would have to be outside any particular stage to see the whole. Otherwise, you're still just seeing life from one perspective. You'd have to imagine or project what the poet Eliot called the 'still point of the turning world.' "

"So Norton's mountaintop view is his 'still point'?" asks Augie.

"Yes, it serves to put a frame around his theory. And it has another use."

"It's good that eternity has so many uses," says Augie. "Let me hear."

"People change from one generation to another. Look at our attitudes about women's rights, the independence of nations, freedom of speech, what it means to be an individual. If Norton puts so much emphasis on choice, he needs to find something other than choice to anchor this process. Those who have reached the ethical stage of midlife might see in the elderly this capacity for recovering not only the meaning of their personal past but an independent order of value rooted in a universal and eternal past."

"Does he mean," says Augie, "that the last stage of life is no longer an ending but a return to a beginning?"

"Exactly," I reply. "The tension of time is released in old age because it is no longer needed for fulfilling aspirations and goals. The person is no longer invested in relationships as part of realizing his or her own personal development, but now experiences sympathy and fellowship in affirmation of others' lives without the need to change them, simply accepting them. The elderly rediscover their common humanity."

"We lose something, we gain something," says Augie. "It's a trade-off."

"Yes," I reply, "Norton has the idea that the elderly must actually let go of the goal of actualizing their individual potential. It ceases to be a vital source of meaning. This leads him to regard the older person as reflecting the course of life as a repeating cycle—and this is how he believes the older person can serve other generations by representing the universal, cyclical past."

"A past that is always present," says Augie, shaking his head. "No wonder you want to spend time with us old folks. We, the representatives of the eternal. But, tell me, does this philosopher, Mr. Norton, say how he knows all this? Is he an old man, too?"

"When he wrote the book? Middle-aged, I think. He says he's observed this in the everyday life of his grandfather." I expect to get the eyeball treatment, but Augie remains still. He's intrigued, so I continue. "Norton describes his grandfather, an elderly gentleman who smokes a pipe, uses a favorite penknife, and takes daily afternoon drives to the store. These gestures and habits symbolize, for Norton, meaningful repetition. They are, he implies, the mundane equivalent of rituals, like that of tribal elders in religious ceremonies."

"Does it mean you hope to become an old man with a pipe, a pocketknife, and a lonely life taking daily drives to the grocer or the pharmacist?"

"No, Augie," I answer. "But with your goal of achieving eternity, I thought you would be interested in Norton's version."

Both of Augie's eyes open. He sits up and turns toward me. "That's quite a story, Ron. I think it's good he admires his grandfather. But, you know, middle age is like that. You want to imagine there's a time for contentment before you die."

"Who knows?" I respond. "Maybe like you, Augie, the grandfather was really going to visit a lady friend his grandson never knew about."

Augie laughs. "Ja, I hope you're right. But something bothers me here. Mr. Norton doesn't seem to have any loyalty to his country."

"What?" I exclaim, baffled by Augie's sudden conclusion. Didn't he think Norton paid taxes? "I'm sure he's a very good citizen," I reply.

"No, his loyalty is to ideas, to the mind. He could be a Frenchman or a Norwegian. But we in Denmark know eternity belongs to the soil, the clouds, the fjord. And we have the powerful gods Odin, Thor, and Freya, and the savior Jesus to back us up."

"What are you talking about, Augie? Is this a streak of nationalism?"

"Not nationalism. History," he answers, sitting down on the edge of the bench. "Let me tell you about a conversation I had recently with the beautiful woman we are going to meet." He glances at his watch. "Ja, we must soon go, but first I'll tell you a story."

I sit back, rest my head on the stones, close my eyes, and enjoy the warmth of the sun.

TANTE INGER

"You see, our Mrs. Bolton is my mother's cousin, Tante Inger. She's not really family, but I've always called her Aunty."

He's surprised me again. His Tante Inger? Apparently, I jumped to false conclusions. Or has Augie purposely led me on?

"Have I told you the story about Tante Inger's eightieth-birthday party? It was held in Lar's and Jette's big farmhouse a couple years ago."

I cannot place the story and shake my head.

"You know the tradition in Denmark for birthdays." I did. They were like national holidays. Out in the countryside, there would be Danish flags hoisted on the flagpole, coffee parties with songs and speeches, and lots of eating and smoking. "Well," Augie continues, "I walked in and found a huge crowd in the big living room. We had layer cake, strudel, three kinds of cookies, and plenty of good, strong coffee. Then Cousin Lars opened a box of cigars. I was sitting in a corner enjoying a Flora Danica with Tante Inger, who smoked a little cheroot, as is the custom among her generation. She kept looking over at me and nodding, like there was something she wanted to tell me."

"And did she?" I ask.

"Oh, ja, she certainly did. First, she motioned for me to pull my chair closer. I thought maybe Tante Inger was losing her hearing. Then she leaned over and spoke in a gentle voice as if her story was meant for my ears alone.

"She said she remembered how, years ago, on a day just like this, her birthday, her grandfather, Jens Peder, saddled up his horse and rode down south to Ringsted for a meeting of the council of elders. She described his horse, the weather, and the account her grandfather gave after he returned from the long journey. You can imagine how long it would take to get there and return on horseback. She told me about the meeting, who was there, what issues they had to decide, and so on. She described all of this in great detail. She was about to tell me about how some of the peasant farmers were planning a revolt. They wanted to burn down the country estate of the king. But, just then, Tante Inger's great niece—that's my cousin Ulla—came over to show off her youngster and that distracted Tante Inger from telling any more of the story."

"Your aunt has an amazing memory. But Augie what does this have to do with David Norton and the eternal past?"

Augie rests his hands on his knees. "Th, that's what I'm trying to tell you, Ron. Tante Inger's gift for memory? What she described? Ja, this happened more than eight hundred years ago."

"What?" I exclaim.

Augie laughs at my surprise. "That's maybe not the eternal past, Mr. Philosopher, but close to it. Very close. You see, Tante Inger is telling us, eternity is now, is right here in little Denmark. If we let it wander around or float in some philosopher's mind, eternity is of no earthly use. No, if I thought eternity had no purpose, I wouldn't bother with it."

"And did your aunt find a purpose for eternity?"

"Sure," says Augie, "to help her walk up your pyramid of life."

"Prepare for death?"

Augie nods. "If living life to its fullest is such preparation."

"But Tante Inger. Is she? You know?" I touch my forehead.

"Sharp as Grandfather Norton's penknife," says Augie. "Maybe we could introduce them."

"Maybe. But Augie," I complain, "with so many eternities, how can we know which tells us the truth about fulfillment?"

Augie squints into the distance. Low, fleecy clouds skim the landscape of fields and tree-lined lanes leading toward the white-washed farmhouses. "Eternity can mean many things," he says, still gazing thoughtfully. "As a Christian, I should say there can be only one eternity, the mind of God. But from where we stand"— he nods toward the stone wall—"we cannot know this for sure."

Augie gets to his feet and stretches. "Anyway, even if Mr. Norton claims I don't have a future," he says, "you and I have a date with a lovely lady. So let's go."

We walk toward the one car remaining in the church parking lot, Augie's shiny red 280Z. I'm still pondering how Tante Inger's personal past could get mixed up with eight centuries of Danish history. Was it some kind of archetypal unconscious like the one Jung speaks about? Was the idea of eternity always linked to the particularity of history and culture—touched by the soil, colored by memory, flavored with cakes and coffee?

We climb into the car and, moments later, sail across fields of wind-raked barley, rye, and oats, me asking him to explain Tante Inger's remarkable memory, Augie humming one of Grundtvig's hymns.

CHAPTER TWELVE

BELONGING TO THE WORLD

How do we know when we have reached a conclusion? When the form of discourse is explanatory, we expect an analysis of causes and effects to terminate in some final result, like the part of a physics equation that falls to the right of the equal sign. Logically developed arguments usually end with expressions like "Therefore X is the case, and not Y or Z." Sermons that draw on the authority of Scripture reach a crescendo of moralistic passion, then diminish through such prescriptive phrases as "Therefore, I say unto you, always . . . [or never]. . ."

There are other modes of inquiry that rely more on description and narrative, less on concepts and explanations, to offer insights to the reader. Many of these seek through personal involvement to understand a "distant" people—a tribe of Australian aborigines, ghetto youth, residents of a nursing home—while capturing the inquirer's own process of discovery. Yet when is such a description complete, since there is always much more to understand and relate?

Is the end of an account also its conclusion, or just an ending?

Philosophers in the twentieth century have been sharply divided between those who want the discipline to emulate rigorous scientific methods of analysis and objectivity and those more drawn to the arts with their ability to delve deeply into the ambiguities of life and to evoke or provoke a change in consciousness on the part of the viewer, reader, or listener. While this distinction is overstated—in truth there are numerous combinations and variations of this dichotomous pair at work today in philosophy—it brings out the question: What do we expect of a conclusion, and how does it serve us?

My conversation in the cemetery with Augie considered the image or idea we may carry around of an ideal state of life—a telos, or aim, dynamically alive; not a terminus, a death. Old age leads to death, as does all of life, yet death is not the conclusion, though it is an end of sorts, and yet not an end, since we go on in the lives of others. About our own finality we have no certainty, though we may believe many things. Augie and I did not reach any final conclusion, but our conversation gave me a clue about getting to results. I had started out asking about *what* something is or might be—completeness, in this instance, humor or deliberateness, in other situations. As the conversation evolved, I found myself shifting from *what* to *how*—wondering *how* it might be to know the meaning of completeness, humor, deliberateness. In my pursuit to understand the various issues that came up through my encounters with older people, there was often a transforming moment when asking *what* a thing is turned into *how* it might be to experience it.

Now we are going to meet Tante Inger, the person who can remember events of centuries past. Maybe she possesses other talents for drawing conclusions or picturing ideal aims, since she has a vast field of material from which to draw.

MADAME BLUE

We pull into the small gravel farmyard, a barn on one side, a low whitewashed stone farmhouse on the other. Augie turns off the engine and deftly slides out of the car, while I fumble momentarily with the seat belt. Through the windshield, I see a red-painted door opening at the top of a short course of steps. A slightly bent woman with white hair and wearing a dark blue dress just then steps onto the porch. Augie approaches her and makes a low, formal bow as though the woman might have been the queen of Denmark.

"*Daws*," I hear her say to Augie as I close the car door. The greeting is in country Danish, something like our "howdy."

"*Goddag, min ven*," Augie replies more formally, taking her outstretched hand. They stand a moment looking at each other. Then Tante Inger glances toward me. "*Velkommen*," she calls out. They wait for me to join them on the porch, where Augie introduces us. As she holds my hand, Tante Inger says she has heard about me and that as a friend of Augie's I am especially welcome in her home.

We step into a long, low-ceilinged living room that faces the farmyard. The remodeled interior of the old house forms a remarkable contrast to the outside. The floors are a beautifully finished white oak and the furniture, made of chromed metals, handsome leather, and light hardwoods, Danish ultramodern. A television set and hi-tech-looking stereo stand in one corner, and on the walls are mounted contemporary paintings—I recognize the work of several Scandinavian artists. Tante Inger motions us to sit on a couch beside the coffee table. Seated, I look around and notice a few objects from earlier times. An antique, tole painted chest sits against the opposite wall, and a green clock, its pendulum case decorated with bright red flowers and vines, hangs on the wall at one end of the room. Tante Inger brings out cups and saucers, goes to the kitchen, and comes back carrying a blue enamelware coffeepot, a kind I have not seen for many years.

"You will have to excuse me for this," she says, hoisting the blue pot. "I rarely use it. I prefer the stainless thermos or, for fine folk like yourselves, my china. I do this for Augie. He likes the old ways, now and then, don't you, Augie?"

Augie laughs. "Ja, good old Madame Blue. I don't get served this way except when I come to coffee with Tante Inger."

Madame Blue is what the country people call the humble coffeepot from which Inger is now pouring. Watching her movements, I am impressed at her agility, despite her years. I study her narrow wrists and strong-looking hands, several fingers of which are gnarled by arthritis. With a long, narrow face, prominent cheekbones, and deep-set eyes, Tante Inger looks at one moment like a sorceress and at the next like a kindly grandmother you could easily imagine going to visit on a Sunday afternoon in the countryside.

Having filled our cups, Inger takes her seat in a straight-back chair at the end of the table. As she reaches for her cup, she says, "You know, of course, I am not his real aunt."

"Yes," I answer, "you're what family experts call fictive kin."

"Fictive?" She looks at Augie for clarification.

"*Imaginær slægt,*" he translates.

"Oh," she nods, "an imaginary aunt. That is a good way to describe our relationship, because Augie is sometimes fond of telling tall tales about his Tante Inger." She looks at Augie, who smiles coyly.

I give a little cough and stifle a smile.

"Aha," says Inger, "he has told you something, yes?"

"Well," I stammer, "just something about your . . . ah." I look at Augie, who shrugs indifferently, leaving me in an awkward position.

"My what?" Inger puts down her cup.

"Your excellent memory, and . . . uh, knowledge . . . of history."

"*Ach, nej*," she laughs, "not the one about my ancestor riding down south to the elders meeting!" she exclaims, throwing up her hands.

She looks at me for verification, and my silence gives her the answer.

"And, my friend, did Augie tell you it was in a dream? I didn't really believe it happened. Did he tell you that?"

I am startled. Had he purposely misled me? "Augie," I say, "you didn't mention that particular detail."

"Well, I, I . . ." Augie stutters. "It was such a good story. I didn't think you'd care about the details."

"Details!" Inger laughs. "You must think I'm some kind of daffy old woman." She reaches across and pats my knee. "Well, but you know," she adds in a low, mysterious voice, "it could have been true. Yes, yes. You see, among the old ones of my parents' generation, what we call folk memory was quite common."

"Really?" I say, relieved she had not taken offense.

"Oh yes," she replies. "And why not? After all, we Danes grow up from the time we are quite small with the Nordic myths, folktales, and Bible stories. Also, we hear about things that happened in our families and in the region—like Uncle Niels, who ran away to sea at fifteen, the peasant rebellion plotted by some of our local men, animals that can talk, and many other strange things." She makes a circle in the air with her finger. "Over time, they are no longer stories that happened to people long ago; they become part of your life."

"Seep into your personal identity," I remark.

"Practically swallow you up," she enthuses, taking a bite of a cookie.

"Our friend Ronald, here," Augie interjects, "is very interested in the tricks memory plays on us."

Inger tilts her head and considers this idea. Then she slides open a drawer in the table and removes a small tin, which she places on the table. "Smoke?" she asks as she opens the lid, revealing a row of small cigars wrapped in cellophane.

"*Ja, tak,*" I reply, taking one. Augie declines, instead offering her one of his own. "*Nej, tak,*" she responds, "those are too strong for me." A box of wooden matches is passed around, and the room soon grows hazy.

"Oh," says Augie, waving his match to extinguish it, "before I forget, I should greet you from Pastor Mikkelsen."

"*Tak for det,*" she replies, plucking a bit of lint from her dress. "Was his sermon good?"

Augie hesitates. "Not so bad."

"He's a very nice man, Pastor Mikkelsen," she says. Then, leaning across the table and pretending to whisper, she adds, "But, you know, at times he can be a little dull."

Inger glances at Augie. "*Værsgo,*" she says, pushing a plate of cookies toward him. "Now, about these stories," she continues, "shall I tell you how I think about them?"

"Please," I say.

"Yes, well, the way I see it, every generation receives a legacy from its predecessors. They pass along wonderful stories from the Bible, the sagas, legends . . . many, many such stories. When we are quite young, these stories seem terribly exotic. In our enlightened youth and young adult years, we laugh at ourselves for believing such fables. Yet not so many years later, the stories start cropping up in our minds. Maybe they were not so farfetched as we had thought. In old age," she sighs, "we see our lives reflected in these stories. Some people, as I've said, may lose their footing in the present and slip away into olden times."

"These stories have great power in a society with its traditions still intact," I comment.

"Yes," she agrees, "but Denmark is now such a modern country. You wouldn't know the stories made any difference. Television has almost replaced Hans Christian Andersen. Almost. Still, from my point of view, life is more or less the same; just the settings change. Of course, these changes are quite dramatic. Especially in my generation. For instance, unlike my mother, I was not a farmer's wife. My husband had a job in town as a printer. I had a career outside the home as nurse and midwife. I moved out here from town after my husband's death. Renovated the old place." She glances around, apparently pleased with what she sees. Then, pointing to a side window through which we could see fields of knee-high barley, she adds, "The land I rent out to a neighbor. If I were a young woman today, I am quite certain I would be a doctor. But I would still have to make decisions about marriage and family, go through all the trials and tribulations about love, money"—she counts off on her fingers—"God, my politics. Despite these differences in circumstance, it seems a voice once whispered in your ear the story of what you will become. And, mind you, there are only so many to go around."

"But," I protest, "this is a kind of fatalism. Maybe these same stories hold us back."

"Oh," she exclaims, "they do, indeed."

Inger's response makes us all laugh. Is she serious? I press on with my objections. "I agree, it is good to have knowledge of one's traditions. Without these stories from history and legend you would have no background, no bearing. And I love the way people in Denmark continue the tradition by writing lyrics to venerable melodies for songs they share at birthday parties and anniversaries. But the traditional tales have also been used to keep people in their places by making them think it natural they should be poor or ignorant or without certain rights. So we cannot just accept these stories at face value."

Inger claps her hands. "Bravo," she says, "you have passed the first test."

"The what?"

"Tante Inger likes to draw out new acquaintances," says Augie. "She likes to find out where you stand on certain matters."

"Oh," I murmur, a little confused. "Then you don't believe this about how we are all just living out the same cycle of tales?"

"Certainly not," she says emphatically. "There is a good deal of truth in them. Mind you, I'm not for doing away with tradition. We need these stories like we need our mother's milk. They help us to grow up, strong and healthy, and they immunize us against sheer stupidity—as you just mentioned about background and bearing. But we can't be hanging about our mother's bosom all our lives, pleasurable and secure though that may be."

I nod, trying to figure out just what kind of person this Tante Inger is. I should have known that anyone Augie likes to spend time with will have a complex character, and stand with a foot in more than one world.

VOICES

"Now tell me something," Inger says, taking a sip of coffee. "Augie says you work with old people in America and have gotten many impressions from them."

"They've influenced my way of thinking."

"Influenced? In what way?"

"Ronald, here, believes that we old people have finished with growing up and that now we are interested only in eternity and how to get there," interjects Augie.

"Shush," she exhorts, shaking a finger at Augie. "Let your friend tell his own story."

"Well," I begin, "we were just speaking of people who experience folk memory. My experience is a little like that." Inger raises her eyebrows. "I wouldn't describe it as slipping into olden times, rather that other times and other lives have become a part of me. Voices. Over time I found I could hear in my mind the voices of several people who had become important to me. I could summon them, hold council, ask them questions. Usually they would answer."

"Imaginary kin?" she teases.

I smile. "I've wondered the same thing. Yet what is so special is the way the voices ask me questions and tell me things that I can't imagine coming up with on my own." Inger squints suspiciously. "I'll give you an example. A short time ago, I was working on a book and having a hard time understanding where it was going. One day, while I was taking a walk, I thought of an old friend, Dorothy, and decided to ask her for help. 'Dorothy,' I said silently, 'can you tell me how I should think about my book?' And immediately I pictured her speaking to me. 'Etudes,' she replied. What, I thought, études? What could she mean? So I asked again. 'Etudes,' she insisted. When I reached home, I looked the word up in an encyclopedia. I knew it was French for 'study' and had a technical musical meaning. Chopin wrote études. That was the limit of my knowledge. As I read the description of 'études,' I learned these are musical studies that involve variations on complex and innovative patterns of notes and chords. Some are written for teaching purposes, others for developing new musical possibilities. Suddenly, I realized what Dorothy meant. I was exploring variations on a complex pattern of themes in order to understand their diversity and where they might lead. This single word helped me move forward."

"Your older students have become your teachers. You have internalized them," Inger says.

"Yes, that is how it seems." I take a puff on my cigar and continue. "What especially fascinates me, though, is the voices' quality of transcendence."

"Transcendence?" Inger laughs. "Augie, now he's getting religious on us. You had better explain that one."

"The voices are unique and characteristic of the people I've known. They have their own special way of putting things." I touch my earlobe. "Though I am receptive to them, they retain a life and validity of their own. When someone like Dorothy tells me 'études,' this is an idea I wouldn't have discovered on my own, yet there it is, a gift." I sit back, wondering what she will say.

Augie turns to me and asks, "These voices, are they always helpful or do they sometimes give you a hard time?"

"Certain of the voices are more critical than others, and some can be harsh and unpleasant to deal with," I admit.

"Ja," Augie responds, as if to confirm his own experiences.

"Quite a story," Inger says dryly. "Then, like our folk memory people, you do not know where your thoughts begin and end, or even if they belong to you or someone else?" Before I can try to answer, she turns to Augie. "Did you know your friend hears voices?"

Augie gives her a wry smile. "Don't we all, Tante Inger?"

She shakes her head. "I'm going to have to think about this." Then she shifts her gaze to me and says, "Besides hearing voices, have you learned something useful from these people? Perhaps some secrets about aging?"

PAYING ATTENTION

"I've learned it's important to pay attention when people are telling you about their lives, because they are inviting you to step inside a picture of the world you might never have considered. I am especially interested in stories about turning points."

"And by paying attention you have figured out?"

"Figured out that not only do we sometimes come to see the world in a new way but these moments also often signal changes in how we perceive the meaning of time."

"Hmm," she murmurs, stroking her jaw, "this, I think, I understand. As a midwife, I have seen sometimes quite frivolous young women who only wanted to sing, dance, and make love turn into fiercely protective mothers suddenly concerned about savings accounts and their children's future. And as a nurse, I have seen gravely ill people become concerned to ask forgiveness of people they feel they may have wronged years ago. Are these the kind of changes you are talking about?"

I nod. "Yes, changes in how we view the future and the past. But not only dramatic situations or crises that bring change. Ordinary experiences, too, when for some reason you see things from a slightly different angle. Very often these moments come and go before we're fully aware what they might mean. Only later do we realize that something has happened."

Inger taps her cigar against the ashtray. "Can you give me an example from your life?"

I think for a moment. "Well," I begin, "I think of the very first time I got interested in teaching older people. Inwardly, I was struggling with the issues of adult responsibility—marriage, children, a job, my career—all that is part of growing up. Also, I was trying to cope with my father's death and certain feelings of vulnerability about my own mortality. In the outward, public sphere, we were celebrating the bicentennial of our country. The combination, inner and outer, triggered something in me—that I should find some special way to take part in the celebration. This public event, which I didn't take very seriously at the time, got woven together with my personal life. The result was my decision to teach older people."

"You knew what you were looking for? What you would be getting into?"

"Something about old age as a philosophical time of life. Otherwise, it was a leap into the unknown. That this decision would lead to a new career, and bring other changes to my life, still seems unbelievable. And that a small, personal choice would connect me to large, public issues about aging and later life also amazes me."

Inger nods. "So you, too, heard a whisper? Your calling?"

"Destiny, or coincidence," I reply; "I'm still not sure."

"We don't always know the urges that reach into our lives from far and wide."

"That seems truer every day," Augie interjects.

"An interesting coincidence, your maturation and the social mood. How did that give you a different meaning of time?" she asks.

"I became interested in other people's lifetimes, not just my own. That helped me appreciate how people had lived through events and experiences of their earlier years. And that inspired me to learn more about my own family's history. I realized that our separateness from one another is an abstraction. Like the voices, I lived in and through relationships to other people and other times, yet I was still my own person."

"You widened your horizons." Inger studies me, then glances at Augie, who seems to be getting restless. "Augie," she asks, "how do you say in English *fællesskab?*"

"Fellowship," Augie answers.

"Yes, that's it." She looks at me and says, "Sharing time with people—that's fellowship. Is that what you found with these people?"

The word sounds so simple, yet the thoughts and emotions of the time felt complex. "Yes," I respond, " 'fellowship' is a good word."

"And you liked these people, admired some of them, yes?"

"I enjoyed getting to know them, and I admired certain qualities—for example, a person's deep humor that showed me how to embrace life's many paradoxes and contradictions, or another person's way of making thoughtful choices, especially at difficult times. I was fascinated by the ways my older friends had gotten themselves unstuck from unhappiness or found encouragement to recover from past misfortune or error." I pause, looking out the window behind Inger at the metal roof of the barn gleaming in the sunlight. "Early on, I was drawn to people's memories. I believed that by searching the past, we could figure out how we'd arrived in the present moment. If you knew that, and wanted to, you could change your life. Gradually, I began to suspect that revisiting the past could also reinforce what you already believed or that you might just replace one story with another. I didn't mean you had really discovered anything. Remembering must also be a creative venture, I decided. Imagination is the key: revitalizing life, finding a new course of action, redefining your future—they all depend on finding a fresh way to recollect the past."

"These older people offered you important lessons. Yet, I wonder," she continues, "the way you describe your fellowship and the older people. Were they a laboratory for you to conduct studies?"

A laboratory? I hesitate. "Maybe a philosophical laboratory," I respond. "Because many issues traditionally debated by philosophers arose in the stories people told. They didn't necessarily have a vocabulary for describing them that way—which was what made these conversations so exciting and unrehearsed. The concreteness of real-life issues helped me turn back to the philosophers to hear their words in new ways."

"More voices?" she laughs.

"The same voices, only now they were speaking directly to me. And the more I immersed myself in the lives of my older friends, the more I realized that when philosophers write about aging and human development, they are as much telling us about their ideas of time and the meaning of history. Old age is a mirror; that's how it seems to me now."

A SONG

"Interesting," says Inger. "Augie, don't you think what our friend is telling us is interesting?"

Augie nods. "Ronald is often thinking interesting thoughts. He should write a song about them."

"A song? Oh yes, that's a wonderful idea." She turns toward me and says excitedly, "Have you ever thought of that? What would you make your song about?"

I have, in fact, adopted the Danish songwriting tradition and set lyrics to all sorts of tunes for various occasions like birthdays, anniversaries, and even opening sessions of conferences. "If I were writing lyrics for a song?" I play along, rubbing my chin. I think for a moment. "I would put in something about belonging to the world. That phrase used to run through my mind in the early days of working with older people, and I still like the sound of it." I feel a little embarrassed and pick up a cookie.

"You didn't belong to the world before that time?" she asks. Before I can answer, she continues, "No, I suppose in an important way, you did not. You were busy belonging to yourself. Becoming your own story. This theme, 'belonging to the world,' as you put it, what does it mean to you?"

"It means something," I answer, tentatively, "something about making a home of my own. I have a house and family. It isn't that. But I'd long had this feeling we are just passing through life, visiting the places where we live."

"A very nomadic idea. Have you traveled so very much?"

"I've lived in several parts of the U.S. and here in Denmark, but I am not what you call a world traveler."

"Oh," she says brightly, "then this moving around is more in your mind, your mental geography, I suppose."

Her speculation reminds me of the German Romantic poet Novalis, who said philosophy was the urge to be at home everywhere. "You may be onto something, " I reply.

"Perhaps," she continues, "you are a wanderer looking for home. It makes sense because you can't be a wanderer unless you have a home, a place to wander from and back to. Like Odysseus in the Greek myth."

Inger's reference to Odysseus, the Greek for Ulysses, startles me. There is a connection I have failed to make. So preoccupied was I about my journey and my shipmates that I forgot about the place of home, a wanderer's base of operation—even if that wanderer only daydreams or works complicated philosophical puzzles while taking a walk around the neighborhood. This is what Professor Sheppler's wife, Sonja, was referring to when she presented the neglected side, Tennyson's version of the Ulysses story: the homecoming. Maybe these explorations with my older friends are ways to help me find my way home. And not just me, but them, too. To be at home with one another. Home means connectedness, closeness across differences in generations, a way to remember what is important—not only a place, but a moment. Maybe that is why time is so important to me. I know I cannot explain all this to Inger.

"I can see," says Inger, "that we have struck some familiar chord in our conversation. No doubt you will be finding some very good material for your song. Augie, what do you say we go for a little stroll and help our friend, here, with his song. I've made a path through the fields down to my woods and pond. Or should I say,"—she turned toward me—"one that I am borrowing? Would you like to do that, you two?"

"A little walk," says Augie. "That would be excellent. I think I know some melodies Ronald could use."

"I'm ready for a walk," I reply. "And for your help with my song."

Inger changes into tennis shoes and supplies us each with sturdy walking sticks. Then we set off on a path through the field, Augie trying out the melody to one hymn or Danish folk song after another, Inger laughing or moaning in response to Augie's suggestions, and I testing out a line or two as the song slowly takes shape.

References and Additional Readings

The following section contains sources referred to in chapters, as well as related readings that might be of interest to readers.

Introduction

William Stafford read poems from *Traveling through the Dark* (New York: Harper and Row, 1962) and from *Smokes Way* (Port Townsend, Wash.: Graywolf Press, 1978). Stafford's views of writing as a discovery process are offered in his *Writing the Australian Crawl* (Ann Arbor: University of Michigan Press, 1978). The young poet teaching at the senior center, David Romtvedt, would go on to publish several books of poetry, prose, and fiction. See his *How Many Horses* (Memphis: Ion Books, 1988), *A Flower Whose Name I Do Not Know* (Port Townsend, Wash.: Copper Canyon Press, 1992), *Certainty* (Freedonia, N.J.: White Pine Press, 1996), and *Windmill: Essays from Four Mile Ranch* (Santa Fe: Red Crane Books, 1997). Many years after my first encounter with Tennyson's "Ulysses," I read a fascinating account comparing Tennyson's and Picasso's portrayal of old men in poetry and painting in Robert Kastenbaum's "Old Men Created by

Young Artists: Time-Transcendence in Tennyson and Picasso," *International Journal of Aging and Human Development* 28, no. 2, (1989): 81–104.

CHAPTER 1

References to Aristotle are from the *Rhetoric*, bk. 2, chap. 12, trans. W. Rhys Roberts (New York: Modern Library, 1954). For more on Uncle Toby, see Laurence Sterne, *Tristram Shandy, Gentleman* (New York: Odyssey Press, 1940). C. G. Jung's classic essay "The Soul and Death" can be found in *The Structure and Dynamics of the Psyche*, trans. R. F. C. Hull, Bollingen Series XX (New York: Pantheon Books, 1960). I am fond of F. M. Cornford's anthropologically inspired translation of Plato's *Republic* (New York: Oxford University Press, 1941). For a thoughtful, contemporary interpretation of Greek philosophy and Homer's famous couple, Odysseus and Penelope, see Martha C. Nussbaum, *Love's Knowledge: Essays on Philosophy and Literature* (New York: Oxford University Press, 1990), chap. 15. Arthur Schopenhauer's "The Ages of Life," from *Counsels and Maxims*, trans. T. Bailey Saunders (London: Swan Sonnenschein, 1890), is well worth consulting for its wealth of provocative insights into and prejudices about the stages of life and their philosophical implications. For more on Schopenhauer's theories of music, see *The World as Will and Representation*, vol. 1, trans. E. F. J. Payne (New York: Dover, 1969). Professor Sheppler's theory of the unity of time was probably influenced by Saint Augustine. See the *Confessions*, bk. 10, trans. John K. Ryan (Garden City, N.Y.: Image Books, 1960). An excellent article on time and narrative in Augustine is Emmet T. Flood's "The Narrative Structure of Augustine's *Confessions*: Time's Quest for Eternity," *International Philosophical Quarterly* 28, no. 2 (1988): 141–62. On continuity of the self across the life course, see Sharon Kaufman's narrative-based *The Ageless Self: Sources of Meaning in Late Life* (Madison: University of Wisconsin Press, 1986); and John Kotre's "narrative psychology" approach in *Outliving the Self: Generativity and the Interpretation of Lives* (Baltimore: Johns Hopkins University Press, 1984). For more on the theory of the embodied self, see Joseph L. Esposito, *The Obsolete Self: Philosophical Dimensions of Aging* (Berkeley: University of California Press, 1987), chap. 2.

CHAPTER 2

Friedrich Nietzsche's classic essay "On the Uses and Disadvantages of History for Life" can be found in *Untimely Meditations*, trans. R. J. Hollingdale (New York: Cambridge University Press, 1983). Nietzsche's historiographic ideas are not completely original. See, for example, the introduction to Hegel's *Philosophy of History*, trans. J. Sibree (London: G. Bell and Sons, 1914), where Hegel outlines three major types of historical narratives, including "reflective history," which Hegel also calls "critical history." All quotations are from T. S. Eliot's *Four Quartets*, in *Collected Poems, 1909–1962* (New York: Harcourt, Brace, and World, 1963). A helpful rendering of the enigmatic sayings of the pre-Socratic philosopher Heraclitus is *Fragments*, translation and commentary by T. M. Robinson (Toronto: University of Toronto Press, 1987). An insightful interpretation is Philip Wheelwright's *Heraclitus* (Westport, Conn.: Greenwood Press, 1959). For Kierkegaard's views on "becoming oneself," see "The Aesthetic Validity of Marriage," in the novelistically written *Either/Or*, vol. 2, trans. Walter Lowrie (1944; reprint, Princeton: Princeton University Press, 1971).

CHAPTER 3

I have found a valuable resource for this chapter in *The Life of John Stuart Mill*, by Michael St. John Packe (1954; reprint, New York: Capricorn Books, 1970). All references to Mill's *Autobiography* are from the Jack Stillinger edition (London: Oxford University Press, 1971). For more on James Mill's and John Stuart Mill's careers with the East India Company and the relationship of their political views to colonial management, see Lynn Zastoupil's *John Stuart Mill and India* (Stanford: Stanford University Press, 1994). For a psychobiographical view of J. S. Mill, see A. W. Levi, "The Mental Crisis of John Stuart Mill," *Psychoanalytic Review* 32 (1945): 86–101. A helpful book on how philosophers (including J. S. Mill) regard imagination is Mary Warnock's *Imagination* (Berkeley: University of California Press, 1976). For Mill's liberationist views on individuality, see his *On Liberty* (1859), ed. Currin V. Shields (New York: Library of the Liberal Arts Press, 1956).

CHAPTER 4

For Plato's description of the three parts of the soul, see *Republic*, bk. 4, chap. 13, in the Cornford translation with notes. For a useful discussion of the recent history of concepts of the self in light of the postmodernist debate, see George Levine, ed., *Constructions of the Self* (New Brunswick: Rutgers University Press, 1992), esp. "Introduction: Constructivism and the Re-emergent Self." Simone de Beauvoir, *The Coming of Age*, trans. Patrick O'Brian (New York: Putnam, 1972), is the now classic demythologizing study of old age accomplished in the same scholarly way as her earlier *The Second Sex*. For a fuller discussion of the "gerontological self," see my article "In Search of the Gerontological Self" *Journal of Aging Studies* 6, no. 4 (1992): 319–32. For an insightful, often cited discussion on the history of the idea of the self, see Charles Taylor, *Sources of the Self: The Making of the Modern Identity* (Cambridge: Harvard University Press, 1989). Stephen R. Sabat, and Rom Harre, "The Construction and Deconstruction of Self in Alzheimer's Disease," *Ageing and Society* 12 (1992): 443–61. A clear and helpful study of the self in personal narrative is found in Harry J. Berman, *Intepreting the Aging Self: Personal Journals of Later Life* (New York: Springer, 1994). Martin Buber's classic *I and Thou* (originally published in German in 1929) is a rather formal, philosophically abstract work. More engaging essays can be found in the collection *Between Man and Man*, trans. Ronald Gregory Smith (London: K. Paul, 1947). For a detailed exposition of Buber's philosophy, see Maurice S. Friedman's *Martin Buber: The Life of Dialogue* (New York: Harper, 1960). For a Buddhist-inspired approach to end-of-life issues, see Stephen Levine, *Who Dies?: An Investigation of Conscious Living and Conscious Dying* (Garden City, N.Y.: Anchor Press/Doubleday, 1982). A provocative discussion of the concept of multiple selves in relation to aging is found in Richard A. Posner, *Aging and Old Age* (Chicago: University of Chicago Press, 1995), chap. 4.

CHAPTER 5

Sigmund Freud's fascinating views on humor can be found in "Humor," *Collected Papers* (New York: Basic Books, 1959), and *Jokes and*

Their Relation to the Unconscious, trans. James Strachey (New York: W. W. Norton, 1963). Isaac Bashevis Singer's wonderful story "The Spinoza of Market Street" can be found in *An Isaac Bashevis Singer Reader* (New York: Farrar, Straus, and Giroux, 1981). For Aristotle's distinction between tragedy and comedy, see *Aristotle's Poetics*, translation and commentary by George Whalley (Montreal: McGill-Queen's University Press, 1997). On the structure of dramatic comedy, see Northrop Frye, *Anatomy of Criticism* (New York: Atheneum, 1966). The topic of timing in humor is discussed by Mildred Seltzer in her contribution "Humor," in *The Encyclopedia of Adult Development* (Phoenix: Oryx Press, 1993). Norman Cousins' well-known views on the benefits of humor are found in *Anatomy of an Illness* (New York: W. W. Norton, 1976). For readers wishing to further pursue the subject of the therapeutic uses of humor with the elderly, see Francis A. McGuire, Rosangela K. Boyd, Ann James, *Therapeutic Humor with the Elderly* (New York: Haworth Press, 1992), and Lucille Nahemow, Kathleen McKluskey-Fawcett, and Paul McGhee, eds., *Humor and Aging* (Orlando: Academic Press, 1986). For Kierkegaard's theory of humor as life stage, see his *Concluding Unscientific Postscript*, pt. 2, chap. 4, sec. 2, A., "Existential Pathos," subsec. 2, trans. David F. Swenson and Walter Lowrie (Princeton: Princeton University Press, 1968). Kierkegaard's fascinating comparison of Socrates and Christ is found in his *Philosophical Fragments*, trans. David F. Swenson (Princeton: Princeton University Press, 1962). On Jewish humor, see Sarah Blacher Cohen, ed., *Jewish Wry: Essays on Jewish Humor* (Bloomington: Indiana University Press, 1987). Useful discussions of philosophies of humor are found in John Morreall, ed., *The Philosophy of Laughter and Humor* (Albany: State University of New York Press, 1987), and idem, *Taking Laughter Seriously* (Albany: State University of New York Press, 1983).

CHAPTER 6

References here are to Aristotle's *Nicomachean Ethics, Book 6*, trans. Martin Ostwald (New York: Library of Liberal Arts, 1962). William Carlos Williams, *In the American Grain* (New York: New Directions Books, 1956). I am grateful to Professor Arthur Farber's wife, Ruth Farber, and to their son, Daniel, and daughters, Ann and Laurie, for reviewing this chapter and giving me permission to use Art's and Ruth's names. Speaking for the family, Daniel concurred with my emphasis on Art's special qualities. "It was always an inside family joke. Dad did everything with the same graceful movements—table tennis, bowling, 'slicing eggplant'—all had this sort of dip and flow and great concentration about it." The family found it amusing that I remembered him as having small features. "He had large ears and a large nose and unusually big, fat glasses. We suggest you use the term 'prominent features,' " Daniel communicated.

CHAPTER 7

Stanley Cavell, *A Pitch of Philosophy: Autobiographical Exercises* (Cambridge: Harvard University Press, 1994), is a fascinating, richly suggestive, sometimes illusive and daunting blend of life story and academic philosophy. The program I directed, "All My Somedays—A Living History Project," was funded by a grant to the Pierce County Library System from the National Endowment for the Humanities. For a discussion of the All My Somedays project and the authors Hill and Theberge, see my article "History on a Human Scale," *History News*, Sept. 1983, 17–22. Charlie Hill, *Craving for Acceptance* (Tacoma: Pierce County Library, 1980). See Augustine's *Confessions*, bk. 10. Ann Theberge, *From Valdres to Moose Jaw: A Family's Journey* (Tacoma: Pierce County Library, 1980). For a more detailed discussion of the role of narrative and personal history, see David Carr, *Time, Narrative, and History* (Bloomington: Indiana University Press, 1986). For a more detailed discussion of metaphors and autobiography, see James Olney, *Metaphors of Self: The Meaning of Autobiography* (Princeton: Princeton Universtiy Press, 1972). For more on Charles Taylor's notions of a moral ontology, see his *Sources of the Self*. Two valuable sources on the history of autobiography are Georg Misch's *A History of Autobiography in Antiquity*, trans. E. W. Dickes (London: Routledge & Paul, 1950), and Karl Joachim Weintraub's *The Value of the Individual: Self and Circumstance in Autobiography* (Chicago: University of Chicago Press, 1978). An important figure in the "virtue ethics" movement, Alasdair MacIntyre offers the highly readable *After Virtue: A Study in Moral Theory* (Notre

Dame: University of Notre Dame Press, 1981). See also John Paul Eakin, *Fictions in Autobiographies: Studies in the Art of Self Invention* (Princeton: Princeton University Press, 1985).

CHAPTER 8

Arthur Schopenhauer, *Counsels and Maxims*. Norman Daniels adopts a version of noted ethicist John Rawl's "veil of ignorance" in his *Am I My Parent's Keeper?: An Essay on Justice between the Young and the Old* (New York: Oxford University Press, 1988). Susan MacManus offers some provocative research findings on the voting patterns of different generations in her *Young v. Old: Generational Combat in the 21st Century* (Boulder, Colo.: Westview Press, 1996). For a fascinating discussion of rainbows, ranging from mythology to scientific explanations, see Carl B. Boyer, *The Rainbow: From Myth to Mathematics* (Princeton: Princeton University Press, 1987). On the history of Lake Wascana, see *Walks through Wascana Centre* (Regina, Saskatchewan: Wascana Centre Authority, n.d.) and Margaret E. Robinson, "Pile o' Bones," in *History of Wascana Creek* (1975). The character of Mr. Liu in this chapter is partly inspired by Mr. Li Erzhong, president of Hubei University for the Elderly and the comments in his speech entitled "The University for Old People in China," later published in *Proceedings of the Regina Seminar, July 25–27, 1996*, in *TALIS (Third Age Learning International Studies)*, no. 7 (1997): 91–96. Mr. Liu is a fictional character based on a composite of people I met at the conference. A useful book on Confucius is David L. Hall and Roger T. Ames, *Thinking through Confucius* (Albany: State University of New York Press, 1987). For more on education for older adults in the United States, see Ronald J. Manheimer, Denise D. Snodgrass, and Diane Moscow-McKenzie, *Older Adult Education: A Guide to Research, Programs, and Policies* (Westport, Conn.: Greenwood Press, 1995).

CHAPTER 9

Josiah Royce, *The Problem of Christianity* (1913; reprint, Hamden, Conn.: Archon Books, 1967). Christopher Lasch's *The Minimal Self: Psy-*

chic Survival in Troubled Times (New York: W. W. Norton, 1984) and *The Culture of Narcissism: American Life in an Age of Diminishing Expectations* (New York: W. W. Norton, 1978) remain important commentaries on contemporary society. Clifford Geertz, "The Uses of Diversity," is discussed by Richard Rorty in his essays in pt. 3 of *Objectivity, Relativism, and Truth: Philosophical Papers*, vol. 1 (Cambridge: Cambridge University Press, 1991). For more on Richard Chess's experiences in Israel, see his book of poetry, *Tekiah* (Athens: University of Georgia Press, 1994). To explore the metaphor of "gates" in Jewish mysticism, see *Safed Spirituality: Rules of Mystical Poetry, the Beginning of Wisdom*, trans. and introd. Lawrence Fine (New York: Paulist Press, 1984).

CHAPTER 10

I have drawn from Plato's *Symposium*, trans. W. Hamilton (Harmondsworth: Penguin Books, 1952). Edmund Sherman, *Reminiscence and the Self in Old Age* (New York: Springer, 1991), provides a thoughtful overview of theories of reminiscence, including the philosophical importance of that process in later life.

CHAPTER 11

Two valuable books related to issues of fulfillment and old age that have influenced my thinking are Thomas R. Cole's *The Journey of Life: A Cultural History of Aging in America* (New York: Cambridge University Press, 1992) and Harry R. Moody's *Abundance of Life: Human Development Policies for an Aging Society* (New York: Columbia University Press, 1988). For fuller elucidation of "The Fullness of Time," see Kierkegaard, *Philosophical Fragments*. For a helpful discussion on N. F. S. Grundtvig, in English, see Kaj Thaning, *N. F. S. Grundtvig*, trans. David Hohnen (Odense, Denmark: Det Danske Selskab, 1972), and *Grundtvig's Ideas in North America*, also edited and published by the Danish Institute (1983). For Grundtvig's own words translated into English, see *Selected Writings*, trans. Johannes Kundsen et al. (Philadelphia: Fortress Press, 1976). On Kierkegaard's interpretation of the Abraham story, see his *Fear and Trem-*

bling, trans. Walter Lowrie (Princeton: Princeton University Press, 1954). Piaget's notion of the pyramid of development is discussed in Carol Gilligan's *In a Different Voice: Psychological Theory and Women's Development* (Cambridge: Harvard University Press, 1982). For Erik H. Erikson's characterization of maturity in old age, see his *Childhood and Society*, 2d ed. (New York: W. W. Norton, 1963), chap. 7, and, for a restatement, his *The Life Cycle Completed* (New York: W. W. Norton, 1985). David Norton's *Personal Destinies: A Philosophy of Ethical Individualism* (Princeton: Princeton University Press, 1976) is a unique effort to combine classical philosophical ideas of morality with humanistic psychology's approach to human development. Another interesting, though quirky, theory that links stages of life with particular philosophical world views is offered by James K. Feibleman in his *The Stages of Human Life: A Biography of Entire Man* (The Hague: Martinus Nijhoff, 1975).

CHAPTER 12

An important example of the descriptive method and its philosophical justification can be found in Michael Jackson's anthropological study of the Warlpiri aborigines of Australia, *At Home in the World* (Durham: Duke University Press, 1995). I am also indebted to Barbara Myerhoff's eloquent and moving work of narrative anthropology, *Number Our Days* (New York: Simon & Schuster, 1978).

INDEX

elderly (*continued*)
  tranquility of, 11–13
  in writing workshops, xiii–xiv
  see also aging
Elijah de Vidas, 226
Eliot, T. S., 30, 35–48, 50, 53, 54, 104,
    288
Emerson, Ralph Waldo, 156–57
emotion:
  capacity for, 62–63, 65
  meaning of, 126–27
  sharing of, 69–72
  time and, 164
empiricism, 59, 83, 94
enabling dialectic, 175
energy, 50–51
epistemology, 29, 160
Erikson, Erik, 181
Eros, 166–67, 242
eternity:
  bitter, 274, 281, 282, 288
  experience of, 266–67, 270–74,
    283–84, 286–87, 290,
    292–93
  as fulfillment, 274–77, 283–84, 293,
    295
  meaning of, 44, 272–75
  sweet, 274–76, 281, 282, 288
ethics, 13, 29, 110, 124, 125, 160, 282,
    287, 289
Ethics (Aristotle), 135
Ethics (Spinoza), 116, 131
ethnocentrism, 213
"études," 302, 303
Eve, 247
evolution, 80
existence, *see* being
existentialism, 123–24
experience:
  accumulated, 90–91, 166, 193
  arch of, xi, xii, xviii, 27, 31, 81,
    105–6, 154, 185
  of being, 142
  communal, xvi, 210–11
  concrete, 135–36, 152
  of eternity, 266–67, 270–74,
    283–84, 286–87, 290,
    292–93
  examination of, 29

ideals and, 77–81
imagination and, xvii
integration of, 175, 286–87
meaning of, 104, 211–12
personal, xviii, 70, 71, 79
as relational, 100
universals of, xvii–xviii
wisdom and, 90–91

faith:
  completeness and, 253–54, 260–61
  humor and, 126–32
  identity and, 238–39
  leaps of, 49, 275
  will vs., 172
families, multigenerational, 190
Farber, Art, 137–47, 148, 149, 150, 151,
    153
Farber, Ruth, 137–39, 140, 141, 144
fellowship, 305–7
"fictive kin," 297, 302
financial security, 14, 49, 138–39
Finch, Jody, 262
finitude, 132, 136, 279–80
Five Gates, 226
Fleming, Arthur, 181–83, 207–9
folkekirke, 279
folk history, 291–92, 296–307
forgetfulness, xvii, 239
forgiveness, 152, 153–54, 164, 172–73,
    304
Four Quartets (Eliot), 35–48, 50, 53
Four Worlds, 225
Fox, William Johnson, 69
frailty, 95, 97–98, 102, 107, 260
Frank (student), 55–56, 57, 63, 65–66,
    72, 74, 80, 81
Freud, Sigmund, 108, 109
friendship, 70–71, 72
From Valdres to Moose Jaw (Theberge),
    169–74, 179
future:
  absence of, 287–88, 293
  ideal, 74–81
  possibilities of, 54, 61

Geertz, Clifford, 213
gender, 243–44
generation gap, 78–81, 194, 196

332   *Index*